Two
of the
Missing

A Reminiscence of Some
Friends in the War

by Perry Deane Young

COWARD, MC CANN & GEOGHEGAN, INC.
New York

For permission to quote from copyrighted material, the author gratefully acknowledges the following:

From *A Second Flowering* by Malcolm Cowley, copyright © 1973 by Malcolm Cowley, reprinted by permission of The Viking Press, Inc.

From *My Wicked, Wicked Ways* by Errol Flynn, copyright © 1959 by G. P. Putnam's Sons, reprinted by permission of G. P. Putnam's Sons.

From *Gardens of War* by Robert Gardner and Karl G. Heidler, Random House, Inc., as Publisher.

From *Here Is Your War* by Ernie Pyle, Holt, Rinehart and Winston, Inc., as Publishers.

The Richmond Organization for portions of "Those Were the Days," words and music by Gene Raskin, copyright © 1963 and 1968 by Essex Music, Inc., used by permission.

MusicMusicMusicInc. for portions of "The Ballad of the Green Berets" by Sgt. Barry Saddler and Robin Moore, copyright © 1963, 1964 and 1966 by MusicMusicMusicInc., used by permission.

From *The Films of Errol Flynn* by Tony Thomas, Rudy Belhmer and Clifford McCarty, reprinted by permission of Citadel Press, Inc., Secaucus, N.J.

From *The Memoirs of Hadrian* by Marguerite Yourcenar, copyright © 1954 by Marguerite Yourcenar, reprinted by permission of Farrar, Straus and Giroux, Inc.

SBN: 698-10602-4
Library of Congress Catalog Card Number: 74-79685

Printed in the United States of America

To
Henry and Virginia Woodhead

Friends
before and after this war

In Appreciation

A number of people provided the love and support, real money, food and lodging that kept me alive and well during the time I was writing this book. I am especially grateful to George Page; to my agents, David Stewart Hull and James Oliver Brown; and to Karlyn Barker, Mary Bauer, Fernando Casillas, Tom Corpora, Jerry Dilts, David Edwards, Ron Hollander, Dr. Sidney Isenberg, Christopher Isherwood, Raphael and Eugenie Jones, Lewis Lapham, Reynolds Price, Patricia Brehaut Soliman, Tom Timmons, Bill Wright, and, of course, to William.

Before Our Time

Last, and probably most important of all, was the feeling of vitality, of being in the heart of everything, of being a part of it—no mere onlooker, but a member of the team. . . .

I've written that war is not romantic when a person is in the midst of it. Nothing happened to change my feeling about that. But I will have to admit there was an exhilaration in it; an inner excitement that built up into a buoyant tenseness seldom achieved in peacetime.
—from Here Is Your War, *by Ernie Pyle, "America's Favorite Correspondent." (Copyright 1943, Henry Holt and Co.)*

Author's Note

Two of the Missing is a book of memories, dreams, and nightmares arranged in no particular chronology except as the author felt they best told the story. It is not meant to serve as a biography of any of the people involved in the story. It is a reminiscence; the author's attempt to figure out his own (and his friends') involvement in a complex moment of American history.

Two of the Missing

The Reasons Why

Those fuckers, I thought that night when I first heard the news. *They've finally done it—and what a fantastic story they're going to come out with.*

A friend at UPI called up to ask, "Hey, man, did you hear about Flynn and Stone?"

He might as well have been breaking the news that they had just won Pulitzer Prizes. For they had taken the war adventure that final step: they had been captured by the enemy and now they would be seeing it all from the other—far more interesting—side.

> PHNOM PENH, April 6, 1970 (AP)—Five newsmen, including two American photographers believed by other correspondents to be Sean Flynn and Dana Stone, have been reported captured by Viet Cong guerrillas operating in Cambodia.
>
> Flynn, 29, son of the late movie star, Errol Flynn, was free-lancing (on assignment for *Time* magazine) and Stone, 30, was on assignment for CBS News.
>
> All of the newsmen were reported captured by Vietnamese Communists along Route 1 near Chi Pou, close to the South Vietnamese border. Japanese correspondents said Cambodian farmers told military authorities that two Americans riding motorcycles were seized today by Vietnamese Communists just outside Chi Pou.

All of us had yearned for that same experience—always to survive with the story and pictures, of course—and we had worn black pajamas, Ho Chi Minh sandals made of tire treads, captured Viet Cong jungle hats and prized brass belt buckles with the

Communist star on them . . . just as we had once dressed up like the Indians and cowboys we admired. We had lived in open envy of those two women who had done it—Cathy LeRoy and her color pictures of Viet Cong soldiers in the battle in Hue; Michele Ray and her book about her days in captivity in the Mekong Delta.

And it had nothing to do with time or age. Richard Dudman —over fifty, bald, Washington correspondent for the respectable old St. Louis *Post-Dispatch*—has said of his capture in Cambodia and release later that year: "I felt elated at the prospect of getting my first look at the other side of a war I had been writing about for ten years. . . . 'If we get out of this alive,' I said, 'we'll have one hell of a story.' "

And Leo Dufrechou, a crewman on a B-24 bomber in World War II, who came to Arlington National Cemetery December 7, 1973, for a memorial service for five members of his squadron. The five had been missing for twenty-eight years when some Indian tribesmen found their remains in the mountainous jungle near the Burmese border. The old veteran confessed that what he felt when he first heard his friends were missing was not grief but envy. "I thought, 'Now, I've missed a chance to walk out with the others.' "

I, too, was envious of my friends. I was excited by the thought of the two of them riding off on bright red motorcycles—out front and beyond the other correspondents who were being led around on a government press tour of the village.

That night, I called up the old friends and laughed and reminisced about the good-gone times we had shared in Vietnam, the "happy childhoods we never had," as Mike Herr described it in an article about us published in *Esquire* the same week Flynn and Stone were captured. Ah yes, those fuckers, they were surely blowing the collective Cong minds that very night as the rest of us talked about them. Flynn and Stone had best represented the ultimate expression of what we had all come to find in the war. We would go to the edge of danger and often they would take another step to get a better picture—or for more complicated reasons we didn't examine at the time.

Every one of the "droogs" (one in our group had read *Clockwork Orange* and introduced the term without ever explaining it) and "brothers" I could reach that night shared my exhilaration. Flynn, we agreed, would have his captors entranced. He was 6'3", lean, handsome. "Looks like me, but better," his actor father said of him. We could picture a huddle of Viet Cong or Khmer Rouge soldiers around Flynn as he explained the different parts of his Swiss army knife or the workings of his expensive cameras. Behind the glamorous veneer, Flynn was a very professional photographer and cameraman. He had published pictures in *Time* and his news films had been used on CBS network television.

And Stone! He was called "Mini Grunt" by the Marines because of so much restless energy bound up in one tight little body. He was as tough and daring as any of the soldiers and he took more risks to get his pictures than most of the others in his profession. He, too, had become a talented television cameraman—in much the same way his persistence and curiosity made him competent in a dozen other areas. His films were used in the documentary, *Charlie Company*, which won the Peabody Award as well as an Emmy. Stone is a devilish 5'6" prankster who wore glasses, had sandy curly hair, and freckles. His deep-set serious eyes and the harsh lines of his face contrasted with his boyish poking, jabbing, gesturing. I laughed at the memory of the mornings he woke me up waving a lighted match over a trail of lighter fluid up the sheets to my nose. He would surely have the Communists laughing too; poking his thumb in some VC colonel's fried eggs or mashed potatoes. Surely they would love him just as we had when he pulled the same tricks on us. If anybody could survive, all friends agreed, Stone would.

I was so excited I couldn't sleep that night. At the time, I had a dreary job on the New York *Post*, so I wrote a story about my missing friends as I sat in my old tenement flat in New York's Hell's Kitchen, a rundown section between the theater district and the Hudson River. I called the story in for the first editions the next morning. Write a story and get drunk—it was the same reaction I had always had to dramatic events in the news that touched me. After President Kennedy's assassination, after my friends marched for civil rights and then for peace, I would write a story and get drunk. Only the sequence changed as I got older.

In that story about Flynn and Stone, I tried to describe the two of them, tried to explain how they had been the focus of that strangely meaningful experience Vietnam had been for so many of us—who since have been held together by the secrets of so vital an experience which nobody else seemed to care about.

I suppose I was also trying to say that I understood how my friends could get themselves into such a dangerous situation and that more than anything in the world, I wanted to be back there with them. I concluded my story by describing a wire service friend calling with each new dispatch from Cambodia that mentioned Flynn and Stone. "Listen, man," he said, "don't worry. . . ."

"Don't worry?" I laughed. "I wish to hell I were with them."

At first, the only news of Flynn and Stone was bad news. A friend in Phnom Penh wired this message about Stone's wife: POOR SMISER, SHE GETS ONLY SYMPATHY HERE. SUPPOSE YOU HEARD THE REPORT OF TWO CAUCASIANS FOUND TORTURED AND CRUCIFIED IN THE AREA. Reuters had moved a widely quoted message saying that these two bodies were believed to be those of Flynn and Stone. It turned out, instead, that they were two French priests who were executed in an ancient torture ceremony by the right-wing forces of the Cambodian government.

Stone had always called Louise by her surname, Smiser. It was his way of dubbing this plain-talking girl—who never weighed a hundred pounds and stood three inches shorter than he did—from a small Kentucky town as one of the fellows. What he required in a wife was more buddy than helpmate. He couldn't imagine the two of them would ever be "grown up."

"Poor Smiser," I was to learn, was quietly making direct contacts with the forces which had captured her husband. The day after they were taken, however, she still couldn't believe that Dana wouldn't be coming back after a few days (he always had). And, when some of his co-workers tried to go down to the area where he and Flynn disappeared, she stayed in her hotel in Phnom Penh because "if Dana's all right, he'd kill me for being so worried."

During the year since I left my friends in Vietnam, I developed a certain detachment about what I had witnessed during my time as a war correspondent. But, with the capture of Flynn and Stone, there was a new and personal connection—two of my friends were now somewhere out there where those bombs were killing people I had known before only through military statistics.

Flynn's former agent said his capture had everybody in Hollywood talking about the war for the first time. "You know," he said, "my friends and their children were smart enough to get out of going to the war. None of us ever really knew anybody out there; Sean is our only connection to those news stories."

Bob Hodierne had a similar reaction to Stone's capture. Hodierne is a young photographer and writer who dropped out of college in 1966 to go to Vietnam because he thought the war wouldn't last. He worked as a free-lance out of the UPI dormitory—one of a talented group that included Stone and many others. Then he returned home, finished college, only to be drafted and sent back to Vietnam, this time in uniform. He served thirteen months in growing disgust with the war and he arrived back in San Francisco on April 10, 1970, swearing to forget it all and go on to other things. But when he called his parents they told him that his friend Dana Stone had been captured four days before. "And now I am obsessed with the memories," Hodierne says. He has a recurring dream about running into Stone at a cocktail party in Minneapolis. Stone sloughs off Hodierne's questions about the capture (as he would in reality), says, "Ah, it was nothing"; he's been back in the States for six months already. And Hodierne wakes up another morning with the memories.

My own sleep had never been troubled by the memories of Vietnam. We had all dreaded our return "back to the world," but what we came back to face were not endless questions about "What was it really like." We came back to stark indifference about the central experience of our time. If anybody asked—just being polite—we learned to answer quickly so they could change the subject.

But, on the morning of October 2, 1971, I saw Flynn clearly in a dream. We had what seemed like a long conversation.

I was stumbling along, lost and alone in a foreign city. I could see light at the end of a dusty, narrow alleyway between two abandoned stone warehouses. I headed toward the light and some wide worn steps leading up to the top of an ancient stoa whose support arches had been patched up and filled in with bricks and concrete.

There was a paved walkway on top of the stoa and away at the far end of it, I could see the figure of Flynn. Even at such a distance, there was no mistaking him, although he stood in a slouch, his arms pulled down and back as if by shackles that embarrassed him. He wore the faded vestments that had been made for every member of our group by members of a pacifist religious sect whose island community we had visited south of Saigon.

Flynn could see me running toward him, up the steps and onto the walkway, but—typical of him—he did not shout a greeting. It was his ideal of a man's behavior, a daily kind of courage, "cool and detached, free from all physical excitement and impassive as the calm of a god," as a college friend of ours would describe him, quoting the Memoirs of Hadrian.

This classical setting I have fixed in my memory because I know that someday I will see it for the first time in reality and understand its significance in my life. The faint image of another figure seemed to stand between me and Flynn, but it disappeared as I moved toward him. Glancing back at the alley below, I could see it moving backward, apparently hurt and confused, into the darkness.

"Hey, howya doin', boy?" Flynn said, lightly mocking my Southern accent, with the widest possible grin, but without any sort of embrace, not even a handshake. It was reminscent of that last time I had seen him at the bar in Maurice's Hotel Constellation in Vientiane, Laos. After an absence of several months, he had merely grinned and said, "Howya doin', boy?" However calm the welcome, it felt good standing there beside him.

In the dream, Flynn asked about all the old friends. I went down the list—Jack and Mike and Page and Swanson and the others—telling him where each one was and what he was doing. Then I asked him about Stone because of a report that Dana was still alive in captivity, but that he had suffered severe abdominal wounds during the American bombing in Cambodia. This report came from an eccentric Dutch adventurer who emerged one day from captivity himself only to volunteer to return and find Flynn and Stone. According to him, Stone was laid up in a field hospital where the *medics did not have the medicines or the equipment needed to carry out complicated skin grafts.*

"Stone?" Flynn asked, a little puzzled by the question. Then, he laughed aloud as he rarely did. "Stone's all right. He just took a little gaff." He made it sound as if Stone had pulled another prank on his friends.

Flynn's mention of that word, "gaff," ended our conversation abruptly and woke me up. It was a word I had never used and I went to a dictionary, where I found some comfort in the definition: "Rough treatment, abuse." But not death.

I am convinced now, safely back in the world, that I might never have written anything about Vietnam if this hadn't happened to Flynn and Stone; if those two hadn't "gotten theirs" as we were fond of saying about someone who did not come back.

Now, I, too, am obsessed by the memories.

Pursuing an Old Romance

"He's crazy," my friends would whisper in explanation to others. The utter senselessness of going to Vietnam made it all the more poignant for my antiwar friends, all the more fun for me. "*'Perdu' encore*," said Mags, invoking my nickname from our summer in Paris, when I would wander off by myself. "For my own Pierre," she wrote in a paperback copy of *War and Peace* which I carried with me. "May he survive all his wars."

Then I had the actual tickets in my hands—Honolulu, Tokyo, Saigon, all those impossibly distant places now filled in quite neatly under my own name as passenger, who had never before been west of New Orleans. The agent who booked my flight also provided a twelve-page "itinerary." It was his way of sharing a young man's excitement on experiencing the place for the first time.

He wrote that he was very fond of Saigon:

> The Paris of the Orient, for all its faults and fiercely hot climate. War has left its inevitable hideous imprint, but the place is still extraordinarily colorful. There are still the early-morning flower markets, Chinese and Vietnamese pagodas, the lush botanical gardens, an amazingly well-filled zoo, and a national museum with an extraordinary collection of Oriental art. As in Paris, we had our main meal at noon (a two-hour ritual) and sometimes in the afternoon or early evening, a siesta. Aperitifs at a sidewalk café before or after, or a leisurely *cyclo-pousse* ride along the boulevards, watching the slender girls flying by, their baggy pantaloons flapping in the wind. . . .

Extraordinary! I thought. *As in Paris.* . . . I grinned at those around me on the flight; they would probably be getting off and going to their offices in San Francisco. I read over my itinerary once more, then plunged back into the ornate pink-cloth covers of Graham Greene's *The Quiet American,* which I was reading for the third time on my own flight to the setting of that romance. Never mind that all the great literature of war has pointed up its absurdity, the stories have also sustained the romance or at least our interest in experiencing it ourselves.

Kate Webb said she had me paged before we boarded the plane, but I would never have believed it if I had heard my own name called out in the huge Tokyo International Airport. She was one of my new co-workers at UPI, Saigon, a New Zealand girl who had been taking a vacation in Tokyo, her first days off in the ten months since she paid her own way from Australia to work at pittance wages as a UPI stringer writing war stories.

She was short, thin to the point of frailty, and she never talked above a whisper, but I was to learn that she—like me—was never more happy than when she was standing in filthy men's fatigues drinking beer and talking dirty with the fellows.

After flying some few hours in a world of clear blue sea and sky, we passed over the coastline of South Vietnam. I pressed my face into the little window, straining to find the war down there among the patches of brown and green. Kate smiled at my excitement, answering my naive questions with amused patience. She pointed out all the landmarks; I dutifully recorded them in my diary later that day. "The little fires are artillery," she says. "The vegetation is mostly gray from defoliation. The triangle-shaped forts along the roads were left from the French wars. The wide clearings along both sides of the roads are for 'protection.'"

Our flight circled wide and low then eased smoothly onto the runway. Except for acres of warplanes, there was nothing extraordinary about the place. UPI had sent out a special Vietnamese employee with connections to usher us through customs. Then we piled into an open "mini-moke" that wasn't even a jeep, but more like a beach buggy. It fitted our mood as we set off laughing, legs dangling out the open sides. We passed the headquarters compound of the Military Assistance Command Vietnam ("Mac-V," sometimes called "Pentagon East"), a low complex of nondescript, cream-colored buildings I would never have noticed except for the high fences, barbed wire, and armed American MP's at the gates. At the edge of the airbase, we passed two American billboards: WELCOME TO SUNNY SAIGON/PAN AMERICAN and, IN SAIGON, TOO, YOU HAVE A FRIEND AT CHASE MANHATTAN. Then we moved into a confusion of military trucks and jeeps plodding through a million—by official count—Hondas, and thousands and thousands of antique black Citroen sedans and tiny blue and yellow Peugeot taxis left by the French.

The traffic was maddening even on a normal day, but I was told that the city was in the midst of Tet, and everybody was off work, out for a joyride, buying up firecrackers and noisemakers and party groceries. (More diary notes from that day: "Tet streamers are stretched across every block of every street and hordes of youngsters are happily running and shouting in the noise of millions of firecrackers exploding.") The first time I heard a "barrage" of firecrackers, I grabbed the sides of our beach buggy and prepared to leap for cover. Kate Webb whooped with laughter at the nervous new recruit.

Here I had tensed myself for the terrors of war—a quick landing under fire, a mad dash for cover—only to land smack in the middle of the gayest carnival I had ever known. The shock couldn't have been greater if I had arrived at the house of a happy group of friends only to find their bloody corpses splattered about the party room. Whenever anybody asks me what it was really like in Vietnam, I recall my first exposure to the place and smile. What was it like? It was a carnival.

The Vietnamese carnival of Tet was centered on New Year's Day in the Chinese lunar calendar. Of course, most of the Vietnamese are not Chinese. They use the Western calendar and theirs is a history of fighting off the armies from the North. But the Vietnamese also celebrate Christmas with equal fervor even though only 20 per cent of them are Christians.

With their history of hard times, the Vietnamese are not about to offend anybody's god, and they seem inclined to adopt any excuse for a festival. Vietnam is the California of the Orient, where the Eastern cultures run up against the sea and where they have existed in varying degrees of war and bickering—never at peace. Now, the people are mostly Buddhist, but the land was once ruled by Hindus, some of whom became Moslems; and then the Christian missionaries arrived 300 years ago. Even the most modern intellectuals in Vietnam are still influenced by the teachings of Confucius and by the *I Ching* and the Yin Yang. The mountain tribes hold to animism. And in the 1930's, new religions sprang up incorporating all the others with Churchill, Shakespeare, Victor Hugo, and various other Western "saints" included for good measure.

It became a worthy carnival, indeed, when the United States added to the confusion several hundred thousand military men and civilian construction workers, hundreds of newsmen.

Never in my life had I seen or imagined a place so fantastic as Saigon at that moment. There was the clatter and confusion of the Orient, the decadent beauty of the French colonial days. There were stucco villas set in tropical gardens along tree-lined boulevards. More and more of the trees had to be cut down to accommodate the military traffic going to the airport and the docks. There had once been open countryside between the French city of Saigon and the older Chinese city of Cholon, and also along the road to the airport. But the French and then the Americans built an urban sprawl of cheap apartment buildings with hundreds of shacks used as massage parlors and bars thrown in between by the Vietnamese.

We turned left at the enormous Presidential Palace, a glittering white modern American building set in grounds covering several square blocks. We came in behind the cathedral of Our Lady, a red-brick monstrosity that was always there to remind us of those who had preceded us in failing to "save" the Vietnamese. Stretching ten city blocks from the cathedral to the Saigon River was Tu Do Street, the old Rue Catinat, the axis of the city's nightlife. Here were the two hotels where most correspondents lived and had their offices. Here was the Vietnamese National Press Center and the old opera house that had become the "National Assembly" and in between were blocks and blocks of bars fully stocked with numbered girls in white tea frocks.

On a little street off Tu Do, a half-block from the river, UPI's Saigon offices were located in a narrow four-story building, adjacent to the Melody Bar. With all government offices closed for the holidays, it was a quiet afternoon in the office and it looked—the same old desks and typewriters that barely worked—like UPI offices everywhere. As much as I came to detest that office and that company for professional reasons, I realize it was my only possible connection to the war and the circle of friends I met there. Through UPI, I met Flynn and Stone and countless others now so significant in my memories.

UPI provided us a vehicle for witnessing the war which in turn gave us—as Malcolm Cowley has written of the "World War I generation"—"shares, as it were, in a rich fund of common emotions." UPI was to us what the ambulance corps had been to them. And nobody ever questioned their motivation or faulted them for not wanting to be ambulance drivers after the war.

Outside the UPI office, the noise got louder toward nightfall as people kept setting off more and more strings of firecrackers hung from the rooftops down to the sidewalks. My Tet was in January, 1968, but the scene was little different on that day in January, 1966, when Sean Flynn arrived in Saigon in similar confusion, carrying two suitcases, a suit, an attaché case, a camera, and a tennis racket.

Somebody in Paris had given Flynn the address of a hotel, apparently as a joke. He told the address to the taxi driver at the airport, who looked at Flynn rather strangely, but he drove him to the place anyhow. Flynn got out and beheld a gaping hole in a wreck of a building which had been the Metropole Hotel—destroyed in a recent terrorist action. The taxi driver weaved through the Tet celebrants to another hotel, where he found Flynn a little closet of a room with no windows and many cockroaches. The room was cheap at $11 a day; rates in the other hotels had risen to $20 and $30 a day with the influx of American dollars.

After he checked in, Flynn strolled around the city. But his sightseeing efforts were frustrated by the revelers. Soldiers were setting off firecrackers in tin cans for extra volume in the bars and restaurants, and there were constant barrages all around him. He said he was "expecting to be assassinated at any minute," and so he returned to the quiet of his room "to regain my spirits," and to pass the time killing his insect roommates with a rolled up newspaper.

After a couple of days, the city went back to work, back to the business of war. Flynn made the rounds of the government offices to get himself accredited as a correspondent authorized to travel with American and South Vietnamese troops. The formalities seemed endless to him. He said he was as "lost in the war as I had been lost in the city."

However, Flynn's own name was his best introduction. Also, he had a letter from the editors of *Paris-Match* saying they would accept his stories and photographs. Flynn had never worked as a photographer before, although he had bought a Leica camera from "some guy on the black market in Spain." He said he flattered himself that his knowledge of French (the second language of most Vietnamese) would give him an edge on the American correspondents. Later, he said he knew the real reason *Paris-Match* had given him the letter was that they wanted a story about " Sean Flynn, son of Errol Flynn, in Vietnam."

But Flynn and I (with my UPI connection) had it easy compared to Dana Stone in his effort to get accredited after he arrived in May, 1966. He wrote his parents that "neither the Vietnamese nor the Americans wanted me here and I am very lucky to have gotten my papers at all."

Stone spent days "being sent to another office on the other side of the city because 'whoever sent you here misinformed you.' " He said he had signed twenty different documents "saying it's no one's fault but mine if I'm shot or crashed or hurt by the revolving door in the press room."

Nobody had ever heard of him or of *The Valley News*, the newspaper in Vermont which—according to his letters—had sent him to Vietnam. "I didn't meet the requirements for nothing," said Dana. The Vietnamese wanted him to get an agency to sign that they would be financially responsible for him, but Stone somehow got around that. "I think they figured that I really couldn't be here on my own," he said, and "also I took a picture of the official who gave my case a final ruling and this pleased him all to hell."

His letter from *The Valley News* was fine for the Vietnamese officials, Dana said. "They couldn't read the English too well so I had to tell them what the letter said." He informed them his paper was "same-same" New York *Times*. But the U.S. Army officers threatened to block his visa and send him packing home. After much time and talk, he found a sympathetic Army colonel. The colonel agreed with him that there was "no background for combat photography" and suddenly Dana Stone was authorized by the U.S. and Vietnamese military commands to go out and do it for the first time.

Flynn Goes to War

With his press cards in hand, Flynn decked himself out for battle—jungle boots and fatigues tailored to look just right and two live hand grenades ready to throw. He walked into the offices of *Time* magazine to see if he could sell some pictures of an upcoming operation. The bureau chief took one look at those grenades (their safety pins untaped) hooked onto Flynn's web gear, and let out a yell. *What in the hell did Flynn think he was going to do with those?*

"Well, if I'm in the field and I have to jump into a hole in an emergency, I'll throw one of these in first," Flynn explained. The bureau chief exploded. "This is not the goddamn field. This is Saigon, doctor. Get out of here." Somewhat confused about the role he had come to play, Flynn walked out the door.

While I trust this account of the scene—given me by a reporter who was sitting there—it was very out of character for that bureau chief to order Flynn out of his office. He and a number of his successors came to admire Flynn and to seek his company. I think that Flynn—as his father said of himself—brought a dash of color into their routine lives of briefings and deadlines.

At UPI, Flynn got a much more cordial response. Probably nobody there even noticed the grenades and, if they had, they wouldn't have complained. The bureau chief kept pistols in the desk drawers when I worked there and the company hired a number of—usually armed—stringers who also sold their information to the CIA. Like the CIA itself, UPI would buy pictures and information from anything that walked in off the street. Some of these were the most talented, sensitive people I've ever known; others were clearly dangerous.

The soundtrack for our war movie was provided by the Armed Forces Viet Nam radio rock programs. No matter how remote the place or how tense the situation, we were never out of earshot of a favorite hipster disc jockey who would often dedicate the latest sounds from back home "To all you guys out there groovin' on the danger."

Flynn would always warn us—as a reason for staying in Vietnam—that you couldn't go on a combat assault in New York City. He meant there was no thrill "back in the world" to compare with what we felt every time we got into a helicopter to be dropped into combat. There was something very special about helicopters—like flying in a motorcycle. The ride gave you the same near-sexual thrill, with all that noise overwhelming any attempt at conversation and with the wind blowing in the open doors as you sped along. You could imagine it was your own body doing it—that those whirring blades extended from the depths of your own brain. Never will I experience the same sort of childlike exhilaration I felt riding in an open helicopter gunship in Vietnam, skimming the tops of trees in the jungles, making like a powerboat leaving a wake in a narrow river, speeding inches off the ground straight down an abandoned railroad track like an oldtime choo-choo train. The pilots would always try to scare us, knowing we loved every minute of it.

A medical evacuation ("medevac") chopper dropped Flynn into the midst of his first firefight. He said there was a dreadful noise, with bullets whizzing all around him, "mowing down the foliage of the trees, mowing down the men" beside him.

An American soldier was standing on his left, firing his rifle; Flynn stood there taking pictures "like a tourist on the Place de la Concorde." Then there was a deafening explosion in the palm tree over his head. His companion had been hit and fell dead beside him.

Flynn had imagined that the war was always a pitched battle like this one, but he was told the action he saw in "Operation Masher" was the heaviest combat in the war up to that time. He stayed in the field for nearly a week and the military vocabulary of initials and cursewords began to replace the language of Paris and the Riviera. He returned to Saigon to swim at the Cercle Sportif and recuperate.

On March 6, two months after he arrived in Vietnam, Flynn was wounded during a sweep through a Michelin rubber plantation. Suddenly, he said, "the whole world" opened fire around him. There was an explosion near him and he fell. Sittting up, he saw the blood oozing through his fatigue pants and felt the wound in his left knee. Because of the trees, there was no way for a helicopter to land to fly Flynn out for treatment. He was forced to walk on the wounded leg for the rest of the day. Never in his life, he said, had he suffered so much. Back in Saigon, a surgeon told him he would be laid up for two months if he had an operation on his knee. So Flynn decided against the operation and spent only three weeks recuperating. The doctor told him that when he was seventy years old he would be able to predict the changing weather by his knee.

Flynn's friend, the actor George Hamilton, was visiting Lynda Bird Johnson in the White House that night and they used the President's emergency lines to make sure Flynn was all right. His mother had her friend, the actor Senator George Murphy, get more details through his contacts.

During this rest period in Saigon, Flynn made friends with a young Special Forces sergeant who told him he could come along on an operation to insert a unit in a contested area. There were twelve American soldiers, two companies of Nungs (Chinese mercenaries), and Flynn. The Special Forces were very particular about the people they let come along on their missions and they insisted that newsmen carry weapons because "we don't want any liabilities."

The miles and miles of walking through jungles reminded Flynn of Africa. The whole expedition was "like a hunt," he said. "Perhaps it was childish," he explained, but he was caught up in the spirit of the hunt and also with a new fascination for the different kinds of weapons.

He said he became an expert in the use of the weapons they carried on that patrol. He was assigned to carry mortars and a machine gun. At the beginning of the march, the officers had put Flynn in the middle of the column for his own protection. Then, when the brief but violent encounter with the enemy took place, they knocked Flynn to the ground. "I was furious," he said. "I couldn't see anything."

In his first war story for UPI, Flynn told about being with the

Green Berets and Nungs, whom he described as "Chinese mercenaries who wear the skull and crossbones on their sleeves and who hate, really hate, the Viet Cong." They were weaving their way through a bamboo thicket, he said, when they spotted a boy running away from them. They yelled and shot over his head, but the boy kept running. Finally, they ran him down and tried in vain to get information out of him.

Later they captured the boy's father, although the two denied any relationship. Flynn said the American adviser told them to try some "psychological warfare" on the boy. They led his father off to a distance out of sight and told the boy they were going to shoot the father if the boy didn't talk.

"The jungle was silent. The boy looked up with a sneer. The Americans, his expression said, had been bluffing," Flynn said. "Then a rifle shot broke the silence. The boy gasped. He began to cry. The Green Beret let him cry awhile, then asked, did he want to talk now?

" 'No,' said the boy. He was tied up and carried off to the district center for incarceration."

In the same story, Flynn described another civilian, an old man whom they caught without any identity papers, which the Americans considered just cause for interrogation as a Viet Cong. The Green Berets and the Nungs tied the man's feet and strung him up to a tree limb upside down. After fifteen minutes in that position, Flynn said, the old man "confessed" he was the sniper who had fired into a nearby marketplace the day before, killing a baby.

The extraordinary thing about this was that Flynn took pictures of both episodes he described. UPI sent the pictures over its wires worldwide and, as far as I can determine, this was the first time an American photographer had taken pictures of prisoners being tortured in Vietnam.

The Son of Captain Blood

He was Ivanhoe and Don Juan and Jeb Stuart and Captain Blood and General Custer and Robin Hood and Major Vickers and Captain Courtney and Lieutenant Douglas Lee and Flight Lieutenant Terence Forbes and Major Nelson and Gentleman Jim Corbett.

As Jack Warner said of him, "He was all the heroes in one magnificent, sexy, animal package." He was a fantasy figure to at least two generations of Americans, but he was the real father of my friend, Sean Flynn.

You could not look at Sean without thinking of his father. It was not just that his father was who he was, but that the son grew up in his precise physical image.

Strangely, the one thing Sean's friends could never allow him to be was the one thing he most certainly, inescapably had been since birth. I mean, quite simply, he was his father's son. I think we were all needlessly embarrassed for Flynn about his parentage. His father was such a confused and contradictory (his own words about himself) personality for anybody to be born to, but his son's acquaintances tended to ignore all the potential of their relationship.

Sean was not consistent in his own talk about his father. In one interview he said, "You know any father can have a son, but not many can be friends. Dad and I were friends. We didn't see a lot of each other, but I liked his zest for life." In another, he said, "That's all dead and buried and I want to forget it. I never saw any of Flynn's pictures—certainly not *Captain Blood*, which I'm told was a lot of junk . . . . Flynn means nothing to me. I'm me and I don't want people to keep dragging up his name. I'm not particularly proud ot it. . . . We weren't very good friends."

If Sean was confused and embittered about his relationship with his father, perhaps it was the same age-old grief we have all felt about our fathers: that we could not have known them better.

The elder Flynn wrote a pathetic conclusion to his life in the last chapter of his autobiography, *My Wicked, Wicked Ways,* published posthumously. I repeat it here because his son was to pick up the same chase and follow his father, adventure after adventure, until he reached the war.

Errol Flynn wrote, "My father has not been Theodore Flynn, exactly, but a will-o'-the-wisp just beyond, whom I have chased and hunted to see him smile upon me, and I shall never find my true father, for the father I wanted to find was what I might become, but this shall never be, because inside of me there is a young man of New Guinea, who had other things in mind for himself besides achieving phallic symbolism in human form."

He had been "hoaxed by life," Errol Flynn said, but it was surely not life and the various options it opens to all of us, but Hollywood—and his acceptance of the money and fame it offered—that had perpetrated the hoax. It started even with his name and national origin. He was immediately dubbed the "Irish" swashbuckler by the publicity agents, when, in fact, both his parents were native Australians and he was born in Hobart, Tasmania.

It seems that Errol was even passing along the hoax by giving his son an Irish first name and his own second name, which he had dropped because it was for an uncle, Leslie, whom he despised.

Errol met Sean's mother, the French actress Lili Damita, on a boat to America in 1934. He was seeking a $75 a week studio job and she was already "a much beeger star." In her fourteen movies, she had played opposite most of the leading men of her day and her films included *The Bridge of San Luis Rey.* The handsome young Australian pursued and won the famous French sexpot, whom he described as one of the most beautiful women in the world at that time. Theirs was an explosive, often violent marriage, which only enlivened the legend growing up around the star of *Captain Blood* in 1935, and then of a succession of swashbucklers. Once, Lili broke a champagne bottle over his head when he showed up late for their anniversary party; he hit her in the mouth with his fist. Both were hospitalized.

With the success of his movies, Errol was able to build his own bachelor house up on Mulholland Drive overlooking Hollywood. Its most notorious feature was the double mirror over his own bed. He also equipped it with tennis courts and a cockfighting arena. He wrote that Lili was never allowed in the house. After seven years of marriage, she summoned him over to her place one day to tell him they would have a child. He and Lili made several appearances together during her pregnancy for publicity pictures and then they were shown with the baby, smiling for the cameras.

These were among the incidental facts about his parents which Sean and everybody else could have read in his father's autobiography. "Poor Sean, I just felt so sorry for him that summer," one of his teachers told me. "He came home and went to the Coral Beach Club and everybody was in their cabanas reading that book in which his father said such awful things about his mother."

Errol wrote: "On May 10 [the date is listed as May 31 in all other records of Sean], 1941, my son Sean was born. As it happens, Sean and I were destined to become close pals. . . . Out of this impossible snarl of two volatile people there came something good anyway."

Sean was not a year old before his mother began litigation for a divorce. She never made another movie after she married Errol.

As a child, Sean apparently did spend some time around his father's house. There are a number of photographs of him there with his father's two daughters by his second wife. Errol would stage circuses for the children and once he had a helicopter pick him up at home for the children's amusement. The house must have been a wildly exciting place for a little boy to visit and call home. His daddy's pals were not only some colorful characters from Australia but also included the liveliest actors in Hollywood during its most important years. "I always like men about me," Errol Flynn said, "roisterers, fun guys, rompers. . . . For some kinds of fun the friendship that two men can have or a gang of fellows can have simply can't be beat." I have often thought that maybe we were re-creating this group with our group in Saigon. But I think the origins are much further back—perhaps it is that man is by nature a hunter who prefers the company of his fellows, even when there is no hunt or war.

Vietnam Is the Place to Be

Dana Stone arrived in Saigon about a week after Flynn's Green Beret torture story appeared. I'm sure everybody in the office was still talking about the pictures, which caused a small controversy in the States. Nobody could have been as surprised by that as Flynn himself. It was, after all, his first experience from the inside of the news business.

At that stage I don't think he would have done anything to deliberately embarrass his military hosts. Stone would still be teasing him about his transgression years after this. It wasn't that either was political enough to support their hosts, but both came to have a certain feeling for those who were providing the free helicopter rides and the combat show itself. When the time came to be antiwar, they wouldn't see any sense in choosing sides. Traveling with the North Vietnamese troops, they would have taken the same pictures.

Stone also took photographs of Americans torturing prisoners when he first arrived. Some of these he sent to Louise Smiser, who was then living in Spain. I was not able to find out about Stone's first combat experience, but he did tell Louise that it was bloody and terrifying. Knowing him, I can imagine he pushed himself into the very worst of war that could be seen. On their honeymoon, he told Louise he would have left Vietnam after his first impressions of men killing men at close range. But he simply did not have the money.

After he was in the war awhile, he developed a philosophy about photographing everything that happened in front of his eyes. He said once he had seen four men executed "right in front of me. Really stupid. Really stupid. I could have taken pictures; I don't know. I didn't. I was glad I didn't. I wouldn't have used them anyway."

He explained that the GIs, especially the Marines, were all "prim and proper" until they got to know an outside newsman. Then, he said, "You get pet units you keep going back to and they know they can trust you. . . . A lot of the press people, mostly the writer guys, have this philosophy. They're always saying, 'Report everything.' But the guys that are hollerin' this come up with the worst distortions and make the most compromises in the long run." He knew that in the long run he would see more and get better pictures by not offending the unit on his first encounter. He also felt that his presence often kept the GIs from abusing the Vietnamese civilians, especially those stopped for questioning as Viet Cong.

Once, Dana was on a "search and destroy" mission with an American unit which had rounded up a number of Viet Cong suspects. A young American interrogator was openly abusing a Vietnamese woman he was questioning. The woman had her hands tied behind her back and was squatting. The interrogator was also squatting, facing her with his questions and holding a big stick he intended to use on her. Dana watched the interrogator hit the woman with a rock, then he sauntered over in photo range and squatted down with his cameras ready. The interrogator stopped his abuse and the woman was led away to a group of other detainees.

The photo chief for UPI in Saigon when Stone arrived was Dirck Halstead, himself only a few years older than the free-lance photographers whom he paid $10 and $20 each for combat pictures. Bob Hodierne, who was twenty-one when he arrived at UPI's offices just after Dana arrived, says Halstead treated the young photographers with style. He made them feel they were part of a romantic tradition of war photography. He also gave them free beds upstairs in the UPI dormitory. Nearly all the young photographers had read an interview of Halstead in a photography magazine which they remembered (he denies the wording) as saying: "Vietnam is the place to be if you're young and hungry and want to be rich and famous." Dana would always use that line—sarcastically—to explain why he was in Vietnam.

These young photographers had a great deal of competitive spirit.

They would joke that you should never go into combat alone, because if you got hit there would be nobody to take your picture. Another joke involved one young photographer telling about his best buddy's getting hit and dying at his feet. And what did you do? "I gave him two hundred fiftieth of a second at F/11." And, of course, they joked about it, but it actually happened: a photographer's dying words were, "Get my film back to Saigon."

From the beginning, Dana Stone stood out among these young free-lancers. He was more persistent and aggressive, competing not so much with them as with himself. He quickly established himself as one serious about the craft and he became one of the best. Halstead believes Stone was one of the very first photographers to come back with actual combat pictures—that is, pictures taken during the heat of combat, rather than after-action shots of the wounded being carried off.

In July, three months after he arrived, Stone wrote his parents: "My opinion of my progress varies from hour to hour. The damn war has been slow this month and I've not done well—but yesterday I was told that I had won 3rd prize in UPI's monthly picture contest. All of UPI, not just here in Vietnam—tho my prize was only $25 the recognition has done much for my uncertain ego—now I'm certain that I'm as fine a photographer as I suspected I was all along. . . ."

After his early success, Stone was presented a new camera by UPI. The only problem was he didn't know how to change the film and he was too proud to ask. Finally, he was out in the field with Henri Huet—a gentle French-Vietnamese photographer who won the Pulitzer Prize and was killed in action in 1971. Huet worked for the opposition, the Associated Press, but Dana finally had to ask him for help. Stone never forgot that embarrassing moment because Huet was very helpful and never teased him about it afterward.

Huet also gave Dana some advice about combat photography which he passed on to Hodierne and other young photographers who later asked him what to do. This was: Never just stand up and start shooting pictures in combat; always wait until you can see a good shot and then go after it. Stone also told Hodierne that if he ever stopped to help somebody wounded in the field, he should always use their battle dressing. That way, he would still have his dressing if he got wounded later. He gave the same advice to his parents in a tape to them: "So always be sure you carry a battle dressing when you go out in the field. . . ."

One afternoon, Hodierne and Stone were out with a patrol of the 1st Air Cavalry Division. Two men were hit near Hodierne. One died and the other was yelling in pain. Hodierne was afraid the noise would bring in more fire from the enemy, so he spent a half hour treating the man and then the rest of the afternoon carrying him along to a safe place. Stone, meanwhile, was shooting pictures which he later sold. He told Hodierne that you had to develop a feeling you weren't really there, that you were not an influence on the scene. You were just an observer. Hodierne says, "Stone slipped some of the time, too, but by and large, he was a pretty disciplined objective witness to what was going on around him."

Military Training

Because the course of the war seemed uncertain in late 1965, there was a feeling that the Army Reserves might never be needed. And, for a brief time, a new program to give us our basic training on weekends and during summer camp replaced the old system of calling reserves up for six-months' active duty. With the call for more and more combat troops in Vietnam, however, all this had changed by the end of 1966 and, almost a year after I signed up, I was finally called to active duty for basic training at Fort Benning, Georgia.

LETTERS FROM CAMP

Fort Benning (no date)—and so we were herded onto the cattle trucks and then blindly out to Malone Range No. 19, "Infiltration." Marched off the trucks and bunched into straight lines. "Cover down, goddammit."

The sergeant welcomes us on behalf of his staff and gives us a detailed explanation of the course, its purpose, and how it compares to actual combat conditions. He says the machine guns—five of them firing at about four feet across the field we will crawl—will be using live ammo and he has them fire and sets off two or three charges of TNT for theatrics.

We are to crawl the course "dry" (it is four or five inches deep in rainwater) and then wait till it gets dark to crawl it again so we can see the bright red flares that trace so many rounds of machine gun fire. Right face, column of two's from the left. I am about number 500—with my last name—as we march around into the trenches. The movement is mechanical with me now, and I was marching right like the others, 1, 2, 3, 4, and all that.

The loudspeakers blare then, and trooper Young cracks up (on the inside). They are playing an LP of German drinking songs I heard that time in Munich talking with a guy whose father was in the Nazi army. He was proudly showing me pictures of his old man in uniform and translating all the songs I was hearing now blaring out across Malone Range No. 19 as we prepared to make like war.

The dry run proves to be anything but that as I plop across the first wall and splat into a mud puddle that stretches the length of the entire course. It also covers trooper Young, in precise military crawling position, and his weapon—which must never, ever be submerged. Under, over, plosh, groan, "Get yo ass down, sojer," and I am past the machine guns with blue knees and elbows and herded up the road, muddy and cold now the wind is blowing. Chow down. "Eat it now, chew it later."

Then we are marched back into the trenches to wait for darkness; as the loudspeakers blare that drunk and happy music. I asked one of the guys why you reckon they played the music—which reminds me, in that floodlit surreal setting of war, of the execution ("Hark the Herald Angels Sing") in *The Victors*. He said it's to calm us down because a lot of guys used to go berserk and stand up and say, "Shoot me and get it over with, goddammit."

Fort Benning (no date)—My sergeant here is an interesting guy from a backwoods Kentucky town—plain talking, he says we were all standing on a streetcorner, hair down to our knees, no socks, sandals, before we came in and the only thing we have to be sore about is the splinters in our ass from being dragged off the front porch. I heard today he's volunteered for Vietnam and will leave in January.

I have a thing to tell you about the sergeant's attitude on Vietnam. Like, we've received no propaganda at all in support of that war—just the warning that we should take this training seriously because we might go there. One sergeant veteran said the other day: "You'll find out when you get out there, it's either you or him. If you don't get him, he's damn sure gonna get you. He may not believe in the cause either."

A boy who went to the same basic training camp in 1968, when there were more than half a million American soldiers in Vietnam, told me all this had changed by then. There was constant talk about the war as a noble effort, and when the trainees did their morning run, they sang out in cadence:

> I wanta be an Airborne Ranger;
> I wanta go to Vietnam
> I wanta life of sex and danger;
> I wanta kill the Viet Cong.

Fort Gordon Military Police School, Jan. 29, 1967—Most of the guys around me will go directly to Vietnam. Of 240 graduated in an adjacent company Saturday, 200 went to Vietnam. Gives everything a different air.

Fort Gordon—Notes from today's class on vice control: Sgt. says a little boy walks past his parents' bedroom, looks in at them and says, "And they send me to a psychiatrist cause I suck my thumb." He also said Vietnam ain't so bad: they was only 38 killed there Labor Day last year and they was 675 killed on the highways of the U.S. that day. Also this: a Yankee woman says, "You come," a Southern woman says, "You-all come." Call me cop-face.

Fort Gordon—did I pass along this graffiti, scrawled in every john in the classrooms used only by MP's at Fort Gordon? "LBJ, LBJ, How many kids did you kill today?" "Burn pot, not people," and "FTA," which is everywhere and we all know it means: "Fuck the Army."

Fort Gordon—Chanting this one out in cadence as we march across Fort Gordon to "police the area," which is what the Army calls picking up cigarette butts. "Three more days and we'll be home/Drinking beer with lots of foam/Three more weeks and Vietnam/Playing games with Viet Cong."

The following is taken from my notebooks which I saved from the only course we were ever given about Vietnam. The laughter began when the sergeant deliberately mispronounced "guerrilla" as "gorilla." He was a genial veteran of the war who had already volunteered to go back. It was a fun class which promised a fun war.

CHARACTERISTICS OF A GUERRILLA FORCE (slide)
Sgt.—To break it down simply: counter-gorilla warfare is gorilla warfare against the gorillas. Awrite now class, to establish a gorilla force, you first must have what?
Pvt.—Gorillas.
Sgt.—Right. What else?
Pvt.—Equipment. Leaders. Bananas.
HISTORY OF GUERRILLA WARFARE (slide)
Sgt.—Okay, first there was the caveman and then the Indians.

They lived off the land, had their own communications, and made their own weapons. And then Teddy Roosevelt went where?

Pvt.—Cuba.

Sgt.—Right—and that's what he did was gorilla warfare. We learned it from the Indians and then Teddy beat 'em down with it and that's why we're here today.

CIVILIAN SUPPORT

1—Those friendly to the Resistance Movement.

2—Those forced to support it through fear or through coercion.

Sgt.—Awrite, class, now cohersion. That's like if you said I'm gonna cut your mother's ears off if you don't fight. What you gonna do? You gonna fight to protect your mother's ears, right?

Sgt.—So old Charlie comes along saying, "We're gonna burn your little hut down and take your rice." This would have a tendency to make you want to fight. They could draft you. They come along and say, "Well, you're eighteen." And you'd say, "Well, I don't know." Did you realize that Charlie is sometimes only fourteen or fifteen?

Pvt.—Well, sergeant, I mean, I'm only nineteen and they can put me there just as easy as they do him. I mean, it's not like the two of us just starting this thing.

Sgt.—How else can the gorillas get support?

Pvt.—They could pay 'em money. Red China's sendin' 'em arms and money.

Sgt.—Yeah, that's right. We're doin' it too.

Pvt.—Some people'd do anything for money.

Pvt.—Do it ever night.

Sgt.—Yeah. Bend over.

(A question of Sergeant Sikes, who has also been there.)

Pvt.—I heard they was superstitious.

Pvt.—I heard if you got a ace of spades they won't kill you.

Sgt. Sikes—No, cows is the only thing that's sacred cause they don't want you killing off their grandaddies.

Pvt.—What's the biggest problem you ever run into in Vietnam?

Sgt. Sikes—Wimmen.

PROPAGANDA

Sgt. Propaganda is when they show a VC struggling in with rice for the village; and when we fly over with leaflets showing a GI rocking a baby. Course, we don't show him with his hand on the mother's ass. And these stupid ignernt people who don't know how to do nothing but dig in their rice fields, they're gonna believe what we tell 'em.

COMMAND/DISCIPLINE/MORALE

Sgt.—Now, class, what do y'all think this means for the gorillas?

Pvt.—It means you follow me or I'll skin you alive.

Sgt.—Yeah. We'll cut yer pecker off and stick it in yer mouth if you don't behave. Some of you may like that though, right?

Sgt. (quieting laughter)—Now, you punks going to Vietnam better listen to this shit; you're going to need it.

When I arrived in Vietnam, less than a year after this class, the first Americans I saw killed were military policemen shot during the 1968 Tet Offensive in Saigon. I checked with their units and found that most of them had been at Fort Gordon when I was; perhaps they'd had this same fun class.

As for Dana Stone's military background, it ended before its time and with Dana's usual touch of irony and humor. He had surely joined the Navy with some romantic notion of sailing in and out of the world's exotic ports. What he found was day after day of tedious make-work assignments that became more and more frustrating. He would polish the brass and then be told to polish it again. The only exciting moment in his career was when the ship he was on left port with a mysterious destination none of the the low-ranking seamen knew about. There were wild rumors they were sailing toward Cuba as support for an invasion force. But Dana said he didn't believe any of the talk until they were actually there and pulling survivors of the Bay of Pigs out of the water.

Although he had worked for a summer on ships on the Great Lakes, Dana developed a violent form of seasickness in the Navy. To emphasize the seriousness of his illness, he once vomited on the head of an officer coming up a ladder. The Navy finally put him in a hospital near Boston where he could be studied in a continuing program to find a cure for seasickness in the Navy.

Dana lived generally as an outpatient while they ran their experiments on him. He liked the work he was assigned to do in the laboratories. He also liked talking with the more educated doctors and researchers. After months of testing him, the doctors found Dana had a heart murmur. Dana had known about this before he entered the Navy. But the doctors thought their tests had caused it. They offered him the choice of an early out or a pension for the rest of his life if he finished his three years. Dana kept quiet about his medical history, took his discharge papers and went home.

Sean Flynn got his draft notice after he was living in Europe. During a long drive to the designated Army examination center, he twisted his back. He complained about his sore back to the doctor examining him. This was before the escalation of the war had increased the demand for draftees. So the sympathetic doctor smiled and said. "You don't really want to go in, do you?"

Flynn said no and the doctor put through his medical deferment.

More Marine Than He Is

After so much time in the field, Dana Stone became a recognized authority on survival and military tactics. When he was out with a patrol, a platoon, or even a company, he wouldn't besitate to let a commander know if he thought he was making a wrong move that could endanger the unit—and Dana Stone. Many of the young commanders had just arrived in the war and most would have only two or three real combat experiences during their thirteen-month tours, whereas Dana Stone went from one action to another.

Once, he was with a unit hiking along the edge of a shallow river. Stone kept telling the commander that somebody had just been in the area and maybe they were still around. But the officer ignored him and prepared to camp for the night. Stone walked back along the river on his own search mission. A North Vietnamese soldier, in full battle gear, jumped out of the water right in front of him. He'd been hiding underwater and had run out of breath. He surrendered, even though Stone was armed only with his cameras. Stone shot his picture and yelled for help. When they searched the area, they found several other enemy soldiers. Dana always felt he should have been allowed to keep the one he found.

Another time, Stone was with an armored unit operating near the demilitarized zone—in close range of artillery in North Vietnam. The lead vehicle hit a mine and its wreckage blocked the entire convoy for the night. The young commander didn't seem to know what to do. Dana Stone did. He ordered you-and-you-and-you to set up a perimeter; others to install claymore mines around them. The commander, probably relieved Stone had taken charge, never said a word.

In a letter to his parents, Stone mentioned a particular Marine officer who "knows better than to try to make a Marine out of me because he knows I already consider myself to be a lot more Marine than he is."

But, in a tape home, he said, "I don't know. I don't think huntin' will be much fun anymore. Sure like to see some of these sporty people I've met at home and in California. Sporty fishermen. They oughta come over here—fishing with a hook in your mouth too, it's altogether different. But, I do understand, especially after you've been walking and sleeping in the rain for four days and you haven't eaten much and didn't get any letters from your girl and the sergeant's yellin' at you. You see why people'd be quick to shoot."

He stood witnessing the ultimate war wound and wondered—for maybe a few seconds—what he should do with his cameras.

And then Dana Stone started snapping pictures of the young Marine clutching at his shattered groin, his face contorted in pain. After a while, they calmed the boy down and had him wrapped up on a litter. When he could talk, he yelled for Dana, who was certain he would ask for the film. But no, he wondered if he could get copies of the pictures.

After he had proved his abilities as a photographer, UPI put Stone on a retainer so he would report in regularly with pictures. It wasn't long after that that he simply disappeared for six weeks without telling anybody where he was going. There was a big "movement" board on the UPI wall and for several weeks—as a joke at first—Dana Stone was listed as MIA.

"Finally," said Bob Hodierne, "I realized after a month that they were serious and we started looking for him. Everywhere we went, we got conflicting reports: 'Yeah, we saw him two weeks ago.' 'No, we never seen anybody like that.' The general drift was that nobody had seen him in a month and he had been in an area where there had been some fighting."

UPI sent Tom Corpora, a writer who was a close friend of Dana's to Pleiku to try to find him. The information officer at the 4th

Infantry Division said he last saw Stone hitchhiking into town after dark—against all good advice.

And then one afternoon, Stone sauntered back into the UPI office as if he'd been out to lunch. Hodierne said, "He never really offered any explanation and he didn't have a good story, but he had enjoyed his stay with the Special Forces."

Dana described the trip in a letter home: "I had fun traveling with them and their Montagnard troops. Learned about cooking rice in a piece of bamboo and cooking dogs by simply hitting them on the head and throwing them in the fire. I learned about eating eggs that were already half chicken and I could possibly transplant a banana tree. I also learned forty different ways to make a man tell you things he'd rather not. I learned that there ain't no way at all to sleep in a hammock when it's cold and not be cold yourself . . . . UPI didn't think too much of my spending a month in the field but I figured I needed a vacation." He did tell his co-workers that among the "forty ways" of torture he witnessed, the mercenaries had attached electrical wires to a man's testicles and cranked an old telephone box to give the suspect a jolt.

Stone took hundreds of pictures of this excursion and they were quite valuable to him. But he could never negotiate a sale to UPI because they wanted an accompanying story ("Just a bunch of words," he said) and he knew it would end up a hackneyed translation of a meaningful experience.

Looking for Happy Camp

One afternoon I met with Harry Black, a young lawyer in White River Junction, Vermont, who had been Dana Stone's best boyhood friend. We met in a quiet corner of an elegant bar and at first Harry was talking as if to a judge.

He said that he and Dana had known each other as toddlers. They got caught sneaking a look at a blasting site—he got punished, Dana got to go to the movies because his parents never found out. They were also students at Kimball Union Academy in Meriden, New Hampshire, during the same years, although in different classes. Dana had been expelled from public school because of some "incident on the playground." His parents had to send him to Cardigan Mountain School to repeat the eighth grade because the headmaster at KUA said he was just too small to mix with the other boys there.

Harry said that Dana was fiercely competitive in athletics and a special star in long-distance running. By his senior year, he was captain of every team except hockey—and that team's captain had been chosen before he tried out.

Louise had told me so many stories about Harry that Dana had told her. I was determined to get him drunk, relaxed and—this most important of all—reciting poetry to me as he used to do for Dana. So I led the way, belting down shots of whiskey and chasing them with gulps of beer. Harry caught on and pretty soon we were laughing and catching onto bits of his memory, running backward.

One time he said, laughing, he and Dana and another buddy were riding around in his car and arguing about the existence of God. Harry stopped the car and said, "Okay, we'll just swear He doesn't exist and then if He does exist, He'll strike us dead.'' The reason he remembered the story was Dana's nervous reaction. He coaxed the others out of swearing and changed the subject.

Another time, they decided they would go after a lighted cross on top of a nearby mountain. They got right to the foot of the cross, where their objective had been to cut off the light, but once they were there Dana made excuses again: they hadn't brought any wire cutters and they couldn't find the right wires.

At KUA, Dana was called ''Roman'' by a number of his friends because he would shout out that greeting to one and all: ''Hey, Roman!'' Harry said Dana never explained why.

Between his junior and senior years at KUA, Dana ran away from home to get a seaman's job on the Great Lakes. He brought back his papers to prove to Harry and any doubters that he had successfully lied about his age and got a job. Harry finished a year ahead of Dana and got a summer job unloading trucks before he went on to college. Dana stopped by to see him on the job and said, ''Yeah, when you get your degree, maybe they'll let you drive the truck.''

After Dana graduated at KUA, he convinced Harry to go back and commit a crime with him. The young lawyer hesitated before he told the story and then said—seriously—''Oh well, I suppose the statute of limitations has run out.'' Harry said Dana just wanted to see how it felt to be a criminal. So, they ''broke into'' the school's locker room. (Dana had saved a key.) They stole jersey No. 1 from the hockey team's supplies and then fled. Much to their confusion, nothing happened. Dana concluded that it didn't feel any different.

Harry and I left the Woodstock Inn and made the rounds of every available drinking place in Woodstock and in White River Junction. Stumbling out of the bar in the old Coolidge Hotel, we staggered, arms on each other's shoulders, down the sidewalk toward a breakfast diner. I looked over at him and knew the time was right. ''Tell me a poem,'' I said. He rared back, laughed and started reciting from ''A Shropshire Lad,'' Dana's favorite poem:

> The time you won your town the race
> We chaired you through the market-place;
> Man and boy stood cheering by,
> And home we brought you shoulder-high.

After Dana got out of the Navy, he talked Harry into hitchhiking with him to California. Harry says the trip wasn't anything to talk about. They got one ride from St. Louis to Los Angeles and slept most of the way across country.

In Los Angeles, they checked into a cheap hotel room where they had to use the curtains for bed covers. Dana got a job in a button factory, but Harry couldn't find work and the adventure was mostly uncomfortable for him. He wired for money and went home. He was later drafted and assigned to a base in Germany where for a long time he would get letters from Dana about his rambles up the coast of California to San Francisco and farther north. Once or twice, Dana included some short stories he had written. Harry read them and threw them away; he doesn't remember what they were about.

While he was living in San Francisco, Dana was looking at a map of Northern California. He spotted the town of Happy Camp up near the Oregon state line and decided it was a great name for his next move. On his way to Happy Camp, he stopped at a county fair in Yreka. Here, he talked with some people at a booth for Weed Community College. They told him there was no tuition at the school and he quickly decided to become a student again. (He had spent a few weeks at the University of Vermont.)

There was one professor who took a special interest in Dana. He liked his quick wit and his energy. They shared a love for roughing it outdoors. The professor invited Dana along on a fishing trip to Sawyer's Bar—a ghost town beside the Salmon River, nearly surrounded by a federal wilderness preserve of thick redwood and pine forests.

The name came from a sandbar in the river where there had once been a sawmill. Sawyer's Bar had been a thriving town of 4,000 during the busiest gold rush years. By the time Dana Stone arrived there, no more than forty people lived in the entire area—some loggers, some forest service workers, some leftover miners, some troubled city people escaped to the quiet countryside.

Getting there was a treacherous journey on a narrow dirt road that wound around and back and over a pass that was above the treeline. In the winter, the pass was often blocked by snow. The postman drove in and out every other day and he was the main link with the outside world. Locals called his car "the stage," because he would bring in medicines and bread and various supplies which the disagreeable woman who ran the general store refused to stock. Aside from the store, the only other buildings still being used were the post office and the bar—a grungy place the size of a small warehouse. The bar functioned as a community center and nearly every resident passed through at least every other day. The loggers' cleated shoes had chewed the floorboards to sawdust and the windows had probably never been washed. There was an antique juke box which could be freely manipulated by sticking your hand through the broken front.

The other gray frame buildings—hotel, whorehouse, and church—stood there rotting from neglect. The church was tilted because some overzealous gold-seekers had dug the ground from under it.

Sawyer's Bar was to become the most important reference place in Dana Stone's life. Once he had been there, everything and every place would always be measured by what he had seen and done there. He came back another weekend after the fishing trip with the professor. He was driving his own Volkswagen and intended to go back to college after a few days. But, standing in the bar he met two other young men who shared his disillusionment with college and his yearning for adventure.

Tom Mage and Brian Bundy had left school and come to Sawyer's Bar, pursuing the romance dreamed about by every boy since Mark Twain—of living in the wilderness and mining for gold. They invited Dana Stone out to their cabin for the night and he stayed two months, becoming one of the "Haywire Boys."

They had a lease on the old Haywire mine which—if they had ever finished building it—would have operated on a hydraulic system of flumes built from a stream on the other side of a steep hill. They never called it that, but everything the three of them set out to do ended up as a competition. Even when they carried a stack of lumber up a steep hill to build the flume, it became a race to see who could carry more boards faster.

Dana said he could walk more than sixty miles to the town of Eureka, and Mage took up the challenge. Mage lasted about twenty miles, but, to his amazement, Dana kept plodding along and called up the next afternoon to say he had made it—walking through a rainstorm, straight through for twenty-two hours, his feet bleeding, tears streaming down his cheeks from the pain.

Mage is philosophical about Dana's "physical thing." He says "I went out for track quite a bit and I know what Dana was trying to do. Actually, I think Stone in a way was always pushing toward getting himself into the situation where he is now. If anybody can make it through the kind of situation he's in now, I've really got a lot of confidence in him. It's like he's asking for an ultimate test."

Mage remembers that in their late-night talks at the cabin, Dana spoke of Schopenhauer's philosophy of pessimism, that man alternates between two states—frustration and boredom. Everything Dana said in those days was "shit this" and "fuck that." (And Louise says he once mentioned to her that he seriously considered a vasectomy while he was in the Navy because he felt the world was such a shitty place he had no right to bring another child into it.)

Dana's boredom and frustration threshold in these early adventures would be reached—almost by pattern—at the end of two months. After two months, he dropped out of two different colleges. After two months at the Haywire mine, he went back to San Francisco. Mage and Stone both had more running to do, but Bundy lives to this day with his wife and children on his own land near Sawyer's Bar.

Mage says he expected Dana to go to the war, but he never could see himself in that situation—anyhow, not after he nearly died in the desert south of Mauritania. That was his last adventure. He was traveling with two other Americans in a Land Rover and their gas supply was used up much faster than they had planned, leaving them a hundred miles from the nearest town without any gas. "We sat on the desert for five days waiting for help. One evening a plane came out and circled our position and dropped us some water. Then, the next morning, three or four Land Rover trucks came out and found us on the desert. We could see for miles and miles, we thought, but all of a sudden we were surrounded by all these trucks. Before anybody said anything, one of the Arabs ran to the back of a truck and cracked us some cold beers from an ice chest. I had had the hell scared out of me.

"A few months after that, I read of a similar experience. Some Germans got lost thirty miles out from Cairo—and they died. These adventures were the result of seeking adventure for adventure's sake. It just hasn't seemed necessary for me, Tom Mage, to do that anymore. It had been a compulsive thing to do."

Learning from the Green Berets

It is difficult now to recall the exotic image of the Green Berets. My own copy of Robin Moore's fictionalized version of his adventures in 1964 with the Special Forces in Vietnam ("America's #1 Best Seller") was published in April, 1966, the same month Sean Flynn was in the jungles with them. On the cover of the book is the handsome face of Sergeant Barry Saddler who wrote and sang "The Ballad of the Green Berets," which in another time they would have described as the song all America was singing.

> Fighting soldiers from the sky
> Fearless men who jump and die
> Men who mean just what they say
> The brave men of the Green Berets.
>
> Silver wings upon their chests
> These are men, America's best.
> One hundred men we'll test today
> But only three for the Green Berets. . . .

I think President Kennedy deliberately encouraged the romance of the Green Berets because he saw them as an American foreign legion, expertly trained in counter-guerrilla warfare, which he may also have hoped would be the scale on which we would fight our future wars. The Special Forces men were ordered to take off their berets and dress like other soldiers for Kennedy's visit to Fort Bragg. His first question, I am told, was, "Where are the berets?" He told them to wear their berets as a "badge of courage." (One suspects a devious speechwriter with a taste for irony was at work there.) Whether the assassination of Kennedy was a military coup in fact, it certainly was in effect. After his death, the war quickly expanded beyond the function of our legionnaires and I never heard that song sung in 1968 except in vicious parody.

While a number of Green Berets would curse Flynn for giving them bad publicity with his torture pictures, their superiors apparently were not upset. Just two months after the pictures were published, they invited Flynn to join a super-secret and very dangerous mission to go back into the Ashau Valley where the North Vietnamese had taken over a Green Beret camp in early 1966.

Flynn had never told me about this mission, but he had mentioned an officer in Danang who sometimes had him over to dinner in 1968. Flynn would come back shaking his head about the stories he heard from this group—which conducted secret forays into North Vietnam—because he said a lot of their "reconnaissance" was done on home leave back in the U.S. When I finally located this officer, now retired, he sent me a formal report entitled "Shaun Flynn" (at least he pronounced the name right, most of the other GI's called Flynn, "Seen") which I quote here in full:

Detachment B-52 (Project Delta 5th Special Forces Group (Airborne) 1st Special Forces in May of 1966 was deployed east of the Ashau Valley; its mission—to determine enemy strengths and capabilities.

The command was engaged in conducting reconnaissance patrols and ranger operations against the North Vietnamese Army forces who were holding the valley which is astride the border between Laos and South Vietnam.

A call from our higher Hqs. alerted us to the arrival of a US correspondent, Shaun [sic] Flynn, and requested we extend all courtesies. Shaun arrived the next day without fanfare; dressed in combat gear; and requested he get a "firsthand view" of our operations; his intent—to accompany our "ongoing" operations.

After talking it over with one of the reconnaissance team leaders then on alert—"in the icebox"—it was agreed that he would allow Shaun to join and accompany his recon team but with the understanding that Shaun would have to carry his "weight." Following briefings and rehearsals, the team was infiltrated by helicopter on top of one of the several hills overlooking the valley floor. The operation lasted three and a half days with the team and Shaun was a success; and I must add, both the Vietnamese and Americans held Shaun in the highest esteem.

Three days later NE of the valley, one of the other recon teams made significant NVA contact and called for an exploitation force. Shaun was at the operations tent at the time when the decision was made to commit one of our US/RVN led Airborne Ranger companies. Again, Shaun requested to accompany the operation. The American commander readily agreed—well realizing that Shaun could more than take care of himself. The company was committed at "last light" and after a two-day sweep, made significant enemy contact in achieving its assigned objective. During the entire operation Shaun accompanied the command group. Had he been military he would have been cited for bravery, but as it was all we could do was buy him a scotch upon return to base camp.

Two years later Shaun visited our Reconnaissance Hqs. at Danang. He met many former acquaintances. We wanted him to stay but he had other campaigns to cover up in the highlands.

The former Army officer told me the Green Berets had a big party for Sean when he returned to the base camp. "He kept up on both missions; he took his turn on watch, just one of the guys in both cases. The guys fell in love with him; they thought he was the greatest thing going. They identified with him because he was willing to take his share of the chances."

Flynn was in Vietnam almost four months before he ever sold any pictures or offered any stories for sale. His first story, with pictures, for UPI appeared on April 27, 1966, and his one and only story, with pictures, for *Paris-Match* was published the next month. All his friends say that Flynn did not write any of these stories, but he did provide the information. When I read them, I was moved by the incidents he had chosen to describe. His was hardly the eye of the heartless swashbuckler.

Flynn and the captain stood looking at the Vietnamese child, his stomach cut apart by shrapnel, his intestines hanging out into the mud. But the child wouldn't cry; he just kept smiling and saying in American, "Okay. Okay." Tears welled up in the captain's eyes, spilling down his cheeks.

"That's the last time I cry over Vietnam," he said.

Flynn said, "One feels so stupid, so useless."

It was almost last light, but the sergeant told the lieutenant they shouldn't camp there because the Viet Cong might sneak in under cover of the noise made by some cattle grazing nearby. So the lieutenant called on the radio and got permission for the sergeant to shoot the cows. But the cows still didn't fall; they just kept standing there staring in terror at Flynn. For as long as he lived, Flynn said, he would remember their enormous uncomprehending eyes. And so he took out his own pistol and finished killing them one by one.

With each shot, he said, he had learned a little more about the stupidity of war. If he hadn't killed those cows, they might have caused his own death.

Among the childhood heroes of Sean and his friends in Palm Beach was a man who operated a small gun shop and who also ran a rifle range further inland. He had been hunting in Africa and was said to have trafficked in guns among various revolutions around the world, all adding to his stature in the boys' eyes.

The man idolized Errol Flynn and would have done anything for his son. He taught Sean to shoot—something for which his mother was grateful because "It was something I couldn't do," and something she also felt every boy should know. He helped Sean acquire a large collection of customized weapons—including a nickel-plated .357 magnum, a carbine with an M-1 kit on it; a .44 Winchester, and a Thompson machine gun.

"Sometimes we would pretend we were in a war," a friend recalls. They would go to some property Sean's mother owned, and, "Particularly Sean would like to play war. We would pick out a pine cone or a bottle and pretend it was the enemy." Once, another friend said, Sean picked out a palm tree in the distance and mowed it down as the enemy. Others in Palm Beach told me that two or three cows were shot in these war games.

The Son of Lili Damita

The swashbuckler's life (in or out of films) was hardly what Lili Damita envisioned for her only child. Once the son was born, she wanted to get as far away from Hollywood as she possibly could. The boy grew up looking "exactly as I wanted him to look." But she didn't want him to adopt any of Errol's "horrible faults."

She wanted him to become "everything I ever dreamed of." She wanted him to grow up in Palm Beach, Florida, where she bought a small house in 1942. Even the Kennedys were "persona non grata" in those days, she says, and her son would be reared there among what she considered "the very best of families." Then she wanted him to go to the best of schools and enroll at MIT and become an engineer as her father and grandfather in France had been.

After visiting in Beverly Hills and in Palm Beach, I can't see all that much difference in the places—except that some of the Beverly Hills people are better looking and still work for a living. Palm Beach is one of those little enclaves of the rich, most of them beyond sixty, that sustains itself—dinner parties and drinks at the club—on the members' own exaggerated sense of self-importance. It is an island of people who want more than anything now to live out their days in warmth and comfort. There is little energy left to their lives. They have been everywhere, done everything they wanted to do. And, with every possible option left open to them, there is no new place they want to go, no new thing they want to experience. I cannot imagine a less stimulating environment for a lively boy to grow up in.

I was surprised to see that the house where Sean lived as a child was a neat little bungalow that could have been taken off a street in any American small town. Behind the house, there was a one-room maid's quarters, a separate building. This had been Sean's private apartment from the time he was a little boy. It was another way his mother taught him to be independent. A friend from Sean's grade-school years told me it was a rather barren room, with one bare light bulb hanging from a cord, a bed, and a chest of drawers. The only thing unusual he remembered in the room was that Sean had a photograph of his mother and dad beside his bed. "The last thing that would have occurred to me when I was six or seven was to have a picture of my parents by my bed," he said.

The Palm Beach Private School, which Sean attended through eighth grade, was within walking distance of the house. I stopped by there and found two teachers who remembered Sean. They echoed what many others had already told me about him as a child: "Such a beautiful boy with such perfect manners," as if to say that he was never the hellion one would have expected Errol Flynn to have sired.

One of the teachers said that Errol Flynn would always address his letters to his son in care of the school. They came about one every six months and they would always promise some kind of Italian scooter or motorcycle which never seemed to materialize. Sean would share the letters with his friends and then wait in vain for the promised gift.

Sean's name was not among those painted on the wall of the school lobby for honors in scholarship or athletics during the years he attended. His French teacher told me he was not an outstanding student in any way. "You know, that's why I was so delighted when I read that he had gone to Vietnam," she said. Whatever did she mean by that? "Well, he was so handsome and he had such beautiful manners. It all just came so easily for him; I just didn't think he would ever do anything serious or worthwhile with his life." She remembered that his mother would attend the annual Parents' Day at the school and once, in the father-son relay race she fell flat on her face she was running so hard.

Apparently Sean's father ultimately did come through with the scooter because one of his friends remembers the two of them used to ride side by side all over the neighborhood. He graduated from the scooter to a fine Triumph motorcycle. "He had the only black leather jacket in Palm Beach," a friend recalls. "There may have been a few in West Palm Beach, but his was the only one over here."

After the motorcycle, he had a glowing reddish-orange—actually, a sort of pink that was fashionable that year—MG which had every visible part of the engine chrome plated. His next car was a 1954 Austin-Healy with "16" still lettered on its sides from the time Phil Styles had raced it at Sebring. Sean told an interviewer in 1963: "Funny thing, millions of kids all over the world rated my old man their hero. Great! But me, I wanted to race cars, that is what I wanted to do! Moss, Fangio—they were my heroes. I never knew my old man. And that is OK because he never knew me. And that made us quits. But Fangio and the others, they seemed much more worth admiring. They had that quality which seemed to set them apart."

Every year, Sean and his friends would travel together to the races at Sebring—usually partying all night the night before at his mother's house. Sean loved to drive fast and dangerously. The exhaust on his Healy came out the side. Once, when Sean was trying to see how close he could come to a car he was passing on the right, his exhaust left a streak down the side of the other car.

After the Healy, Sean had a 1957 Chevy—the ultimate cool car of the Elvis Presley era. The car was all-white on the outside with an all-red interior. It had four-valve carburetors and glasspacks and moon-disk hubcaps. "It was really great for picking up girls," says Sean's friend from those days, Steve Cutter, who is now a successful young real estate man in Palm Beach.

"We were always trying to outdo each other trying to look nifty," Cutter says. Even with ducktails and flattops in fashion in the fifties, these two stuck to the more conservative short haircuts. They wore narrow-lapel, one-button sport jackets and short-sleeved shirts.

Steve and Sean were best friends during the summers of their high school and prep school years. Steve says that Sean was the best friend he has ever had. They spent a lot of time talking to girls at the Coral Beach Club and running around in their cars. Sean was very good about loaning his car to Steve and once when Steve wrecked the MG Sean didn't say a word.

Steve helped Sean get a summer job with him doing construction work. The job was stapling insulation into the rafters of houses being built. They were both in such good physical condition—lifting weights and doing exercises every day—they didn't use ladders, but hung onto the rafters with one hand and used the stapling gun with the other.

At the end of both summers, Steve and Sean saved the $1.50 an hour they made and blew it in Havana. "We'd go down to Cuba and screw our asses off," Steve recalls. "We didn't drink a lot—neither of us had ever been drinkers."

I had talked with Lili—she prefers her first name and pronounces it from deep in the throat like Dietrich's "Lola"—by telephone from New York while she was in Fort Dodge, Iowa, where she and her second husband live out-of-season from Palm Beach. An actor friend of Sean's had described her as a formidable woman, the kind who would stand on her head to show you she was still in good shape.

The house which Lili had built in 1960 is a two-story, gray-painted, rough board-and-batten Thai house with roof-to-ground panels that slide open to the breeze. It is down a little street just before you get to the estate of Marjorie Merriweather Post. You can see a tower of the Post mansion from a bedroom sundeck Lili built into the top of a banyan tree.

She yelled a friendly hello down from the upstairs and then hurried down the open stairway to extend a firm handshake—something I'm sure she taught Sean was very important on meeting new people. She looked incredibly young and lively for her age. She had to be in her sixties, since she was older than Errol when they were married in 1935.

She sat across the room from me and stared me down, almost menacingly. She quickly made it obvious that she did not care to speak of her late first husband; and neither did she wish to dwell on Sean's going off to the Vietnam war. "It broke my heart," she said. "It has made an old woman of me. You see me. I sleep with the phone beside my bed; but I don't sleep—I worry all the time."

I asked Lili about Sean's paternal grandparents because he had told me about spending a summer with them on Errol's plantation in

Jamaica. The grandfather was a distinguished marine biologist, awarded the Order of the British Empire for his work. When he died in 1968, he was a dean of Trinity College in Dublin. I showed Sean an obituary someone sent me from New York and he said, "Oh yes, somebody told me he had died." Had the grandparents been an influence in Sean's life?

"Absolutely not," Lili said. "I was mother, father, everything to him. I did it all myself." Among other things, she saw to it that he was baptized and confirmed in the Roman Catholic Church, where she has asked for special prayers since his capture. I asked her if Sean's father were also Catholic. "Fleen?" She spat out the word. "Fleen was an atheist!"

At the time I talked with her, Sean's mother had not seen her son in five years. Yet, as she showed me around the house, it seemed that he had just left and she was expecting him back any day.

In 1962, Lili married Allen Loomis, an easygoing, responsible businessmen. He manufactures Eskimo Pies and other ice cream specialties. And seems the genial opposite of her first husband. The mail box is lettered "Lili and Allen Loomis."

Upstairs, the rooms were all white—carpets, walls, ceiling, furniture—in the manner of the 1930's starlet which I had a feeling Lili had remained. Among the decorations here were many color photographs of the son—from babyhood on up to the time of his last visit. The pictures are of Sean hunting in Africa, standing with his mother and stepfather. Not one of them shows him in Vietnam; not one of them shows him with his father.

After Being There Awhile

After he had been in and out of combat for a few months, Dana Stone wrote his parents: "I'm without holes in me and my work is going well. If it would stop raining for an hour or so, I could smile again. I'm in Saigon hoping for some election terrorism or rioting . . . lots of big things are happening to me but it's too much trouble to write it all down—I'll send some more pictures later." Bob Hodierne says "fortunately" the Buddhist riots that summer gave them a lot of work.

In another letter home, Stone said:

> After being here awhile your chances of getting shot decrease tho they increase if you stay too long. I now know a good deal about not getting shot but mostly I guess it's just luck or lack of it that decides your future . . . tired, tired, tired. Walked all over the damn country with the 1st Inf. Div. who had promised big things but couldn't even find an open area big enough to set down a resupply ship to get food and water into us—no VC, no food, no water, no pictures, no damn good for me. Going to bed forever.

Hodierne had been in college in 1966. "It occurred to me at the time that by the time I got out of college the war would blow over and I would have missed it." He considered it "the biggest single news event that would take place during my lifetime and I just didn't want to miss it—that coupled with a fascination with what war was about." He was also fascinated by the "mystique of violence and here was the biggest ongoing laboratory of its kind. Vietnam was a good news story, on the front page all the time, and if you have any instinct about the business at all, that's where you want to be."

Like Flynn and Stone, he had, however, never worked as a photographer before he went to Vietnam. "With a lot of bluff and self-confidence, I was able to do it," he says, "and there are not many stories you can do that on." The art of photography in Vietnam, he says, was "knowing where the war was and being able to keep your eyes open and point the camera in that direction."

Almost everybody who worked closely with Dana in 1966 and 1967 says that he was after something more than a page-one photograph. "His motivations seemed deeper, more inner-directed," says Hodierne. Dana would often stay out in the field longer than he had to and lose the "play" on his pictures because competitive photographers already had theirs back in Saigon. He was genuinely troubled about losing this freedom when he decided to accept UPI's offer of a staff job in the fall of 1967. He told one friend he didn't really like the idea of having to report into the office every day. This friend felt that Stone's prime motivation in accepting the UPI job was to save up enough money so he could get married.

Once when Dana was out in the field, a company commander called in air strikes on some huts, from which someone had been firing on the Americans. When it was all smoke and rubble, the captain said to Dana, "That takes care of that."

"Yeah," said Dana, "gives everybody a fresh start."

The Son of Bob and Connie Stone

The town of North Pomfret is a geographical area of rural Vermont. Not only does it lack any sign of neon or hamburger drive-ins and motels, it doesn't even have a bus stop. The bus took Louise and me as far as Rutland, where we were shifted—bag and baggage along with the two other passengers—into a bus company station wagon which then took us to an unmarked corner in Woodstock where everybody knew the bus always stopped.

Bob and Connie Stone had driven the fifteen miles over to meet us and they were waiting in their comfortable car, bundled up against the biting cold. He was a genial portly fellow; she was a stiff but friendly New England mother. Both greeted us in the warmest good manners, although somewhat awkwardly. It wasn't just that they hardly knew their daughter-in-law. In me, I know they were expecting something akin to a visitor from another planet. They were like my own family in this regard, having no earthly idea who this creature was who had grown out of them and gone off to exotic places and sent back strange postcards, pictures, letters, and tapes telling Mom and Dad even this: the joy of watching a war.

There was a light snow blowing and by morning it would add another inch or two to two feet already on the ground. Even though it was after dark, I could see that these people had an unusual respect for the beauty of the land they lived on. There was none of the clutter that had made my own hometown—in an equally beautiful setting of mountainland in North Carolina—an eyesore, an obscenity in the face of nature.

Almost before we had finished answering how we were and how the trip had been, Mrs. Stone started telling us about the renters. A

66

nice young schoolteacher had booked up the apartment over the kitchen for another year. The Christmas people—three families of skiers who had taken over the house every holiday season since the Stones bought it in 1960—had been there again. It bothered me at the time, but I think it was natural for Mrs. Stone to talk about these people who would be coming back for sure, instead of dwelling on her own children who might not return. She was a rigidly controlled woman and she had long ago adjusted her life to the absence of her oldest son.

Mr. Stone was not so unemotional about his missing son and several times at dinner that night I thought I could see tears welling up in his eyes as Louise and I talked about Dana as if he were just off on a trip around the world. Neither of the parents seemed particularly curious about the efforts to locate and free the missing journalists in Cambodia. That, too, would have been disrupting something they had already learned to live with.

Except for the modern kitchen fixtures, nearly every piece of furniture in the white frame house dated back to the time it was built in 1798. A log fire in the arched fireplace gave off a warm glow on the aged patina of the wide floorboards, the worn windsor chairs and rockers, the tall grandfather clock. Above the fireplace hung a sword lettered "Spirit of '76," which Mrs. Stone's ancestor had carried in that war.

The Stones moved to this picturesque place after Dana had gone to the Navy. The farm consists of 125 acres with a tiny old schoolhouse built in the early 1800's, a big red barn, a trout stream, and a duck pond. The house where Dana actually grew up was located in a crowded residential section at the edge of downtown White River Junction. It was a small, peculiar-shaped house on a corner near the school, with dormer windows sticking out at right angles from two sides and a porch that wrapped around the same sides. From here, Mr. Stone could walk to his job at the post office. For twenty-eight years, he walked a mail route. He never bought a car until he had the house paid for, and they didn't buy the farm until they had the car paid off.

Mrs. Stone named Dana for her father, Dana Hazen, a prominent dairy farmer who had inherited a large square frame house out from White River Junction. "They were nailing the last shakes on it when they heard the shots fired at Lexington," she said, as if that war 200 years ago were the only one that had ever affected anybody around there. Her people, the Danas and the Hazens, were among the original Puritan settlers who moved up from Connecticut. Mr. Stone's father had come from England as a boy. His family was Roman Catholic and Dana was baptized as a baby and sent off to church for instruction. The father said Dana "was never very interested in the church," but Louise says he was bitterly opposed to Catholicism and all other organized forms of religion when she first met him.

The Stones had two other children—a daughter, Roberta ("Bobbie"), named after her father and born a year after Dana; and a son, Tommy, born thirteen years after Dana. When the last baby was put into the television room, Dana protested that it was unfair to Brownie, the name of a succession of family dogs regardless of kind or color. The dog had always slept there and they had the dog before they got the kid, Dana argued.

Dana always called him "Jones," but the kid brother idolized Dana, and he talked of nothing but going to sea, going to Vietnam—finding his brother through his experiences if not in reality.

Dana had obviously been a little runt of a fellow all his life—inheriting his father's wit and stature, his mother's face and will. He loved to get out of the house and camp out. His father would tease him about his size, saying he ought to get wheels for his backpack so it wouldn't drag the ground. Dana would splutter and fume at the teasing and storm off into the rain.

Surely because of his extra energy, the Stones were always a little in awe of Dana—or so it seemed as they told me about his days with them. They also felt he was more intelligent than the other children. Bobbie would work and hard and still come home with B's on her report card. "She does the best she can with what she has," the mother would say, scolding Dana for coming in with the same grades after little effort. I asked them how they knew Dana was more intelligent and they said a teacher of his had seen his I.Q. scores and said, "It's a honey," and that was all.

Dana's father was delighted when I asked if I could ride with him one morning up to the North Pomfret post office. He had been made postmaster there the year before. This saved him the drive into White River Junction and all that walking once he got there. The post office was the end of the counter in Stu Harrington's store and gas station, a red frame building perched between the narrow road and a steep ravine. For years, Harrington himself ran the post office, but he got so blind he couldn't tell a ten dollar bill from a single.

That day, Rene Chase was filling in for Mr. Stone. She told Irwin Rogers—a ruggedly handsome man in a red plaid coat—that Jud Fischer's Saint Bernard had twelve pups. Rogers said he reckoned it would make the papers; did the last time.

Sitting on a rail fence beside the store, I asked Rogers (town constable at $100 a year) if any of his neighbors ever talked about Stone's missing son. He said no, he had never heard anybody say much about Dana. Likewise, he said nobody argued much about the war or about the recognition of Communist China. Gun control was the gut issue, he said. As I was shaking hands good-bye, he said, "Just don't come after my guns." I laughed and said, "Man, I don't want your guns." But Irwin Rogers didn't crack a smile.

Riding back home, Mr. Stone talked about his military service. He still hadn't been drafted by 1944, when he met a member of the draft board on the street and asked him why. The official checked and found that Stone's file had been removed along with that of another Robert Stone who had left the area. He said he wanted to do his part, so he joined the Navy and was sent to San Francisco. He spent the remainder of the war living in a hotel in San Francisco and working in the military post office. He said proudly that he had carried mail onto every kind of ship going into the war in the Pacific. Then he said, "But don't write anything about that—I wouldn't want people to think I was trying to be a hero."

One night I was sitting at the old dining room table going over some of Dana's letters to his parents. The others had all gone to bed and I figured that maybe Mrs. Stone had chosen this time to confide in me some special feeling she had for her son. But no, she didn't volunteer anything and I couldn't come up with the right questions. I don't think it was that she had no feelings. I think she just felt it was impolite (or even a sign of weakness) to express them in front of others. Her son would always make a joke in the face of sentimentality; the mother masked the moment with a stiff untelling stare.

I asked Mrs. Stone why none of the letters she showed me were dated prior to April, 1966. Well, she explained, that was the last time she had seen Dana—as if it were sufficient answer to the question. "I save them until I see him and then we talk about everything and then I can throw all the letters away."

Did that mean she never expected him to come back from the war? "Oh, no," she said. "I never expected him to come back from California that time."

He Likes to Kid People Along

Dana Stone had the most unusual sense of humor I have ever encountered in a grown man. His pranks were often sophomoric and might have been painful to the recipient if Dana hadn't executed them with such good humor and even affection. If you were never the object of one of his pranks it meant he didn't know or like you.

Bob Hodierne says he didn't especially respond to Dana when he first met him. "His abrasive New England-accented personality put some people off," he recalls. Stone had a tendency to "kid people along, sometimes rather harshly." Once, the two of them were stuck in the safety of a rear area base when one of the young clerks started talking with them. The boy had just been issued a weapon, had never been in actual combat. But he started telling stories about how dangerous their position was. Dana started putting the boy on, telling Hodierne he was scared and maybe they ought to get the hell on back to Saigon. Hodierne asked him about it later and Dana said, "What the hell, that kid can go around now telling people how he scared two war photographers with his stories."

Tom Corpora remembers another time when he was with Stone covering a Marine amphibious assault. "We were going in on amtracks and as we waited to get on the tracks, Dana started teasing—almost baiting—the Marines about what they were about to get into, which I think Dana already knew was nothing. Underneath it was affection and the troops always sensed it. Dana became a kind of legend with grunts of all kinds. Wherever he'd been they all remembered him and remembered him simply as 'Dana.'" For their convenience, he kept his first name lettered on his helmet, flak jacket, and camera case.

Stone would always insist that Corpora read his mail. And this was how Corpora picked up on two jibes that would always cut back at Stone. One was Louise's nickname for him, "Danie," which was all right from her but not from anybody else. In another letter, Corpora found that Dana had written a friend about how he "found himself" in the war.

So, whenever Stone would introduce him as "a thirty-year-old hack for UPI" (a fear Corpora expressed on his birthday), Corpora would tell the story of the brave photographer named Danie who had "found himself" in the war, but still had to take sleeping pills out in the field. Dana had been with a unit once and—after walking all day, soaking wet from a heavy rain—the medic had passed out Seconal so the troops could get a good night's sleep. Dana thought it was such a good idea that he carried the pills with him from then on.

Once, a friendly scuffle between Corpora and Stone in the UPI room at the Danang Press Center ended up in a serious fight with the two of them throwing C-ration cans at each other. A solid hit could have badly injured either of them, but one can went flying through the screen door. Corpora ran outside, picked up the can, and threw it back at Stone. Just as he did, the new commander of the Press Center walked up. When he went back into the room, Corpora found Dana hiding in the bathroom, "giggling as if the colonel had been the headmaster of our school."

Some of Dana's most memorable pranks took place at the press center. He would spread fritos or potato chips in the sheets where he knew some weary friend was looking forward to sleeping after a day in the field. He even "short-sheeted" the beds one night.

Once, Flynn was attempting to read and Dana kept trying to distract him. Flynn ignored him, so Stone went outside and got his motorcycle, rode it into the room, and revved up the engine until Flynn had to take action. He grabbed a big fire extinguisher and chased after him, Dana yelling, "Help, he's after me with a giant can of Mace."

A favorite prank was to tell another correspondent about some big action that they ought to cover. Once, he and Flynn had returned from the field, tired and dirty. Flynn went into his room to shower and change. Stone came running in with the report that there was heavy fighting somewhere and they should be going. Flynn put his combat gear back on and sat waiting in the jeep—while Stone showered in the adjacent room and stood laughing at Flynn through the window.

Keith Kay was a very special friend of Dana's in Vietnam because he was not only an expert cameraman, he had also worked as a logger near Sawyer's Bar. Kay says, "You probably have as many personal opinions as to why Stone ties shoelaces together as you have stories. Deeper motives be damned—he just likes fucking around with people."

On one trip, Kay was bracing himself to jerk all one hundred pounds of his gear—rucksack, sound camera, shoulder brace, canteen belt, and battery pack—onto his back. He got his arms in the shoulder straps, then heaved and fell flat on his back. Dana had tied his pack to a tree. But then, Kay was a special friend so he suffered more.

Flynn Honored His Father in an Old-Fashioned Way

After Palm Beach Private, Lili felt that Lawrenceville was the only school for Sean, even though he had to take some special summer courses to get in. She gave Flynn a Brooks Brothers charge card for his clothes and his friends say he dressed just like every other prep school boy of the time.

George Hamilton, the actor, says he and Sean went to a party with Error Flynn during this time. Hamilton had also grown up in Palm Beach, where he met Flynn at a traffic court where one was being charged with reckless driving in a car, the other on a motorcycle. The party was given by the Gabor sisters. Hamilton says the contrast between Errol and his son was striking. Sean was wearing a plain corduroy jacket and looked really scruffy beside the old man, standing there as dapper as always, the focus of every female eye. Every time the elder Flynn moved, Hamilton says, he would be surrounded by "chicks. When he would go to get a drink it was like a herd of buffalo going for water."

Sean, meanwhile, went virtually unnoticed. After the party, Hamilton met the two Flynns at El Morocco. Sean was sitting with a hooker his dad had picked up for him. Hamilton says it was a delight to watch Sean, the perfect gentleman even with a whore—lighting her cigarette, always being so polite and considerate. "I don't know whether he even knew what she was."

Flynn would later tell a friend about working so hard to make All-American in swimming at Lawrenceville because he thought it was something that would impress his father, who had once tried out for the Olympic diving team from Australia. The father was unimpressed. The son was disappointed, so much so he would repeat the story years later.

In the fall of 1960, Sean enrolled at Duke University, in Durham, fifteen miles from Chapel Hill, North Carolina, where I was entering my sophomore year at the University of North Carolina. Nowadays, the schools and the students are as close as the mileage would indicate, but in those days there was a bitter class rivalry between the schools—one that included not just athletics but social activism as well. Many of the students at Chapel Hill were already involved in the civil rights movement and would be in the vanguard of the first sit-ins which started in North Carolina that year. The Duke student body was not integrated until the mid-sixties. Most of the Duke students were from out of state and they were decidedly upper middle class. A large percentage of the students at Chapel Hill were on self-help scholarships, as I was.

It never occurred to me, then, that Sean and I would have any mutual friends from those days. But, like so many other things I discovered while researching this book, I would find there had been connections even then. A young advertising executive whom I had known for some time in New York told me at a party that he had been one of Flynn's roommates at Duke. Unlike the hundred or so others who've also told me they knew Flynn, my advertising friend admitted Sean had never liked him.

He and Sean and two other students shared a suite of rooms in Dormitory H. Sean never spent much time in his room after he unloaded an enormous amount of luggage, including a rifle he kept locked in a closet.

Flynn only used the room to sleep in and often he wouldn't even do that. When he studied, it was in the library. His name had been a handicap at Palm Beach Private and at Lawrenceville, but at Duke he was a big man on campus even before he arrived. His colleagues in Dormitory H convinced Sean to run for president of the freshman class, arguing it would be good for dormitory spirit. My advertising friend had saved a hand-lettered campaign badge from those days: IN WITH FLYNN.

Steve Cutter said Sean was so surprised at all this attention that he wrote him a long letter, enclosing a campaign button.

1960 was an exciting year in North Carolina. There were civil rights demonstrations in every sizable town; a young liberal had won the Democratic nomination for governor and he seconded John

Kennedy's nomination at the party's national convention. The Reverend Martin Luther King, Jr., was in and out of Chapel Hill and Durham, along with all the other civil rights leaders.

But all this was taking place outside the low rock wall surrounding the Duke campus, a 1920's replica of a Gothic college, built by American Tobacco money. When my friend sat down to draft Flynn's campaign speech, he focused on school spirit. I asked him about civil rights and national politics and he said, "The truth is, we weren't even thinking about those things then."

Flynn was only a year older than most of his classmates, but he was a generation older in experience. He never fitted into the Joe College routine and nobody ever tried to force it on him. It was an honor council offense for a Duke freshman to be seen without his blue beanie. Flynn never wore his and no one ever mentioned the violation.

One of Sean's girlfriends was a glamorous blonde who was competing for homecoming queen. She had a private room in the dormitory and always came out with her face and hair fixed. Even to walk down the hall to brush her teeth, she would wear expensive negligees. The other girls tried to find out if she wore false eyelashes, but they never could. When she heard the editors of *Glamour* were on campus to take some pictures, she appeared before them, ready for the cameras. She was crushed when they chose some "more natural-looking" coeds. The night before the homecoming queen was chosen, she broke down and cried openly because she had been disqualified and expelled from school. The whispered reason was that some of the girls in her dorm had reported that a man (they said it was Flynn) had stayed in her room overnight. After she left, the other girls found a list of names of men she had conquered—including Flynn—scotchtaped to her wall.

My advertising friend met me on the street in New York one day and said he'd thought of another person who'd been close to Flynn at Duke—Sally Hobbs. I had also known Sally during that time, so I was pleased to have an excuse to talk with her again. I located her in Richmond, Virginia. It was a clear sunny morning when I arrived at her high-ceilinged rooms in a weary Victorian house near the University of Richmond, where she was studying to become an occupational therapist. She was delighted to see me, but more than a little confused about these new connections—Flynn, her, me, the war.

Sally is a small, gentle soul and the war had been a distant ugliness she had never thought about in terms of people she actually knew. (Although it did not surprise her that Flynn had gone off to the war, or that he had been captured.)

Sally said that much to everybody's surprise Flynn had been a genial, very ordinary college boy. The two of them had bit parts in a play and she remembers he never tried to hog the spotlight, never tried to be his father's son. At their initial introduction, Sean had made some serious remark and Sally had quipped, "Oh, you can think, too." His looks were legendary after only a few hours on the Duke campus. Some instructors from those days—male and female—still talk about seeing him sitting alone or sauntering across the campus.

Sean apparently liked Sally's spirit, for he would often have serious discussions with her. They were never lovers or even college sweethearts—she was one of a succession of friends who happened to be girls. The last of these discussions took place three months after Sean had enrolled at Duke. He saw Sally outside one of the classroom buildings and said he had to talk with her. They went to the Dope Shop and he told her he'd just been offered the starring role in a Hollywood sequel to *Captain Blood*. The director and the screenwriter for the original—which had launched his father's career—had seen Sean at his father's funeral the year before. They had concocted a nostalgic plan for resurrecting some of the lost romance of the late Errol Flynn, and surely in the process they hoped to restore some life to their own fading careers. What they might do to the life of a nineteen-year-old college boy doesn't seem to have been a consideration. After Flynn explained the offer to her, Sally said, "Do you really want to do it?" Flynn said, "I don't know."

"I asked him if he wanted to do the same thing his father had done all over again and the gist of what he said was that he really didn't but felt he had to. It was something he was going to have to do sooner or later. He honored his father in an old-fashioned way, I think. Because he was his father, he had to take his life seriously. He had to do honor to the validity of his father's life, discover the terms of it, try the same things out himself. He said he would never know how he would feel about it until he had tried.

"It was the first time in my life I had seen somebody I cared for doing something I thought was bad for them. 'What if you go out there and do this movie?' " she asked Sean.

"I'll probably stay out there and get into that whole moviemaking scene," Sean answered.

"After that, what?" Sally asked.

"I'll probably get very bored with it."

"After that?"

"I'll go sailing around for a while."

"After that?"

"I'll go to Africa and do some hunting."

"Then what?"

"Then, I'll probably find some way to get myself killed."

Sally was about as far removed from the war experience as anybody I knew and I was intrigued by her attempts to intellectualize the experience now that she knew two people who had been involved. We talked about why men have to do these things—fulfilling our mothers' expectations, continuing the impulses of the frontier, chasing after our fathers. We talked about courage and whether that was the right word to describe risking one's life in a war that made no sense.

She pulled down a copy of Marguerite Yourcenar's *Memoirs of Hadrian* and read these lines to me:

> But that period of heroic foolhardiness taught me to distinguish between the different aspects of courage. . . . The semblance of such courage which I later employed was, in my worst days, only a cynical recklessness toward life; in my best days it was only a sense of duty to which I clung. When confronted with the danger itself, however, that cynicism or that sense of duty quickly gave place to a mad intrepidity, a kind of strange orgasm of a man mated with his destiny. . . . I smile with some bitterness at the realization that now out of any two thoughts I devote one to my own death, as if so much ceremony were needed to decide this worn body for the invevitable. . . .

Later, when we were talking about wars and why we have them, Sally picked up another book, the *Complete Poems of Cavafy*, and read from "Expecting the Barbarians." The villagers wait and worry that the barbarians attack; there are no speeches in the Senate that day, life is simplified in the wait. Then it becomes apparent by nightfall that the barbarians are not coming. "And now what shall become of us without any barbarians? Those people were a kind of solution."

Flynn's last day at Duke, Sally presented him with a copy of a book of Richard Wilbur's poems. He said good-bye and left. She never heard from him again. Some of Flynn's friends in Palm Beach are bitterly resentful that he never kept in touch; Sally seems to have expected it.

His mother fought his leaving school right up until he quit. He assured her he could always come back and could continue to read and study on his own. Lili engaged Hollywood's most prestigious law firm to inform the agent negotiating with Flynn that the boy was underage and she would never approve a movie contract for him. The agent was Hy Seeger, who had also represented George Hamilton, and he was able to calm Lili down by explaining to her that if she stopped him, Flynn would resent her interference for the rest of his life. Lili relented and in early 1961, Flynn arrived in Hollywood to begin the long search for his father and for himself.

He lived very quietly when he first arrived—staying part of the time at George Hamilton's apartment on Sunset Boulevard and other times at his agent's apartment. He read a lot, swam a hundred laps a day, did his exercises faithfully, and took stunt lessons from some of the best men in the business, who had also worked with his father. He became proficient in fencing. Sean may also have taken speech lessons because—in private and in his films—his enunciation and pronunciation were so deliberate, so precise.

His agent had decided there would be no publicity until they were sure Errol Flynn's son was getting a contract. So, Sean went through his first screen tests as "Steve French." The very first makeup man tried to put a mustache on him—as long as he was trying out for a pirate's role, and since he looked so much like Flynn. "I think he could have become a motion picture star more quickly if we had stuck to the Steve French thing," the agent says now. "He was probably the most beautiful nineteen-year-old kid I had ever seen in my life."

Hy Seeger was fifteen years older than Sean, but he says young girls suddenly took an interest in him whenever he would appear with Sean. He says Sean had a number of girlfriends while he was staying in Hollywood, but there were no long-lasting affairs. The ones who lasted apparently were just friends. One was John Payne's daughter, Julie, who was sitting beside Sean—fondling a rifle with both hands—in a *Life* photograph later that year.

Even his agent says Sean was "not that enthused" about doing a sequel to *Captain Blood.* But, "He thought it was the quickest way for him to get into films and he had kind of a strange pride in the identification with roles his father had done. He had never seen *Captain Blood* until one day at the house it was on television and he watched it. He had only one comment: He said his father could never have gotten away with that kind of acting if he tried to do it now.

Yet, sadly, that was precisely what young Sean set out to do. If "that kind of acting" was not outdated in his father's time, it certainly was by the early 1960's when Sean was beginning his career.

His friends there say Sean never liked Hollywood—the ghost of his father was too overpowering, and he would later describe those months as the "most miserable time of my life." Hamilton says, however, that Flynn was beginning to build a mini-version of his father's legend—firing a flare gun with Tuesday Weld from the roof of Hamilton's apartment building, sporting around in a brand new Jaguar, wearing the plumed cap of d'Artagnan. He bragged to Hamilton that he didn't need any insurance on the car and the next day he smashed it into a bridge abutment.

After several months, Sean signed a contract giving him $1,000 a week for work on *Son of Captain Blood.* The publicity buildup began on a grand scale. *Life* featured several pages of pictures of him in Hollywood, "Swatch off the old Swashbuckler." Louella Parsons interviewed him. He told her he definitely wanted to be a good actor, then proceeded to interview *her* about his father. Louella wrote, "I couldn't help but think it was such a pity that Errol couldn't have known this boy better—he is so much like him. Some way, however, I feel there's a more serious streak in the son and I doubt if he'll ever be as much of a madcap or as wild as Errol."

When Sean left for Europe in late 1961 to begin filming in Spain, he would only return to Hollywood on one or two brief visits. His mother gave him her mother's apartment on the Rue Nicolas Chuquet in Paris and that became his home. Although *Son of Captain Blood* was shot in 1962, it was not shown in Europe until 1963 and in the U.S. in the fall of 1964 when it was "teamed" with Jerry Lewis' *The Patsy* and was barely mentioned in reviews.

Of Sean Flynn, the actor, the New York *Daily News* reviewer said: "An engaging lad with a lopsided grin, Sean is not yet sufficiently seasoned to be convincing as nominal leader of a cutthroat band, an honorarium conferred by brigands who served with the deceased captain." While praising his abilities with a sword, the New York *Post* reviewer said, "As a pirate, he leaves something to be desired. I just don't believe he can be as ruthless as Errol used to be. He was brought up in Palm Beach, you know. At that age Errol was cheating cheaters in the South Seas and preparing himself to make the world his oyster. Sean still seems like a nice boy, which is going to be his handicap for some time to come."

One can only speculate about what effect this accusation of gentility, of being a nice boy, had on the son, but I think it stung. Certainly, Sean become more belligerent in his interviews, less and less "nice" in his talk about his father and about his career. He would say he was ashamed of his father's name and only did the movies for the money.

All Sean's films were low-budget European productions and all made a profit for him, although many were never shown in the U.S. Even his agent couldn't remember the names of the first three in which he was still representing Sean. These were all done with his father's first director, Harry Joe Brown, and all played on the theme of the son's chasing after a dead father. In the only one I ever saw, Sean played the son of a Basque nobleman who had left his wife and gone to Mexico. The son goes in search of the father, only to find he has been killed. The reviewers had said it right: Flynn was terribly stiff, too nice a boy to be playing those cutthroat roles. The scripts were also decades out of date. As his friend, I grieve that Sean isn't around to see the revolution in filmmaking that quickly made obsolete so much that he detested in Hollywood.

Errol Flynn unwittingly spoke his own curse on the son when he talked about himself and his legend: "The worst thing that can happen to you is to be typed after or compared with some insurmountable legend which has preceded you." Sean really had outlasted his father's legend by the time he was captured. Several times that year, GI's would come up to him and ask, not if he were Errol Flynn's son, but if he were Peter Fonda, star of *Easy Rider*, a film Sean could have done as well as Henry Fonda's son.

After three or four years in and out of the film business, Sean did get bored with it and followed the pattern he had described earlier to Sally Hobbs. He sailed for awhile on the *Zaca*. Then sometime in 1965 he set off for Africa. His mother, his friends in Palm Beach and in Hollywood, all refer to these as his "white hunter" days. But Flynn later told several of his friends in Vietnam that he was actually working as a game warden in Kenya and the shooting he had done was in the interest of preserving game. He also said he had been afraid in Africa. Why? "The feeling I was going to get killed never left me," he said.

He had often talked with his agent about how he wanted the ultimate confrontation—man and beast. He wanted to kill a tiger, not with a gun but with a spear. He had also talked with George Hamilton about wanting to see an elephant die. He did get his tiger, though not face-to-face and certainly not with a spear. He was brought into a village in East Pakistan to help kill a man-eating tiger that was menacing a village. Sean was positioned in a blind in a tree, while below him the tiger's most recent victim was left as lure. He later told friends he never saw anything in the war to match the horror he felt sitting there watching while the beast tore open the man's stomach and started eating his entrails. He shot the tiger from above. His mother now has a color photograph of him with the beautiful animal in her Palm Beach house.

Whatever he was doing in Africa, Sean did bring back a number of furs and hides to decorate his grandmother's old apartment in Paris. There were skins on the bed and an elephant's foot served as an umbrella stand. Later, he installed smoked mirrors, pyramided in the ceiling above his bed. With a coincident interest in acid rock and the war, he plugged in two electric guitars he never learned how to play and mounted a loaded M-16 above his bed.

By the end of 1965, Flynn had obviously retraced most of his father's ventures and found them wanting. He contacted the editors of *Paris-Match* and they agreed to buy his stories and photographs if he paid his own way out to the war. He had lived in France for four years. According to *Paris-Match's* foreword to Flynn's story, he had "inherited from his father a famous name and a taste for adventure." But, the story said, the adventures Sean had known were confined to the make-believe of films.

Now, Flynn told *Paris-Match*, he could not resist the chance of discovering, *"La seule grande aventure: Celle de la guerre et de la mort."* Once in the war, though, his story and his photographs were printed under the same old heading: "Son of Robin Hood in Vietnam." And the only Flynn among hundreds of names in the *World Almanac* list of American actors that year was Joe Flynn, born in 1928 in Cincinnati.

More Reasons Why

There was an old oak tree at the edge of the woods down behind the big farmhouse—seven drafty rooms tacked onto a one-room cabin, as the family had grown until it reached me, thirteenth and youngest, last and weakest. That is really where all this began for me, sometime in the early fall—no precise year or date to put on it, just the memory of that lonely feeling that would come over this male child every year when the others would be down there lined up forty or fifty feet in front of that tree.

It was as predictable as autumn—that brief gaudy pall nature pulled over the land, a deceitful cover, I always thought, for the long drab winters that followed in the Appalachian mountains where I was born and from where I never had the strength or means to escape until I fled to the University of North Carolina when I was eighteen.

Those others, the "older boys," would tack up an orange license tag, if the one from the previous season had become too rusted or bent to still make a good target. Then, one by one, they would fire the awesome death-weapons, as terrifying and thrilling to me at five, six, seven, and eight as first sex or near-death itself.

Only once did they ever let me try it. They fitted that big 12-gauge shotgun into my shoulder—which winces at the thought of it even now as I write this twenty-five years later. Then, they helped me aim; showed me just how to squeeze the trigger, real slow. I held on tight as I could, shut my eyes in fear of the awful blast that did knock me flat on my ass when I jerked the little trigger thing. I wet my pants, was sore for a week, and missed not only license tag but the entire tree. But I was still proud that I had done something for once just like the big boys.

Next day at school, I told all the others in second grade, all those in overalls and undershirts who had snickered at the short pants and piano lessons—that would have been all right if I hadn't taken them seriously and dressed up for the recitals with the girls. Only after I had done it could I laugh about shooting a gun.

For several years, I tried out for the teams: nearly fainted just in the warm-ups for junior varsity football; missed net, goal, and backboard during first, second, and third tryouts for basketball; and likewise missed every fly ball that came to me, stuck with careful consideration in centerfield so right and left could cover for me. And never in my young life did I own or ask for a bat, glove, or ball of any sort. That would have been risking the outright failure the others sneered at. I dreamed only of growing up as big and strong (which I did) as the others and someday, somehow, making the team. I would prove them wrong, those boys in eighth grade who yelled that word I barely was old enough to understand, except to know it was the worst that could be said by one boy of another. My little buddy Frankie yelled back a word he knew, but the others only laughed: Anybody ought to know that "whores" are girls. I just took another path from then on.

Hunting in the fall and an interest in sports were about the only real traditions my old man—who never read an entire book in his life—had to pass on to me. But, during the years I might have learned, he was humbled by a sequence of heart attacks and strokes that left him—a 6'4", 240-pound giant of a man—hobbling on a cane. His last months were lived between the TV set, the bathroom, and his bed. When he would fall somewhere in between, I was the only one left to pick him up . . . a thing so painfully embarrassing to both of us we could never look at each other while I was helping him. And then one morning in the dead of winter he died without ever teaching me what he knew about becoming a man, about shooting with the other fellows in the fall.

He died when I was seventeen, so he wasn't around for my late decision to join the Army Reserves after six years of dodging behind a student deferment. He saw no reason to leave his wife and family and fight in World War I, and had told me his own daddy lied about his age to avoid conscription in the Confederate army. By his silence, he endorsed what four of his sons—who were of age and in good health—did to avoid service in World War II.

My mother was the one who would fill my head with heroic tales of her granddaddy, who refused to give up his Confederate coat to some Yankee raiders, of this and that one who was so handsome as he set off for World War I and then World War II, of my brother David's joining the Navy. It was after Korea by that time, but she would cry for days about his sacrifice, about the possibility of his dying at such a young age. And then when Vietnam came along, she wrote me (July 28, 1965):

> David says, "I can't really explain why I feel like I have to get in this and I guess if I did explain even I wouldn't understand." We are getting horrible news pictures of what is going on & what our boys are doing so of course the rest of the world is getting even worse. You wouldn't know, Perry, but Ethiopia was swallowed by Fascists—Poland, Austria, etc. by Hitler. The world sat by and said, "Ain't it awful?" But England did nothing until they & France were practically eaten up—Russia was falling too—we still sat back until Pearl Harbor. . . . Well, people who have lived thru all this just feel that no country is small enough to let fall to Communists. Yes—Two world wars in my time and two America has *had* to go into or be swept off the globe along with all the countries who are now yelling, "Stay at home." . . .

Another day in 1965, she wrote:

> I almost got an attack last week walking up town. I had to pass the *!!?! punks carrying the anti-Viet signs. One of the reporters asked one of the bewhiskered so & sos if he didn't think he was hampering our efforts and causing a loss of morale at the front and he said, "Well, that's the general idea!!!!" They say just because it isn't a "declared" war they aren't committing treason! Nobody likes war except the ones who get rich on it. But when we are in it, I think a nice little treatment of living under the other rule might help. Will you please write. Love Ma.

I received that one the day before I was to be sworn into the Army Reserves. I wrote back, November 3, 1965:

> Dear Mom: as one of the punks who will at 1 A.M. Nov. 4 raise my right hand and swear simply to uphold the laws of this country, I say

to you that you are blindly misunderstanding the most exciting years in this beautiful country's history.

The freedom demonstrators, under whatever banner, in whatever dress, and shouting whatever profanity, are holding onto the grandest part of our tradition in this country. . . . It is a very lonely time for people like me. We see this ugly awful thing around us and we see the people who shout for more of it. And yet I'm not brave enough to march or burn my draft card or myself. . . .

I record these letters here with some embarrassment because they clearly tell me now that I was fully aware of the choices very early, but I lacked the courage of my convictions. And in the end, I, too, had to go to Vietnam.

In reality, I was not one of the punks, although I knew in my heart they were probably right. Our letters do represent some of the confusion of the times. She was trying hard to understand my questioning of values she had never doubted. "I'm too involved in 'my country right or wrong,'" she wrote. And yet, in my own questioning, I couldn't bring myself to break the law, to actively contradict what my mother herself believed.

In another letter, she said:

I am sure you remember the first time David left for the Navy—I wanted to die. I would feel the same if you have to go. I don't really think I could take your being in this mess. But David has developed into the sort of person who is in the middle of a fight no matter if he is on the streets of Asheville or in battle. He says that Vietnam is the most beautiful country he nearly ever saw, says it looks a lot like western North Carolina and it's such a shame for it to be torn up. . . .

Underlying all her sympathy for my doubts was still this unshaken faith in what she had always been told. My brother David was still held up to me as a man unafraid to do his duty, and Mother was proud of her boy in uniform. In spite of her spoken fears, I know that she was never more proud of me than when I finished my basic training in the Army and when I went to work "over there" if only as a correspondent. Although I've sent her several pictures of me in the fifteen years since I left home, the only one she now carries in her wallet shows me (clean-shaven head and face) in the uniform of a military policeman.

Louise and Dana in the Garden of Eden

Louise and Dana first met in San Francisco in June, 1962. She was a graduate of Randolph-Macon Woman's College and had a good-paying job teaching a reading dynamics course. One night, she and some friends were holding forth on various intellectual topics around a table in a prominent Beatnik hangout called the Coffee Gallery in North Beach.

This was the first time she had ever seen Dana. The two were immediately attracted. He snarled cracks in and out of their conversation as he paced back and forth from the jukebox to the doorway to the bar. "You're full of shit," or, "Gee, I'll bet you people went to college."

"He was four months older than me," Louise says, "but he really looked sixteen. I thought he was adorable. I have always liked small men. I was very attracted to his muscular build—beautiful arms and stubby, strong hands, straight good nose, and a deep dimple in his chin. I was watching him as he was watching me. He said later, 'I decided to go after you when I saw the way your little ass twitched when you got up to go to the john.'

"So it was a meeting of the bodies first, then a meeting of the minds—and Dana really knows how to handle the mind business. I have seen him do it many times since. A person may go away furious with him, but they never forget him."

His interruptions, she says, were as if he "put his finger through a gaping hole in what we considered an airtight philosophy. He made me very angry, but of course he attracted me because he was right and I couldn't argue my way out of the verbal traps he laid for me."

Dana volunteered to give Louise and her date a ride home that first night, and then he said he would pick them up and take them to a lecture by Aldous Huxley the next night at the San Francisco Library. After the lecture they went to the Anxious Asp bar in North Beach. Dana grabbed her hand under the table and started knocking her over topside with stories of the adventures he had already accumulated at age twenty-three.

Louise's date finally stormed out of the bar, telling her to "go with Dana, that's what you want anyway." Dana took her home to an apartment she shared with another girl. He called her a "bitch and a tease" because she wouldn't sleep with him. "But I knew this was going to be an important experience for me and I didn't want any back-seat-of-the-car or kitchen-floor seduction. It worked out perfectly and I think Dana would agree."

The next week they found the proper romantic setting—a motel room that came complete with a fireplace and an enclosed Dutch bed. "Our lovelife has always been a joy. Dana is totally uninhibited, no hangups whatsoever. I have never met anyone like him in this respect. And it is a very difficult thing for others to understand. I always think of animals when I think of making love with Dana: two cats cuddling, licking each other. We are very affectionate in public, a very unconscious affection. We have always gotten a great deal of pleasure from a sensual, animal kind of contact."

Soon after this, Louise's roommate moved out and Dana moved into her apartment—but not officially. Louise made him keep his three-dollar-a-week room in the old Golden Eagle Hotel where Lenny Bruce was staying when he either fell or jumped out a window. She insisted on this dual arrangement because she didn't want her parents to know she was living with a man.

Sometimes Louise would stay over in Dana's hotel room. He spent a lot of time staring out the window. The hotel was right next door to Enrico's, another popular place in those days, and the view was always interesting. His curiosity and interest in people—all people—was another aspect of his personality which drew Louise. "I have always been one to become totally irate and intolerant when confronted with a bigot or know-it-all," she says. "But not Dana. He would tell me, 'You can always learn something, even from the biggest fool in the world.' We would meet somebody who would say something like, 'Niggers have such hard heads you can hit um with an ax and it won't hurt um.' I am ready to attack, but Dana would be kicking me under the table to make me shut up. Then he would begin asking the man questions and would always end up learning something—about raising bees, the local irrigation system, the Korean war.''

Louise majored in art in college and had always had a talent for drawing and painting. She was so excited by the free experience with Dana that she decided to depict them and their life together in a mural on their apartment wall. It was of Adam and Eve—Louise and Dana—in the Garden of Eden, both innocent and naked as they were born. Friends told her Dana's likeness was especially accurate, the tight muscles in his shoulders, arms, and legs as finely drawn on the wall as they were in his body. "Little Body" became her nickname for him.

But their relationship was not always so happy and innocent. Given his extra energy, Dana was not an easy person to live with. "I have never doubted that he loves me," Louise says, "but he is torn between having me with him, an anchor dragging him down, or being free and missing his anchor. So when his frustration with this problem reaches the eruption stage, he strikes out—at me. Over the years, I have come to expect a blowup about every two months—an argument will start over nothing and he will hit me. I never feel it is directed at me. I remember saying once, 'You shouldn't hit me like that, you might really hurt me.' He stopped and said. 'Yeah, you're right—I might.' It was as if I had told him something that had not occurred to him.''

She recalls one particular argument: "It was one of those times when you're just so exhausted and you feel like you've been over the same thing so many times. We kept arguing and I just said, 'Well, why don't you shoot me?' ''

Her father had given her a pistol when she left home and she always kept it loaded. Dana picked up the pistol and pressed it against her temple. She didn't flinch, didn't show any fear at all. In fact, she says, she was so tired and they had already had such a good, full life together, that she sat thinking death might not be so bad. "Well, go ahead and get it over with," she said. But Dana reasoned he really could not live without her; if he shot her he would have to kill himself. So he put the pistol down.

Louise and Dana were both frightened of marriage. "Maybe I was more than Dana," she says. "I had seen too many of my friends marry, have children, and—from my viewpoint—be trapped. Marriage meant settling down, joining the establishment. It doesn't, but that's the way it looked to me then. I did not want a home in Daly City and I also knew there were things Dana wanted to do, to see, experience, and I didn't want him to feel I had trapped him. I feel now if we had married when we first met it wouldn't have lasted. I was a coward and it took Dana to make me brave, to take chances with adventure. He taught me because he wanted to. He wanted me as a companion, not because he had no choice, not because I was his wife. When my parents found out we were living together, Dana wanted to get married to end my suffering. But I wasn't going to marry for that reason. There has always been a joke between us about growing up. When Dana would do something foolish, he would say, 'Hey, Lady, am I ever going to grow up?' "

And so, after their first two months together, Dana was restless. He had heard about the wheat harvesters who went up through the Midwest into Canada. He decided that was an experience he should have and so he left Louise and went to Nebraska. After a few days, he started missing her. He called up to say she could have a job as the crew's cook if she could just get to Nebraska. Louise says she would not have hesitated later, but at that time she was afraid to give up the security of her nice apartment and she also worried about not knowing how to cook.

Dana wrote her about the "Big, big sky, Lady," and how you could see the storms coming straight at you across the prairies and you would have to work faster to harvest before the rain. When he came back to San Francisco they were much closer than they had been. She learned very early that this was a vital part of his character—always to be learning new and interesting things. "With most men I feel far superior," she says, "With Dana, I don't. He is so honest and perceptive. He never plays a role. He doesn't have to prove himself in any way to anybody. If he feels like crying, he cries. He climbs a mountain because he wants to see what's up there, not to say he climbed the mountain."

After this, Stone and Louise settled into their own apartment in an old house on the side of Nob Hill. They bought some furniture at the Goodwill Store, and made tables and shelves—painted in bright colors—out of wooden boxes they picked up off the streets in Chinatown.

But it was never all happiness and sunshine in their little garden. Once, they quit their jobs, went to Sawyer's Bar, and spent all their money, thinking they could easily find new jobs back in San Francisco. But they couldn't, no matter how hard they tried. One afternoon Louise came home from another rejection to find Dana delirious with fever. After much searching, she found a doctor who would come and treat him.

She sat by his bed day and night until he recovered. The doctor was very young and very conservative. He asked if they were living together and Louise told him, No, she was just taking care of Dana while he was sick. This lie was to figure in a later episode with the same young doctor.

By this time, Dana had got a job as a soda jerk—convenient to the drug supplies. Among other items he took for their home use was a quantity of Dexedrene. On Saturday morning Louise woke up feeling listless. She started taking more and more Dexedrene to get through her housecleaning chores. Then she walked down to meet Dana at the drugstore. They stopped off and had a drink. As they started home, she became weak and dizzy and almost fainted on the sidewalk.

The young doctor came and gave her some tranquilizers to counteract the Dexedrene. Then he raided their shelves of everything resembling a drug. He also insisted Louise come by his office for a talk the next afternoon. The doctor accused her of living with Dana just to hurt her parents. She explained that the pill-taking had been an accident. But the inexperienced doctor proceeded with his own analysis. He said he really ought to report her "attempted suicide."

When Louise told Dana what the doctor had said, he was furious. He wanted to go punch him in the nose. "It's no business of his how you are living," Dana said. "It's your business and my business. We know what we have with each other. Fuck what he says."

The only time Louise ever saw Dana drunk was once when he did it as retaliation for her coming home drunk. He went to a gay bar that night and had so much fun he had to take Louise back with him the next night. He had made a hit with everybody in the bar and all the fellows called him "dear" and "darling" and argued over who would buy his next drink. Some of them told Louise she really ought to make herself more attractive—fix up her hair, take care of her nails, use makeup. "How I wish I could do what you are supposed to be doing with yourself," one told her.

Louise liked to go to the gay bars with Dana because he was never jealous of her there. When they first started living together he would get angry if anybody offered her a drink when they went out. In the gay bars he never seemed to mind who she talked with or how many drinks she accepted.

In the spring of 1963, Louise and Dana decided they would go to Sawyer's Bar, find a cabin and settle in for a long stay. They bought a 1949 Plymouth and "adopted" two very shy German shepherds who were afraid of cats, among many other things. The date was St. Patrick's Day, 1963, so they named the dogs Sean and Moira.

They found a one-room cabin—abandoned for fifteen years—about ten miles out from Sawyer's Bar. It was in a clearing, surrounded by a thick redwood wilderness, just up from the Little North Fork River which runs into the Salmon River. Rising up behind their place was English Peak, the highest mountain in the whole area. Louise was so overwhelmed by the beauty of the place she was almost speechless. Dana interpreted her silence as disappointment, but she soon convinced him she was genuinely happy there.

Turning the place into a livable home became the focus of their lives. They covered the inside walls with cardboard and insulating paper painted white. They spread out the carpets from their San Francisco apartment and had wall-to-wall carpets. They found some old gas lamps for lighting. Dana rigged up an old sink with a handpump inside so they didn't have to run out every time they wanted water. In another cabin, he found a huge old wood stove that Louise says looked more like a crematorium.

When it came time to build a bed, Dana decided he would re-create the enclosed bed they had first made love in. He was never one to sit still long enough to read, but he loved to have others recite poetry to him or read whole books while he was working. Louise read *Of Mice and Men* to him while he built the bed. As she got closer and closer to the sad ending of George and Lenny (the fond descriptions of the farm they are never to share), Dana's work got slower and slower. Finally, he was just standing there looking out the window. When she finished, Louise saw that he was crying.

Because the floor and the ceiling of the cabin were both uneven, Dana decided the only way to make a level bed was to nail the boards in place and saw off the top as level as he could. He used a big clunker of a chainsaw he had bought cheap, secondhand. Dana held it above his head and Louise was afraid he was going to drop it and cut himself up. She was so afraid he would hurt himself, in fact, she couldn't stand to be in the cabin while he was using it. The saw became a real character in their lives, "like an obstinate friend," she says. It would break down routinely and Dana would spread out the parts on their only table. Then he would get furious that he couldn't fix it and throw the parts around. He would take a walk and Louise would have to pick up the pieces.

Dana called it "The Day of the Death of the Chainsaw" because it was a dramatic moment in their stay in the woods. "Dana had worked so hard on that damn thing and it died with a bang. Here we were, surrounded by this beautiful redwood forest and the silent wilderness and there was that ear-shattering whine of the chainsaw. And then one day it suddenly stopped, leaving 'a silence you 'most could hear.' " Dana said they should have given it a tombstone.

When their money ran out and Dana couldn't get a job, the dogs were the only ones who suffered—eating only boiled chicken feed. Louise and Dana lived, quite literally, off the fat of the land. He would kill salmon illegally, diving into the river and spearing them. A spear was just as sporting as a hook—to the fish, he would say.

Louise could net small trout. And they also dined on venison nearly every day. Whenever they ran out of meat Dana killed a deer. He and Louise would skin it and cut the meat off the bones, and store it in gallon jars in the icy river. One deer usually lasted two weeks. She became quite proficient at cooking game and they had deer and salmon every possible way she could fix it.

There was always the danger of game wardens catching them at their shopping. Once, they were cleaning a deer on their table in the cabin when they heard a car drive up in front. Dana grabbed the deer head and carcass and ran out the back door, leaving Louise with a bloody table to explain. Luckily, it was not a game warden, and

Louise teased Dana about what she would have said, "Deer blood? Ha, ha, ha. Of course not, officer. I just killed my husband."

Another time Dana and Louise were skinning a deer by lantern light. It was a doe and they found she was carrying a fully developed fawn. Louise recalls, "Dana examined everything about it, saying 'Look, Lady, eyelashes and hooves. It's so perfect, so beautiful, and so dead. And I did it.'" From then on, he would always get close enough to be sure he was shooting a buck.

The only work available in Sawyer's Bar was at a small sawmill that never needed more than ten or twelve men. But with his usual persistence Dana did get a job as a night watchman and later moving logs on the millpond. "Dana walked every day for over a month to the mill, which was a good eight-to-ten miles away and finally got a job. The foreman said, 'Anyone with as much perseverance as you have deserves to have a job.'"

It was Dana's job as night watchman to clean out the sawdust bin every night. One night he was shoveling the sawdust into the furnace, when he saw some cats. The mother cat and part of her litter had already been thrown into the fire before he saw them, but he was able to save two of the kittens. The cats were always sickly and Louise worried about them. One morning, she saw the spread-eagled footprints of one of the cats where she had tossed him out the night before. "It looked so funny. I called Dana over to look," she says. Dana didn't laugh. I looked at his face and knew something terrible was the matter. He said, 'I killed the kittens this morning.' I didn't believe him. 'How could you do it without asking me?' 'Lady, I didn't want you involved; they were too sick to live long and I couldn't watch them suffer any longer.' Then he told me how he had shot the first one and then the second one came up and smelled the muzzle of the gun, and how hard it was to kill that second one. He was crying and suddenly our roles were reversed. I couldn't be angry with him any longer. I had to comfort him, help him come to terms with what he had done."

"He hadn't thought about how he would feel afterward," Louise said, using identical phrases Dana would use later to describe some men in the 101st Airborne Division in Vietnam who shot an old farmer in front of him. "So they just shot him. Pow! No reason. They just shot him and afterwards I think everybody felt all guilty about it . . . and they had been in pretty good spirits."

For several days Dana talked with Louise about walking across two mountain ranges, to the town of Happy Camp. It was much farther and much rougher hiking (there was no trail) than his earlier walk beyond Tom Mage. The night before he was to leave Dana came home with blisters all over his palms where he had burned them grabbing onto a steam pipe at the mill. Louise was certain he would never attempt the walk in his condition, but when she woke up the next morning he had already left. He had told her to be in Happy Camp to meet him in the car the next afternoon, roughly thirty hours after he started walking.

Louise, like everybody else in town, never thought he would make it by 2 P.M. And so she was two or three hours late. When she arrived, he was sitting on a curb in Happy Camp, fuming because she was late and because she had all his identification cards with her. Even after his walk, nobody would serve him a beer because he looked so young. But he came back a hero to the folks in Sawyer's Bar. Where a lot of the old-timers had never quite accepted these city people living in sin, they now smiled and waved. The Forest Service men were especially friendly because they knew how rough the mountains were where Dana had walked.

Among Dana's best friends in Sawyer's Bar was an old man named Jay Webb—a veteran of World War I, the son of a judge, a Socialist left from the 1930's who had escaped to Sawyer's Bar presumably to hunt for gold after his wife ran off with a truckdriver. Others in the community regarded Webb as just plain weird; Dana thought he had something to say.

Louise thought Webb looked like Picasso—the same leathery skin, hooked nose, and bald head. Whenever she would tell him this, he would sigh and say, "Ah, if I had ever done anything to match 'The Master.'"

Webb lived several miles outside town, six miles over a rough trail from the main road. He had stopped caring about everything in the way of appearances and cleanliness. Once they found him in the back room of the bar. He was standing there naked, watching his filthy clothes burn. Bears had broken into his cabin and ripped apart his cook stove trying to get at the grease. Old Jay never fixed it; he just kept cooking on the part that was still intact.

Each month, Webb would walk into town to pick up his veteran's pension check. He would buy a supply of groceries and then spend everything left on his monthly drunk. He stubbornly refused to buy powdered milk just because it was lighter, and he was getting too old to carry two cases of canned milk. So, every month, Dana would help him carry it back to his cabin.

After so many months of friendship, Jay Webb presented the young couple with the only thing he had of value, a gold nugget. It became a symbol of their love—Louise kept it when things were going well, Dana got it back when they weren't.

A year or so later, there was a snowstorm that left many of the people in Sawyer's Bar stranded without food. Supplies were being flown in by helicopter, so Dana went up from San Francisco to help. He asked about Webb and nobody had seen him during the storm. Dana made it up to the cabin and found his old friend lying dead on the floor.

This period in Sawyer's Bar, from March through December, 1963, was the longest the two had ever spent together—truly the golden time in their relationship. But there was also a great deal of friction between them after living in such close quarters for so many months. By late November, they were getting into real rights and Louise was coming out the loser more and more frequently. "I loved the place, the life, everything," she says. "The problem was that I was becoming Dana's slave—mentally, I mean. In San Francisco, if we had an argument, I could walk out, there was somewhere to go. But in Sawyer's Bar, to walk out meant to walk into the woods, where you can stay just so long without getting hungry or cold. I finally realized I had to get away or lose my own personality. When I said I was leaving, Dana said, 'Good—I want to see if I can live alone here.' Later, he denied saying that."

On December 20 she loaded up the old car with her possessions, including the two dogs, and drove to the nearest telephones in Yreka. She called her parents and asked if they would take the dogs. The shepherds went by train and lived out their days on the farm in Kentucky. Louise told her parents she would be home for Christmas. The parents may have thought this meant she was through with roughing it, through with Dana Stone (whom they have still not met). But Louise was barely in San Francisco before Dana had gone over to Yreka to call her up and ask her to come back. When she wouldn't come to him, he went to her and they got another apartment in San Francisco before she went home for the holidays with Mom and Dad.

Back in San Francisco, Louise found a job with a publishing company. Dana could never find work he liked, so when spring came he went back to Sawyer's Bar and got a job as a "choker setter" with a logging team. He was handling enormous redwood and pine logs and the job of setting a cable and choker onto them was very dangerous. Once, a big redwood log rolled right at him and the only way Dana saved his life was to dive over it. Louise would visit him and stay in the logging camp on weekends.

Because of the fire danger, the loggers had to stop in the late summer. So Dana came back to San Francisco where, after a few weeks, he was bored again. He hitchhiked to New Orleans and back—a trip memorable only because he fell for one of the oldest tricks in a thumb-tripper's diary. The driver gave him money to buy them some coffee and then drove off with his gear.

His next job was sorting mail bound for Vietnam in the military section of the San Francisco post office. Dana would always call this his first "war-supported job." Although Louise had always been far more politically-minded than Dana, both had focused their attention mainly on the civil rights movement during the early 1960's. Like most Americans, they did not see Vietnam as the specter it became in the ensuing years. They did march in several anti-Goldwater demonstrations late that summer—but these, again, were mainly focused on civil rights. Dana voted against Goldwater that year, the only time he has ever voted.

Their relationship was touch-and-go during the next year. By the spring of 1965, Dana had got a job as a storekeeper on MSTS ships carrying troops and cargo to Vietnam. He came back raving to Louise that nobody realized how serious the situation was over there. The more sensational civil rights stories had obscured the reports from Vietnam. And yet, he had seen the troops jammed onto the ships, seen their camps out from Danang and Saigon: just like it was in the films of World War II.

Dana was already busy at work at being a good photographer. His aunt had left him the money to buy the cameras and he used a free photo laboratory in San Francisco. Whenever his ship docked in Vietnam, he explored as long and as far out as he could.

Louise would look at the pictures, listen to his stories, and then—after only a few days in port—say good-bye to him again. After months of this, she decided that if Dana could go to sea, so could she. She kept telling him she was going to leave, but he never really believed her. Then, one day in September, 1965, she got a call from a Scandinavian line telling her her application for a stewardess' job had been accepted and she could leave on a Danish freighter called the *Helle Skow* in three days.

The *Helle Skow* was scheduled to go to Bangkok and then return to San Francisco in two months. But once in Bangkok, the ship changed course, went through the Suez Canal, and on up to Europe instead. Louise never got back to California.

She was the only woman among a crew of thirty-six, plus a dog, a cat and millions of cockroaches. She became seasick and already started plotting ways to get sent back as the ship passed under the Golden Gate Bridge. But she was told to keep working and after a while she got her sea-legs and was never seasick again.

Louise had never done that sort of work in her life, but she soon learned by scrubbing, lifting, washing. After a few days she could heave two cases of beer up on top of a high refrigerator. "After I adjusted to the work," Louise says, "I don't think I ever felt healthier. It was fun in port, but I found myself yearning for the routine of the time at sea."

Technically, the job consisted of serving meals, cleaning up after the officers, and washing and cleaning all the rooms on the upper deck. But the captain also expected her to service him in bed. She explained very bluntly that he had hired a stewardess, not a mistress, and he left her alone after that. In Bangkok, the captain locked himself in his cabin with two Thai girls, and Louise would leave his food outside the door. She made friends with the girls the other seamen brought back on the ship and answered their many questions about her clothes, her hair, her job. She still had to work from 6 A.M. until 8:30 P.M. in port (for $60 a month), but every minute in between, she rambled about the city, staggering back just in time to go to work. When the ship reached Bremerhaven, Louise quit and went ashore. That was two days before Christmas, 1965.

Meanwhile, Dana wrote his parents in January, 1966, that he had made and spent a lot of money, "and will probably wish I had made a few more trips with MSTS, but I'm bored and want to go some place other than Vietnam. Right now!"

Not long after that he changed his mind and decided Vietnam was the place he wanted to go—only this time he would be a photographer. To earn his plane fare, he got a job on the *T/S Antigua*, a banana boat going from San Francisco to Panama to New York. He had two big windows in his own cabin, with curtains, closets, and a dresser, "just like white folks." This time, he was able to get a job on deck. "I like this—especially I like the bridge and steering the ship tho I'm not always too sure of what is expected as I never get an order completely in English and I don't speak a hell of a lot of Swedish. I get along the rest of the time as the crew is too drunk to understand any language most of the time."

Dana made one last visit to his parents in North Pomfret—the last time they saw him—then flew to Tokyo where he bought some more expensive cameras. When he went on to Saigon, his mother burned his California letters and started saving those he sent from the war.

Louise and Dana continued to write during this time. And after some months teaching at an arts school near London, she realized that they had patched up their differences when, one day, the gold nugget from Sawyer's Bar arrived in the mail. She then moved to Spain where she lived in Torremolinos from September, 1966, through October of the next year, sharing an apartment with a black American girl. The two made jewelry and sold it to tourists to pay the rent and buy food. Then, in October, 1967, she got a job as librarian at the American airbase in Seville which is where she was when Dana wrote he was on the staff of UPI and he would like for her to come be his wife. She had saved up her own money for the trip because she didn't want to get there and find the two of them had changed so much in two years they shouldn't get married.

Dana later admitted he worried about the changes, too. He said he stood back in the viewers' gallery at the Bangkok airport, waiting to see if she still looked the same before he rushed up to meet her. They spent the afternoon making plans to be married at the American Embassy on January 11, 1968. They found a jeweler who melted down their gold nugget and poured it into two cuttlefish molds. Much to the jeweler's consternation they left the bands unpolished. Louise has worn hers since that day, but the sweat under Dana's caused a fungus infection and he wasn't able to wear his in Vietnam. Louise now has hers on her finger, his around her neck on a gold chain.

The first night they stayed in the Oriental Hotel—Bangkok's oldest, most elegant establishment. Dana borrowed a jacket from one of the waiters the next morning and they were married at the Embassy. They went to an expensive American hotel on the Gulf of Siam for an old-fashioned honeymoon.

All the other guests stayed clear of the honeymooners and grinned as they walked by. Dana wrote I LOVE YOU with suntan lotion on Louise's back and the words stayed with her tan.

They were happy in love again and it didn't seem either of them had changed. But, gradually, Louise realized that something about Dana *had* altered—if nothing else, it was his language. He talked of "firefights" and "landing zones" and "smoke" and "air strikes." He told her American GI's called napalmed babies, "crispy critters." He told her about two helicopter gunners. One says, "How can you shoot women and children?" "Well," the other answers, "you just don't lead them as much."

Louise began to worry about being a wife in the war. She wondered if she would ever learn when to laugh.

The Ratio of Terror to Boredom

In early January, 1967, Dana Stone was hospitalized with his first attack of malaria, which he said, "doesn't hurt as much as I thought it would. When I'm in bed I'm bored and bitch until they let me get up, then once I'm up I realize I'm not as well as I figured I was and don't want to do anything anyway." He would have recurring attacks of malaria for the remainder of his stay in Southeast Asia, and he always carried quinine tablets with him.

Except for that "vacation" with the Special Forces, Dana stuck with the war without a break for almost a year. Then in April, 1967, he wrote his parents:

> I'm not sure whether or not I'm finished in Vietnam—it looks as tho the war will last awhile, a long while, but I'm not sure that I would, and the risks were getting way out of proportion to the gains. I seemed to be getting the same pictures that I had made many times before and as I became more accustomed to the war what had initially been interesting and exciting became dull and frightening. Six or 8 days of boredom and 3 or 4 hours of pure terror. Well, anyway I did it for almost a year and that's a good deal longer than I've done anything else and that's reason enough to go do something different—next year for sure I'll settle down and amount to something we can all be proud of.

And so, Dana wrote, "I ain't going to war no more—for awhile anyway. I'm back on a boat that's called the *U.S. Conqueror.*" He sent home a prized 500 mm lens which the Soviet News Agency Tass had awarded one of his pictures along with a medal given him as third prize in another international contest, "in Holland I think, the Hague or something like that." The picture that won this last prize shows a little Vietnamese boy crying from the pain of a bandaged head wound.

UPI noted in its in-house newsletter: "DANA STONE, our expert free-lancer who took 3rd prize in the Hague World Photo Competition has left Vietnam. He went as he came . . . crewing on a ship and now is floating somewhere between Saigon and Manila."

It was as if Stone had chosen the wackiest ship in the Orient so he could come back to Vietnam and amuse his friends with a new batch of stories. The *Conqueror* had three different captains and six different mates in only two months.

In Taiwan, one crew member was run over by a wagonload of pineapples being pulled by a cow. "Another guy punched a taxi trying to hit the driver," Dana said. "Broke his hand and the company did something with him. Another guy went crazy and he is gone too. The day before we left Taiwan, the chief mate quit and when I came off the ship sick the captain was just quitting."

Apparently his sickness in late May was another bout of malaria. He wrote from the hospital in Hong Kong: "They don't yet know what's wrong with me—whatever it is I'll most likely be over it or dead of it before they have come to rest in an official verdict—tomorrow I think that they will start treating me for malaria."

During one stopover in Saigon, the ship's cook went berserk and took a fire ax to one of the officers. An American seaman decided he was going to get rid of two foreigners who had been working illegally on the ship. "They promptly told him what he could do with his Americanism," Dana wrote, "so he went and got his knife and a karate-type Japanese-American and the two went to war against those who would seek to take from us our basic freedoms, etc. Well, justice triumphed—god is on our side you know and the Belgian and the Norway guy left the ship that night. The bosun left the next day."

The ship was back in Saigon in June and Dana wrote: "I'm all set to jump ship if only the thing would sail. I can't leave while it's still in port, they might come looking for me." He and the captain got into an argument in front of an American embassy official "and I have somewhat of an excuse for jumping ship."

The shipping company owed Dana more than $1,200 and apparently he never was paid. "So I think it's nevermind (about the pay) and anyway I miss the war."

He took the staff job with UPI then, with the understanding that he wouldn't have to report into the office all the time, could more or less stay in the northern provinces and go where he wanted to. The big war story at the time was at the U.S. Marine outposts along the southern rim of the demilitarized zone. Stone wrote his parents:

> I just came in today with pretty good stuff but it's not a game anymore. The NVA artillery and mortars that are pounding our ground troops all the time—goddamn awful to hear a mortar tube pop or a muzzle blast from a field piece and know that you have about 3 seconds to find a hole and then to hear them continue to boom at you for goddamn ever. And you only lie there just waiting to see your legs disappear and hope it won't hurt too much or that you won't blow your cool and cry too much over a minor wound . . . so worry about me, my family. . . .

Stone took the one picture which best illustrated that incredible moment of terror in the muddy uncovered trenches in Vietnam. It was perhaps the ultimate moment in that war, where hundreds of Marines crouched in the fetal position waiting for death. Dana's picture shows one Marine crouched in a trench at Con Thien, and it was used as a *Time* cover in October, 1967. It was a significant recognition of his work, because the magazine had to use a black and white cover, something it has rarely done in recent years.

In the three days Dana was at Con Thien there were 275 Marines wounded at the tiny outpost. "It just amazed me the way stuff was coming in," he wrote. "I wandered around and I knew I was getting good stuff . . . so I got my pictures and I went back to Danang and I was pretty happy."

These would have been the first pictures of Con Thien, one of the Marines' major disasters in the war. But Dana sent his pictures by another correspondent to Saigon. "So I was goofin' around and the next day I called 'em and I asked how they were, if they'd moved any of them, and they said they han't gotten 'em and I was screamin' and yellin'. Stamp my feet . . . go on up there and about get blown away and then lose the pictures.'' He said it was his own fault because the other correspondent didn't know he was supposed to notify UPI about the pictures and he had just kept them in his hotel room. Eventually the pictures did turn up, but meanwhile Stone decided he had to go back to Con Thien. He told the AP's Henri Huet and the two went up together.

Even the headquarters base at Dong Ha was taking incoming rounds when they landed there. At Con Thien, a friend of Dana's told him, everything had changed—for the worse. It was that day Stone took his *Time* cover photograph. ''Those trenches were good for pictures,'' he said. Once they were at the outpost, he wandered away from Huet, trying to take some pictures of a young corpsman.

Then, other Marines started yelling ''incoming'' and telling the two of them to ''get in the hole, get in the hole.'' Dana lingered a bit and the platoon leader gave him a shove into a trench. Some rounds hit nearby and they could hear men yelling for the corpsman. Dana said he thought, ''Somebody's got hit near where Henri was. . . .Oh, Christ, he's gettin' all the good pictures. So I went runnin' up there and I saw 'em takin' these wounded guys out of the trench. I forgot about Henri and started taking pictures. Pretty good stuff—guys pretty torn up. Then, all of a sudden I heard Henri cry out. He was sayin', 'Dana, Dana.' But I couldn't see him. He was on the other side of the trench. I'm thinkin', That last guy really got torn up, got his arm blown off, and I was thinkin' Henri got it the same way. Anyways, there he was—a couple little holes, didn't seem like much to me. Course it is if it happens to you. Actually, it turned out to be a pretty serious thing.''

The others were helping get Henri on a stretcher, and he was taking his cameras off and telling Dana to take a picture of him with his own camera. That way his picture would run, not with a UPI credit line, but with his own employer's name on it. And that is how it was printed in *Time* the next week.

Getting a picture on the cover of *Time* was, in Dana's words, ''about the biggest thing that's ever happened to me.'' He seemed to have an endless supply of the covers—sending them to friends and family, replacing one on the UPI office wall that Tom Corpora kept tearing down and hiding. *Time* paid him $300 for the picture; UPI gave him some extra money and raised his salary $25 a week.

UPI also told him not to accept a higher salary from anybody else without first checking with them.

And so Dana was the success he had always wanted to be as he sat there in his expensive Hong Kong hotel room talking into a brand new tape recorder to his mom and dad and little brother.

Goofing with Tim Page

During the summer of 1966, most of the photographers were following the Buddhist struggle movement in the cities, rather than pursuing the jungle fighters. In many ways the street fighting was more dangerous than combat in the jungle. It was, anyhow, where Tim Page got his second (of four) major wounds.

Page was unquestionably the wildest of the characters Flynn and Stone met through UPI. He had left his middle-class home in Orpington, a suburb of London, when he was seventeen. His bourgeois background was always obscured by the crazier stories of his more recent adventures. He was born May 25, 1944. His father was killed while working as a merchant seaman on a ship delivering supplies to Russia during World War II. An accountant and his wife adopted Page and reared him as their own son.

There are vague stories of Page's adventures when he first reached the Orient, but as early as 1964 he was already working as a photographer. He was able to sneak out the first pictures of a coup d'etat in Laos in January, 1965. He sold these to UPI and then on February 2, 1965, he arrived in Vietnam as a staff photographer for UPI.

A large part of Page's reckless reputation stemmed from his early and open involvement with drugs. Correspondents who smoked grass in those days didn't talk about it. One young UPI photographer was fired on the spot when a single joint was found on him in a search at the airport in Saigon. To show how quickly the corporate attitudes changed, another UPI employee was convicted of smuggling forty pounds of hashish into the U.S. in 1969 and never lost his job.

Page was a lovable, charming little boy at times. On other occasions he could be an ogre, clinically watching others' suffering. His "toys" included the weapons of war, along with the model boats, planes, and racing cars he and Flynn would build. He could recite whole chunks from what he had read and at the most appropriate moment. I marveled at his poem-soliloquy on farting—only to discover later he had borrowed it from Genet. His language was generally a put-on—full of puns and Cockney rhymes and phrases he had picked out of books. He had read Anthony Burgess' *Clockwork Orange* and he would often employ the language used by the brothers in it.

Page was a spellbinder in the best tradition of storytellers. I have seen real pacifists entranced by his melodic descriptions of the joys of war. In the face of those normally outraged by the American side of the war, he could talk on and on about "the bloody dinks"—and get away with it.

Page was also a very fine photographer. He published more than eighty pages of pictures in *Life*—probably a record for a free-lancer. But the magazine never put him on its staff because of his uncompromising craziness.

He was first wounded during Operation Starlight near Chu Lai in September, 1965. He received, in his words, "three pieces of shrapnel in the bum." By the time of his second wound, he and Flynn were the closest of friends, and they nearly always traveled together.

The second wound came during the Buddhist riots in Danang in late July, 1966. Page and some others had been lured into a sniper's line of fire between the government troops and the demonstrators. Page was hit in the hand and in the face. Blood was spurting all over him. Flynn ran through the firing to get help. He came back with a Marine officer and a jeep from the press center. They ripped off a door, strapped Page to it, and then tied the whole contraption onto the front of the jeep in World War II fashion. There are some dramatic photographs of Flynn helping to carry his wounded comrade: There is no masking the love and concern in his eyes.

After this wound, Page was taking fairly easy assignments. One was a routine cruise aboard the U.S. Coast Guard cutter *Point Welcome*. Once again Page became a casualty of war when American F-4 Phantom jets strafed and bombed their own ship on nine different passes.

Two Coast Guardsmen were killed, one died later from his wounds, and nine others were wounded. Page survived, but he had 800 pieces of shrapnel in him this time. His wounds were more serious, slow in healing. He spent three weeks in the American military hospital in Saigon. Civilians must pay upwards from $45 a day in these hospitals. Page had no money himself, and there was no agency legally responsible for his bills. But the military hospital kept sending him the bills and Page saved every one of them. Finally, he stapled them all together, along with *Time's* Press column report of the incident, and sent them to the commander of the U.S. 7th Air Force in Vietnam. He never received another bill.

It was while Page was recuperating from this incident that Flynn invited him to come to Singapore and be an extra in his last movie. This one was called *Cinq Gars Pour Singapour* and it was about five American Marines in Singapore.

Page was in some of the bar scenes and he says it was all a "goof," one of his favorite words. The movie crews and cast took over a beautifully decadent old hotel just outside the city. The hotel's patio stretched out to an expanse of sometimes seawash, generally filthy-stinking mud. There was only one news story about the filming. At one stage, the "models" hired to work as bargirls walked off the set because they insisted they weren't *that* kind of girls and their contracts didn't include kissing.

Whatever Flynn's attitude had been in the beginning ("I want to be a good actor") by this time he was dismissing the movies simply as a means to make more bread in order to stay in Vietnam. He had arrived there in mid-Janury, 1966, planning to stay two months. After three months he wrote in *Paris-Match* that he was just beginning to learn about war and death, so he thought he would stay awhile longer.

The Singapore trip apparently was Flynn's first attempt to leave the war. When he returned to Vietnam, a co-worker at UPI recalled

Flynn looked like a "man who's just come off a drunk and is anxious to get back to work and straighten himself out."

Later, Flynn's friends were still teasing him about one incident he was involved in after he came back from Singapore. It was in late November, and Flynn was with an Australian army platoon near the coastal city of Vung Tau. The story was in all the newspapers and one of the magzines said Sean was "now getting his kicks covering the Vietnam war as a free-lance photographer." The platoon was moving through the woods when Flynn spotted the wires to a claymore mine. He yelled "Claymore! Claymore!" And, as one magazine reported it, "The Aussies gratefully hit the dirt while Sean calmly snapped pictures within range of the deadly device. In the nick of time, his comrades spotted and shot the Viet Cong who was about to set off the mine, and only then did Captain Blood's boy stop to ponder. What if the thing had gone off? Choosing a line from practically any of Errol's old roles, Sean said, 'I would have been finished.' "

This was how we talked about it at a party at Stone's house in Danang in 1968 (transcript of a tape recording):

PAGE: The headlines were, SEAN FLYNN, ERROL FLYNN'S SON SAVES AUSTRALIAN PLATOON.

FLYNN: It's a company, too.

PAGE: And it was just like talking to Flynn. He was very stoned and he got everything fucked up. You listen to Flynn.

STONE: Those guys were gonna kill you, too. You don't know? All I know is one day I was sitting in the UPI office when these three grumpy Australians—

PAGE: They wanted to kill him.

STONE: They didn't know where you were.

FLYNN: Yeah, and I wasn't there.

STONE: Yeah, you were. One time they came in and wanted to kill 'im and then another time they came in and you were there. They didn't know what to do when they saw you. They hadn't counted on you being there.

FLYNN: I hadn't counted on 'em coming in. I'd been staying away from the office for a week.

SMISER: What actually happened?
FLYNN: Well, actually, the story—
PAGE: Actually!
FLYNN: Well, it's true, I just can't tell it.
PDY: I was the hero they said I was.
FLYNN: That and the NVA—well, that's hard to say. I mean, in this war, what their motives are. You know, I mean, if the guy ran away, you don't know whether he was afraid or, you know, killed. Right?

Flynn was the only real movie star in Saigon, a town starved for anything glamorous. He and Page were invited to a very elegant New Year's party given by some wealthy French people. There were two or three ambassadors there with their wives and then there were Flynn and Page. "We thought, *What would the Viet Cong wear to a New Year's Party?*" says Page. So the two of them turned up in black pajamas and sneakers, goofing again.

Friends of Page's tell me he had no plans to leave Vietnam, even after his third serious injury. A number of his buddies and employers got together and talked him into accepting $1,000 from *Life* for a ticket back to London. Later, he stayed with Flynn and another friend in Paris, then he got his own place on the Ile St. Louis.

Flynn left Vietnam a second time in February, 1967, and from all I can find out he did not return for another year. Page flew back from Los Angeles after Tet, after he heard that Flynn was back in Saigon. The premiere of Flynn's last movie was in Paris in the spring of 1967. He and Page and about six or eight friends got stoned beforehand and then jammed into a 1952 English taxicab Page had. "We were really stoned," Page says. "Everybody was in evening dress except us in Levi's. Flynn really didn't care two fucks for it. Then we went out and scored some more stuff."

In February and March of 1967, Flynn made his last visits to his mother in Palm Beach and to his friends in Hollywood. His mother has pictures of him and her husband with her as they met at the airport. She says he didn't want to talk about Vietnam, and certainly he didn't mention anything about going back.

It was the first time his old friend, Steve Cutter, had seen him since Sean left home for Duke University. "It was so exciting," Steve says. "It had been like eight years." Steve had since married, but he and his wife had a friend who took a liking to Sean and the two couples went to the Coral Beach Club, dancing at the discotheques and out to a rifle range to try out some new weapons Flynn had got from his friend at the gun shop.

Flynn packed up his guns and carried them with him when the four flew over to Freeport for a few days. He gave Steve a .44 Winchester he still has. Flynn had planned to fly to Europe from the Bahamas, but he changed plans and had to go back through customs into the U.S. He had just started wearing a "Zapata" mustache and the customs checker happened to be a Mexican. Flynn made jokes about his mustache and carried his weapons on through.

Steve says that Flynn seemed to be very tired when he came back, saying, "It's so peaceful here in Palm Beach," and that he was "so thankful to get off all this—to be away from the war and the drugs and all. . . ." Steve said he kept watching for changes in his old friend, but "to me he was the same as always."

After his visit in Palm Beach, Flynn flew to Hollywood. He talked to his agent about resuming his acting career in the States. The agent says now he could have got Flynn back in the business—starting with television parts and then going on to the movies. But what Flynn wanted to talk about mostly was a documentary film about Vietnam. There actually were people interested in backing such a film, but the agent says Flynn left before any contracts could be signed. Years later—right up to the day of his capture—Flynn would still be talking about that film and he had filed away a number of reels for it.

Back in Paris, Flynn assumed a new career as a fashion photographer. He had bought two expensive Hasselblad cameras in Singapore for that purpose. He met a number of models. One German girl—whom Page called "Baby Nazi"—wrote to him after he returned to Vietnam.

Flynn had a Triumph Trophy 650 scrambler motorcycle he rode around Paris, wearing a deerstalker cap. He also bought a Cooper minicar, bright red, that he outfitted with drag tires on the back, bucket seats, and a stereo tape deck. He and Page lived a wild life in

Paris—two young adventurers come back from the war. Dozens of people glimpsed them only briefly at one of their fabled parties and they recall vivid images of Flynn sitting there stoned, of Page making out with a girl in the bathtub while the party proceeded in another room.

The Six Day War between the Arabs and Israelis caused a brief interruption in their partying. There were no regular flights into Tel Aviv that week, Page says, but Flynn rushed down and volunteered to drop in as a paratrooper if he had to. Somehow he was able to get in on a flight the second day of the war. Page missed the flight and got only as far as Beirut and Amman working for *Life*.

Flynn wrote Steve Cutter that there were so many staff photographers covering the Sinai campaign he knew he would never sell any pictures. "So I have to content myself with seeing devastation the likes of which I never saw in Vietnam." One thing he and an English correspondent did in that war only added to Flynn's legend. "But," he swore a year later at a party in Danang, "it's all true. I've got the pictures."

He and Don Wise of the London *Daily Mirror* had rented a Volkswagen bug and had skirted the Israeli guards as they went down through the Sinai looking at the destruction left from the fighting. They had been laughing with Mandie Rice-Davies (who had gone on from the Profumo scandal in London to marry an Israeli captain and open a discotheque in Tel Aviv) that they would bring her a souvenir. They spotted a 106 mm recoilless rifle mounted on a carriage. Wise reached out and pulled the weapon out of a minefield and the two hitched it onto the back of their Volkswagen. The gun was quickly confiscated by the Israeli guards at the first checkpoint they reached on the trip back.

When they got back to Paris, Page presented Flynn with an Arab legionnaire's headdress. Flynn gave Page a Russian helmet. After this, Page and Flynn also spent some time in London. George Hamilton says the two showed up at his hotel room one night dressed in Viet Cong black pajamas. Flynn had told me about sitting in Hamilton's room, dialing the White House, and talking to the President's daughter—the ultimate goof.

Dana Stone found out about Flynn's wearing the black pajamas in London and Paris and teased him unmercifully. Every time Flynn would start to tell a story about something he had done, Stone would interrupt to ask if he were wearing his black pajamas when it happened.

Flynn stayed on in Europe, but Page went off for his first visit to the United States. While he couldn't go on a combat assault in New York, he did get busted with The Doors during a concert in New Haven. Page stayed in the U.S. and Flynn stayed in Europe and the two didn't meet up again until the next year when they were back in the war together.

Keeping House in Danang

Throughout his war days, Dana Stone was a specialist in I Corps, the military designation for the northernmost provinces in South Vietnam. (It was pronounced "eye" Corps.) He had always lived and worked out of a tiny cot in the UPI room at the Danang Press Center. But for his new bride he rented a two-room villa on the other side of town, and he bought a Honda motorbike for the family car.

He had told the cleaning girls and waitresses at the press center that he was going to get married and they rushed out to meet Louise the day she arrived in Danang. They came up and touched her—especially her long braid of hair reaching down to her thighs. One cleaning girl unpinned her own hair to show Louise hers was just as long. Louise says it was the first time she had ever felt big and awkward around anybody. The Vietnamese girls were not only as thin as she, and inches shorter, they were also the most graceful people she had ever encountered.

Their first day in the new house, Dana went off to the war and left Louise to begin housekeeping. She went to the central market, a confused maze of stalls and shops. She was trying to find some whitewash for the inside walls of their house. A young boy who spoke English saw she was having trouble, so he helped her find the right place and negotiated the price for her. Then he gave her a ride home in his truck. Louise tried to pay the boy for his help, but he said no, maybe someday she could help him. She never saw him again.

Late on the afternoon of January 29, 1968, the eve of Tet (the same time I arrived in Saigon), Dana got back from several days in the field. Although he was very tired, he told Louise they ought to get out and see all the festivities. They got on the Honda and rode among the happy crowds—old relatives getting together and laughing, young children throwing confetti and clanging noisemakers, everybody setting off huge strings of firecrackers. In Saigon, I was starting on a round of parties and barhopping.

Louise had become used to the noise of the planes taking off and landing at the airbase near their house, and there was the additional noise of the Tet revelers. But, at 2 A.M. January 30, she was shaken out of bed by the loudest noises she had ever heard. Dana was sound asleep and Louise had to wake him. He told her it was definitely "incoming." He dressed and rushed off to the press center to find out what was happening—leaving her alone with the radio, which was broadcasting yet another sound she had never heard: "Redalert-redalert-redalert-redalert."

For two hours Louise waited, not even knowing what to fear. Then Dana came back to get her on the Honda. He told her there was a fire at the edge of town but it was too dark to get any good pictures. The rockets had hit the airbase and the military was providing a bus to take correspondents out to look at the damage. Dana sent Louise on the bus and he went back to the fire—which turned out to be a firefight, the front ranks of a full battalion of Communist troops who could have marched on into town, but for their own ineptitude.

Dana still didn't know it was a firefight and not a fire when he went to the airbase and got Louise. He told her about seeing three bodies sprawled in the street—one with its head blown off. Louise tried to prepare her mind and stomach for the scene because the only dead people she had seen previously had been in funeral parlors, painted up to look as if they were alive.

Some South Vietnamese soldiers yelled "Stop!" as they neared the scene of the action, but Dana drove on past them up to the bodies. Louise says she felt sick and her muscles were so taut she was sore the next day. Dana explained to her that an American M-16 rifle fired at close range had knocked the head off one body. Louise tried to hold the camera as Dana had showed her, but she couldn't keep steady, and just as she had the bodies in focus, bullets started whizzing by them from both directions. Dana yelled for her to get down. But Louise was quite literally scared stiff and she just stood there. Dana knocked her into a gutter and told her to get on the motorcycle and go back to the press center. She knew she could never manipulate the motorcycle in her condition, so she walked back down to a crossroads and hitched a ride.

An old Southern colonel was leading the cheers on the dock at the press center, where a crowd had gathered to watch the American planes dive-bombing in the area where Louise had just left Dana. The colonel kept shouting: "Get 'em, get those little bastards," as if he were cheering on Ole Miss or LSU.

The war had never been so convenient to the Saigon telephone lines in the press center communications shack—a plyboard A-frame building in the middle of the compound. After two hours in the near war, the correspondents came back truly elated with the stories they were yelling (as if by megaphone) into the long distance lines to their offices in Saigon. ("Mac-V," "Working working working—working, goddammit," "Tiger could you get me. . . .")

A young Marine sergeant on duty in the shack kept getting up and wiping off the wall where an AP reporter was leaving bits of blood and brain that had stuck to his back. Dana also returned with somebody else's blood on him. He never noticed or bothered to explain where it had come from.

After the bombing, Dana insisted Louise get back on the bike and go with him to see how much damage had been done by the bombs. Vitetnamese civilians were pouring back in—trying to retrieve their few belongings and escape the battle area. Louise wanted to stop and help. But Dana told her she couldn't help everybody: if she stopped for everybody who needed help in Vietnam she wouldn't get anything else done. Then Dana stopped and gave an old man a ride. They also saw a huddle of some 200 refugees who had been rounded up for questioning as Viet Cong suspects. Dana explained that the huge "sale day" tags they wore meant they would be interrogated and then either imprisoned or released to refugee camps. None had homes to go back to. The Marines also piled up the thirty bodies of the enemies killed in the fighting and left them in the sun all day as a warning to the villagers.

By dinnertime, rumors had reached the press center that the Viet Cong had taken over the old imperial capital of Hue and were flying the liberation flag over the citadel there. Dana, of course, had to be there. He and Louise went to bed early, in one of the cots in the UPI room. The other correspondents wouldn't let them sleep. There was loud laughter from the other rooms as stories were swapped about the good day's war. And when Louise and Dana were just beginning to doze off, they were tossed out of their bed by one of the celebrants.

Arrived Safely, Happy Tet!

I sent two postcards after arriving in Saigon January 29, 1968. One said: "Arrived Safely, Happy Tet!" The other said: "Rumors, even posted on the bulletin board at the main officer's club, that the airbase may be hit with rockets and mortars."

It is a peculiar notation in my collection of Vietnam memorabilia—documentation of the near-complete surprise with which the Communists carried out the 1968 Tet Offensive. The Americans had expected only a few rounds of incoming at the airbase. The Communists actually hit thirty towns and cities in the offensive's first phase. They took over the city of Hue and hit the ammunition dump at Khe Sanh, causing the Americans' own explosives to destroy nearly everything standing above ground and forcing the Marine defenders underground with the rats.

I spent all my second day in Saigon taking dictation from UPI reporters in Danang, Pleiku, Nha Trang. With remarkably bad timing, the bureau chief had sent out nearly everybody in the office and there was nobody left except Kate Webb to cover the attacks on Saigon that began precisely at 3 A M. the next morning. At that time, Kate was trying desperately to get a flight up to the action in the central highlands when she heard the U.S. Embassy in Saigon was under attack and went there instead.

The guerrillas who had staged the Embassy raid had all been killed by the time I got out of the office for a walk around town. I hadn't expected there would be any more war left, but I could hear some light pop-pop-popping near the Presidential Palace.

Tree by tree, I edged up to the firing, asking each cluster of American civilians—tourists out watching the war—what was happening. The VC were holed up in that unfinished luxury apartment building on the far corner of the block, across from the back gate to the Presidential Palace.

A burly American soldier came waddling up the street, a big grenade launcher on his shoulder. He was yelling in English at the little Vietnamese soldiers inside the palace grounds, "Open the goddamn gate!" They couldn't make him understand that they didn't have a key. Then a Korean officer ran up, pleading with the American not to fire the bazooka—it might go over the building and hit Korean troops on the other side. No communication here: The American swore at the Korean, aimed his pistol at the Vietnamese, climbed over the gate, and started firing.

At the corner lay two sets of bodies—two incredibly small Viet Cong boys sprawled beside a toylike truck loaded down with two 100-gallon barrels of TNT; and two American MP's, their bloody torsos hanging out either side of a jeep that was stopped as if for a traffic light at the corner. Two bantam roosters pecked at the puddles of blood under the MP's and then began fighting. A Vietnamese civilian kicked over one of the dead Viet Cong. His body—rigid and lifeless as a doll—rolled into the gutter, exposing the explosives taped to his stomach.

Some Vietnamese soldiers shoved a high rickety bamboo ladder up against the apartment building and a very drunk American civilian grabbed one of the soldier's berets and led the charge, waving his hat back to some friends crouched beneath the firing. Later, a young medic risked his own life to drag that one's wounded body out of the building. (Recovering in a hospital back in the States, the wounded civilian provided the Associated Press with a heroic description of his actions that day.)

This fight lasted for thirty-six hours—with the Koreans firing from their embassy down the street, the Vietnamese firing from every direction, or so it seemed, and various stray American military men and civilians also firing over the bodies at the corner. The next day I went in behind National Police General Loan and his troops as they stormed the building and found on the top floor one very small Viet Cong man's body with a machine gun and no more hand grenades.

I went from this action directly to the afternoon briefing for reporters. The American military spokesman assured the correspondents the firing near the palace was over and no Amerians had been involved. I went back to my office and pecked out my first war report for UPI. The next afternoon, I was delighted to read a personal message to YOUNG/SAIGON: NEW YORK *DAILY NEWS* SPREADS YOUR PENTHOUSE SIEGE ACROSS TOP OF PAGE THREE. SOME DEBUT. CONGRATULATIONS. But when the story itself came through the mail, I felt sick. It had been rewritten by the same man who had advised me in New York: "The important thing is to get that MACV release and get it on the wire, we'll take care of the writing here." The story was his own creation and—13,000 miles and a day removed from the scene—it had no resemblance to anything I had seen.

Also in the UPI office in Saigon during Tet was a young Marine, a British citizen who had previously worked for UPI in Des Moines. He was waiting for the final word on his discharge so he could shift uniforms and become a UPI correspondent in Vietnam. The staff also included another ex-Marine, an ex-Green Beret sergeant and an ex-paratrooper who had a nice little apartment directly over the apartment of Thankful and Dan Southerland (he was then a UPI writer).

Dan had been at Chapel Hill when I was, although we never met there. He was perhaps the most conscientious reporter I ever knew in Vietnam. His wife, with the very fitting name, was singularly dignified in that wacky Tet scene. She worked every day for three months as a Red Cross volunteer in the main hospital near the airbase; she took care of the numerous relatives of her maid when the city was being rocketed; later, she taught at Saigon University. She was most anxious for me to move in upstairs as soon as she heard that the ex-paratrooper had been wounded the second or third night after Saigon was attacked. He was a burly fellow whom I had barely glimpsed around the office. Dana wrote about what happened to him in another of the unmailed letters he saved:

He got drunk or drugged up and ran a white mouse road block—maybe on purpose, maybe too fucked up to know what he was about. He had a girl in the Melody who was going to marry an Australian. He threatened to kill her if she did. Katey Webb said he took a batch of sleeping pills the night before in an attempt at suicide. Anyhow, he was hit about five times and is in a hospital in the states now—something about all those parachute guys.

Louise was in the UPI room with some of Dana's co-workers when the word came up—not that the man had been wounded but that he was dead. She says there was a brief moment of stunned silence, then everybody dived for the gear he had left in a locker there. Laughing as they divided it up, they said it probably hadn't belonged to him anyway.

The rumors about this guy's thievery proved true when several of Sean Flynn's cameras, that he had stored in the UPI office, turned up among the man's belongings. (Sean had saved the serial numbers.) When I went over to look at his apartment, I found an interesting bookshelf. Two little volumes of Lawrence Durrell's poetry caught my eye. Durrell's characters in *The Alexandria Quartet* are so familiar to me they often figure in my dreams. His poetry, I knew, had been printed in very limited editions. I thought I wouldn't even have to steal them: I would just move in and mix them with my books and nobody would ever know. But before I could go to the hotel and get my luggage, somebody visited the apartment and took not just those little books but everything else of any value left in the place.

Hue

The takeover of Hue was the most elaborate part of the Communists' Tet Offensive in 1968 and it was the most successful. Most of the existing officials were executed and replaced by Viet Cong cadre. The Saigon-appointed province chief hid in an attic until it was safe to come down. For twenty-two days, the flag of the National Liberation Front flew over the thick-walled citadel that surrounded the Imperial Palace and government buildings.

More than any other place in either Vietnam, Hue had come to represent all that was ennobling and refined in Vietnamese culture. Saigon had never been a Vietnamese place; the name came from a Chinese suburb of the older city of Cholon. Before the French made it one of their trading ports in the 1860s, Saigon had been a small Cambodian fishing village.

Hue was where a number of the leading Viet Minh and government officials in North Vietnam had been educated. The university was located there and the place had traditionally been the center of anticolonial (French and American) sentiment. Hue had been the capital during that brief sixty-year period in the nineteenth century, the only time when Vietnam was ever one country. The official language was not that Westernized patois the French priest devised as the "Vietnamese" language, it was Chinese. The Imperial Palace and the emperors' tombs were replicas of the Imperial Palace in Peking. The Chinese emperor had given the Vietnamese emperor eight huge bronze urns (replicas again) to represent the provinces of his domain. The strongest of the emperors had been Minh Mang, who refused to receive the first American emissary sent by President Andrew Jackson. He had also carried out a violent campaign to rid the country of all Western influence, causing 42,000 Christians to be killed because they would not trample the cross, according to a Catholic missal on the subject that I read in Hue. This caused the French to come back into Vietnam—the merchants and planters led by the pious missionaries. In the 1860's, the French finally took over the whole country and a hundred years later—their interests now protected by the Americans—they still own the rubber, tea, coffee, beer, electric companies.

Hue was truly the most beautiful spot in all of Vietnam. The citadel was surrounded by canals from the Perfume River, which separated the old city from the newer sections where the university was. I never saw it except in rubble, but others would tell me about the elegant restaurants, the Cercle Sportif with its terrace built over the river, and life on the sampans. It was considered the most romantic moment in a correspondent's life to make it with a beautiful Vietnamese girl on a sampan in the Perfume River. During the fighting when I saw the place, I couldn't help but laugh at the memory of those tales as I watched the ugliest old hag trying to sell me her body as we crossed the river on a boat crowded with refugees.

Dana Stone was among the first to get in and out of the fighting in Hue. The Communists had blown up the small bridges over the canals and the big steel bridge (built by the Eifel company) across the river. When he first arrived there, nobody could know how much of the city was still in Communist control. From all reports, the only surviving outpost was the MACV compound. Some American civilians were known to have been captured the first day of the attack.

The battle in Hue was perhaps the most exciting in the Vietnam war. The place itself looked like one of those French provincial towns caught in the fighting in World War II. A friend said, "It looked the way a war should look." The fighting there was street by street and it was the same as in the movies, with the enemy flag flying and the American forces moving up and ripping it down.

Dana wrote another of his unmailed letters after he got out of Hue, saying: "I spent a week in Hue and got my fill of street fighting. I liked the looting tho—and think I got pretty good pictures and most of all I made it through in one piece again. . . ." His pictures were published around the world and they showed the American Marines ransacking the beautiful villas in Hue, wantonly destroying classrooms in the university. One group smashed up a row of microscopes in a laboratory. Others ignored a pathetic note on the library door: WE HAVE SCANTY NUMBER OF BOOKS LEFT; PLEASE DO NOT DESTROY. There were no books left. Most of the Marines had never been in such fine houses in their lives and Dana came back with stories about how they seemed amazed to find out that all the Vietnamese didn't live in refugee huts. He photographed one boy opening a bottle of champagne; the first time he had ever tasted it.

By the time I got up to Danang, Dana was already in the midst of the battle in Hue and wounded. Recently, I came across this notation in my notebooks—"Dana Stone, he's up and walking around." I had taken that from a UPI correspondent in Hue and repeated it to Louise, who had worried ever since that first morning when she saw Dana get dressed up just like a soldier—boots, fatigues, flak jacket, and helmet. Somehow, the costume made his job seem more dangerous to her, although it was a very sensible precaution. If a reporter dressed differently from the troops—wearing, say, a white shirt—he would only become a more conspicuous target. The other reporters teased Dana that morning about his wife standing there waving good-bye. They said he would probably be crying to get back by dark so he could sleep with her.

When I first met Dana at the press center in Danang, he had teased me about wearing a "TV" suit which I thought was very comfortable—short sleeves, cool synthetic fabric—and practical, with four big pockets. It was the uniform of the stand-up television men who described the war from the safety of Saigon. In Dana's lexicon, "TV guys" were the worst, "writer guys" were almost as bad. Photographers, of course, were in a category by themselves because their pictures couldn't be taken from some briefer in Saigon.

I don't think Dana ever really accepted me as a member of the team until that day late in the battle in Hue when he met me on the fighting side of the river. The Navy boat I was on carried a number of Vietnamese troops and two big 106 recoilless rifles aimed at opposite banks of the river and fired throughout our slow mile-long trip. I stood behind a machine gunner part of the way, but mortars hit below him, knocking him and me straight back on the deck. Some Vietnamese soldiers standing beside me had their legs shattered in that explosion. Dana had seen me routinely helping lift the wounded on and off a truck when we landed. One UPI man was safely ensconced in the MACV compound back across the river and Dana didn't approve of that. He also sneered at another UPI man who had been close to the fighting but hadn't kept his head up enough to get any kind of a story. We walked down a road, back toward the inner palace walls, partners and war buddies for the first time. We were friends from that moment on.

I wandered on down the muddy streets, closer in to the fighting. The tanks had leveled everything alongside the narrow roads between the picturesque villas. Dana had told me about watching a tank "walk" back over a wounded Marine who couldn't get out of the way. One of the fellows had said, "No more Pancho." Dana had written, "Didn't leave much to send home." (It wasn't that he was insensitive about what he was seeing; he simply knew that this is what war is about and you can't take pictures of it if you keep getting sick.)

It was the last night of the battle when I stayed in a little villa drinking liberated cognac and laughing and listening to stories all night. Beverly Dieppe of the *Christian Science Monitor* was among us. I remember she worried about the Marines leaving behind a boot with a leg still in it. The name of her newspaper caused two Australian reporters to get into a hilarious dialogue about changing the canteen water into wine. Early the next morning, the battle was over. The Communist soldiers withdrew from their last corner stronghold in the citadel. A South Vietnamese unit—escorted by U.S. Marines—was moved up to the flagpole where a nervous one was ordered up to rip most of the enemy flag down.

I got enough names, ages, hometowns for the story, then realized I couldn't get back across the river with it. When I finally did make it across, the Americans had assembled a pathetic huddle of refugees for a ceremony. While they stood there listening to a squawky record of their national anthem, the flag of the Republic rose up the pole across the river. Some anxious soldiers fired off a salute—and shot the flag back down to half-mast: a fitting symbol of the shabby victory that had left the once-beautiful old city shattered beyond repair. ("It was not the Viet Cong who bombed our houses," said one educated refugee in answer to one persistent American newsman's questions about the enemy.)

After an hour or so of maneuvering, I got a telephone line through to Saigon. The AP correspondent on the safe side of the river had already phoned the story in hours before. The UPI deskman would take only the basic facts for a bulletin first lead and then hung up. I never got a line back through and I still have the notes for that story.

We stood waiting at the medevac pad behind the new bleachers at the racetrack in Hue for a ride into the fighting across the river. An NBC correspondent—ex-Marine, ex-policeman, later a bartender in Brooklyn—kept demanding and finally got "three minutes for Huntley-Brinkley." The National Police general walked behind a very important prisoner, handcuffed and blindfolded, to an Air America helicopter. "One day I gonna kill you," he said, grinning to a TV cameraman in front as he shot a "No comment" toward my questions. Two young medics walked through a doorway over which they had lettered MAKE LOVE NOT WAR and started roasting a goose they had liberated from a nearby farm. A small one-engine spotter plane circled low and then—hit by a burst of groundfire—crashed in the trees between us and the river. Minutes later, an ambulance jeep roared up and two smiling Marines hopped out and plopped the bag down in front of us, unzipping it so the body could cool. The sweet odor mingled with that of the goose as the medics sat down to eat.

Note at the end of every military release: NOTE: CASUALTY FIGURES ARE INTERIM AND SUBJECT TO CHANGE. NEARLY HALF OF ALL AMERICANS WOUNDED IN VIETNAM ARE RETURNED TO DUTY WITHOUT HOSPITALIZATION. APPROXIMATELY 85 PERCENT OF ALL AMERICANS WOUNDED IN VIETNAM ARE RETURNED TO DUTY.

After the battle in Hue, I wrote a friend: "I remember the time when I was a kid and I saw a man get his throat cut outside a flophouse on Lexington Avenue in Asheville where I caught the bus out to Woodfin. I had to get off two miles from my stop and walk in the cold air. Another time, a friend was mangled in a car wreck and—in the hospital room—he had to show us his wounds. I had to visit the bathroom and quickly. Now, if I could just describe one street scene in Hue for you. . . ."

Khe Sanh

UPI Saigon said UPI New York was crying for anything out of Khe Sanh—the story was guaranteed page-one play. I was thrilled at the prospect of getting in on such a story, one a number of experienced correspondents had said was just not worth the risk. Hours before dawn every morning at the Danang Press Center, a sergeant woke up those on the list and we dressed in helmets, flak jackets, and packs for the trip to Khe Sanh. A bus would come for us and we rode out to the airbase to wait.

Sometimes we would actually get out to the plane and stand beside the wreckage of another plane that had barely made it back. But for various reasons, it was several days before we got off the ground. By then, a jeep instead of a bus was all they needed to carry the correspondents to the airport.

One quick glance out the little window shattered all my movie-time images of a dramatic jungle setting. Khe Sanh was a sprawling garbage dump—the wreckage of tents and vehicles left in the sterile red dust—and the men crawled about with the rats. "The only victory here," I later wrote a friend, "is getting out alive."

The big gate eased down and we leaped off the plane and ran where a Marine was waving us into a well-built bunker beside the loading ramp. We got inside and stood there uncomfortably waiting. One of those already in the bunker pointed to a deadly sliver of shrapnel—a jagged piece of steel about four inches long. It had cut into the thick wooden frame of the bunker doorway and it was still hot. A rocket had landed there just before we had and these pieces of hot metal could have killed any or all of us. Standing there looking at the little thing, I didn't really know what it was, much less what it could do.

It was hard to tell where anything had been or where anything was (underground) when I started walking down what seemed to be a road through the rubble. I found the old French concrete bunker that was the command post. A friendly major volunteered to take me down to the public information officer. We had taken a few steps when he heard the whirring of incoming mortars. I was straight up and jabbering small talk. The major grabbed the back of my flak jacket and knocked me face down into the dirt. I explained to him that it was my first time in the field and I didn't know incoming from outgoing. He shuddered and kept walking.

The Marine officers all seemed to consider PIO a humiliating form of punishment—this was what they got for not measuring up to the standards for commander of a combat unit. I never met a man more embittered and cynical than the Marine PIO at Khe Sanh. To show his contempt for the press, he had marked off a place for them to stay in a narrow open trench—right beside the old ammunition dump, as close as he could get to the "V ring" where most of the incoming was aimed. Near the hole where the ammo dump had been lay the wreckage of a C-130 plane that crashed two days before I arrived. The young sergeants told me about dragging the bodies of their buddies out of the crash.

The reporters who knew better ignored the old colonel and stayed, not at the "Khe Sanh Press Center," as the trench was labeled, but in the "Alamo Hilton," the name begrudgingly fixed on the safest bunker at Khe Sanh. I wrote a friend from there:

> Khe Sanh, 15 Feb. 1968: The bunker I'm in was built by the Seabees—regular underground house with a tunnel to an enclosed lookout "terrace" outback where I was just called to come watch the gooks walking about on yonder ridge where the U.S. of A. has pounded millions and millions of dollars' worth of bombs and artillery for the past three weeks. A tape recorder blares the rock and roll I've lived by for years and a huddle of Seabees is rolling dice and another group is shouting insults at each other: "Spick, nigger! We ain't prejudiced, you just get the hell outa our bunker." Yes, daddy, just like back home—and outside on the terrace there is a war. A guy just ripped down a dartboard that had become the object of everybody's frustrations. It was already in splinters. My head is still ringing from all the firing today. Around 60 incoming mortars and I figure the return fire is several thousand to one, counting the air show.

The old PIO colonel was amused that I would come to him for a briefing. He gestured grandly for me to sit on a seat he had taken from a wrecked jeep and proceeded to tell me how it had been. Before the first attack, Khe Sanh had been a lovely place. The waterfall just below the base and the high blue mountains reminded me of the Appalachians. "I would get in my jeep and drive out that gate there—with my pistol not even loaded—and go down through the *ville* and then on down to the Laotian border," he said.

He had been whittling himself a swagger stick, and I expected him to use it to draw diagrams of the base in the dirt. Instead, he just kept making a big *X*. Two younger Marines busied themselves clearing out the trench—burning leftover C rations along with a rabbit-sized rat they had just killed. The old colonel tried to describe the survivors at Khe Sanh in the grand tradition of the Corps. He talked about how the enemy had been repulsed on every side. But, he had to admit there had been no patrols in days and they were surrounded, "three hundred and sixty degrees, every way you look."

"Attack?" he asked himself. "I hope he does."

Since it was my first time in the field, I felt I should get with the grunts as close to the "front" as I could. The old colonel kindly answered my questions and told me the front was a line of bunkers on the other side of the airstrip.

Of course, there were no fronts in Vietnam, and in fact the center of the base at Khe Sanh was far more dangerous than the perimeter where I stayed that night. A young corpsman invited me to spend the night in his bunker. Actually, it was a trench barely wide enough for two men to lie down shoulder to shoulder. Above us were two layers of sandbags. A direct hit on a similar bunker the next day went through and killed the young Marines inside.

We went up and down the line, meeting and laughing with various characters who talked about stealing cans of applesauce, about the time the lieutenant was headed for the crapper when somebody yelled, "Incoming!" "He shit in his pants." After dark, we stood in the trench and watched as B-52 "arc lights" created Khe Sanh's own sound and light show. It was not like any fireworks I had ever seen before. It was more like real lightning and thunder. When I lay down on the ground in the trench to sleep that night, I lay awake listening to the corpsman trying to cheer up a friend outside. He tried to get him to sing "Green, Green Grass of Home," but the other one said, "No, please not that." Then they just stood there in silence, watching, waiting. All night long, one of the Marines would cry, "Noooo, nooo, no" in his sleep, twitching violently with his nightmares.

The next day was bright and sunny and I got to know most of the men in this company. When a few rounds of mortars started coming in, I ran from bunker to bunker—getting names, ages, hometowns; asking how it felt. They thought I was crazy and they were right. In one of the larger bunkers, a very sullen young Marine sat playing a guitar and singing: "Where have all the flowers gone?/Gone to graveyards every one." But never once did it occur to me during my first three or four days at Khe Sanh that I could be hurt, much less that I could be killed. Only later, as I began to see the young bodies mutilated and stacked up like waste could I envision the real horror of those innocent-looking slivers of metal. Because of our job, our "objective" roles, I think a lot of us never really thought it could happen to us. At least not until it started happening to so many of our friends.

On a later visit to Khe Sanh, I made these notes in my diary:

At Charlie Med now waiting for a helicopter to come through the fog and carry me out of here with the wounded—31 on the last two choppers. Nine dead here now beside me in those black rubber body bags that make it all seem so clean. Tape recorder plays Donovan, "Sunshine comes softly in my window today." A young medic sweeps the floor with a bloody broom, whistling the tune.

Dana Stone wrote a friend from Khe Sanh:

I wish they would hit this place so I could go see my wife. Today very little NVA troop movement was reported, meaning either they are in position to get on with their attack—or we just aren't able to see them at whatever they are doing. I don't see how we can get much intelligence since we can't run patrols 200 meters outside the wire without Charlie chasing them back in. Too much fog for observation planes—no 123's or 130's were able to land today tho several 130's parachuted supplies in (one load of artillery ammo landed 2.5 miles from the drop zone, too far from the Marines to go get). Only a few mortars. They only shoot at the planes it seems. Shoot at them as they land and take off. I don't know what the writer guys are putting out about here but things aren't bad yet—the few rounds that come in are annoying but not doing much damage, so I expect they must have a ground attack planned.

At Khe Sanh, I met a boy in graves registration who had planted a garden before the siege began, before he got so busy listing the names of the dead. Somebody back home had sent him the seeds and he had planted them behind the morgue tent, labeling each row of beans and radishes and Brussels sprouts and carrots and corn and cabbage. The beans were growing well, then the first artillery barrage got them. The corn seemed like it was going to be all right, but another rocket blast tore up that row.

Remembering the words of the saint who said he would finish hoeing his garden if he knew he were about to die, I asked the boy what he would do. "Well," he said, "I haven't had much time for hoeing my garden."

After seventy-two days, when the 1st Air Cavalry Division moved in and relieved the base at Khe Sanh, it was a "walk in the sun." Although there were some fierce fights in the mountains around the base, most of the enemy troops had withdrawn. We walked as if to a picnic, up through the old plantation to the Khe Sanh base.

There were only some steps where Felix Poilane's house had been; the tea and coffee trees for hundreds of acres around it had been reduced to fine splinters in the powdery bombed-over soil. Along with dozens of memory books full of poetry and love letters, we found a bugle in the North Vietnamese packs left behind. I took some stamps as souvenirs and four or five NVA undershirts to send to my friends. Only one round of artillery was fired on us that day and we laughed and joked as we sauntered through the sterile landscape to the perimeter of Khe Sanh. Some Marines were unloading garbage inside the gate. One yelled, "It's about time" when he saw us coming. Later that day when I phoned in my story, the UPI relay man said, "Keep it short, Martin Luther King got killed today and all the papers'll be full of that."

A friend in North Carolina had a peculiar response to King's death. He wrote me and attacked my "professionalism" for being able to look at something like that and then go back and calmly write a story of facts and figures. I have since come around to his viewpoint, but from Vietnam I wrote:

As for your contempt for the kind you suddenly class me with, may I remind you that I did not sit alone by the terribly pleasant fireside in my room that night in Chapel Hill when our friends went off to march in the cold, get acid thrown on them, and get locked up in the jailhouse. May I also tell you that a great thing, perhaps the greatest, about being a journalist—a "professional" if you will—is that one is able to sit down with a Black Nationalist or a Klansman or a Sergeant Riley who's killed 120 himself, wears one gold earring, no shoes and—the fellows say—hopes to build him a gook when he gets back to New Jersey with the pickled parts he has arranged in jars around his bed.

Vietnam was an appropriate place from which to view America during that cathartic year, 1968. The violence of Columbia and Chicago seemed to flow naturally from the same forces sponsoring the war. After the assassination of Senator Robert Kennedy, I wrote a friend from Vietnam:

I was standing at the Dong Ha airstrip when the news came over a little transistor radio. I quickly got four or five "reactioners" and phoned them into the UPI office in Saigon. An old gunny sergeant looked a little sad at first, said, "Don't really understand that sort of mentality that would do something like that." Then, he thought a bit and said, "But I guess it's the same mentality you have in a war: You don't like something, you kill it."

When the base at Khe Sanh was finally abandoned, I interviewed several of the Marines who had lived through the siege. "It don't make sense," one of them told me. "If they can abandon it now, why couldn't they do it before so many people got killed and wounded?"

Colonel B. F. Myers, the last Marine commander at Khe Sanh, had a desk marker with these words inscribed on it:

> The end of the fight is a tombstone white
> With the name of the late deceased.
>
> And the epitaph drear a fool lies here
> Who tried to hurry the East.
>
> —R. Kipling

One historical footnote here: Ever since the ceasefire in early 1973, Khe Sanh has been an outpost of the North Vietnamese army.

He Was Also Scared

It was always a disarming thing about Dana Stone—especially the longer he stayed and the more his legend grew—that he could so openly talk about being afraid. Perhaps it was a simple thing of the legend outgrowing the reality of the man, with no encouragement from him. Malcolm Cowley has written of Hemingway: "Publicly he was a war hero and a real one, too, considering the courage and instinctive presence of mind he had shown in an emergency. He thoroughly enjoyed the role and played up to it like an old trouper. privately, though, he was and for a long time would remain a frightened man."

Dozens of people have told me how Dana endeared himself to them in some especially private moment in the field when he would suddenly stop and say, "You know, I'm really scared." John Olson was nineteen when he came to Vietnam as an Army photographer. During his stay he also sold several thousand dollars' worth of pictures to *Life* and *Time* under the name "John Stewart." One night, Olson and Stone were sleeping on an open hillside during a clearing mission near Khe Sanh. The rain woke Olson up just before he heard a distant *whir-splat* and thud—the unmistakable sound of incoming artillery. Dana grabbed his camera gear and shirt, but Olson left his as the two ran for cover.

They didn't find real cover, but they did find a big bomb crater which offered some protection. Olson can only remember a brilliant blue flash and a deafening explosion right in the crater where they were. It was a pitch-black night, with fog almost down to the ground. They couldn't see anybody, but they could hear a sucking-moaning noise nearby. Olson was crawling along, trying to find whoever it was when he put his hand right in the company commander's open throat wound. The commander was drowning in his own blood, so Dana and Olson turned him on his stomach. The radio operator had been killed in the blast and the commander couldn't talk. They lit a flashlight and he scribbled the codewords for a medevac helicopter with a pencil.

One chopper did try to get in and they could hear the pilot talking on the radio. "I've got one man hit. I'm losing power." And then the radio was silent as the helicopter crashed. It was fourteen hours before a helicopter could get in, but they had saved the man's life. (At least until he got back to the States, where he later died on the operating table, during a minor operation, when the oxygen supply ran out.)

After the incoming barrage seemed to be over, Dana went back to the makeshift shelter where he and Olson had left their equipment. He came back laughing. Their hootch had taken a direct hit. All of Olson's cameras were destroyed and his shirt was in tatters.

They covered up the dead man with a poncho, then huddled together to try to stay warm. "I have never felt so close to another man in my life," Olson says. "I remember counting off each hour and thinking, 'If we get hit again we'll be killed.'"

Dana confessed to Olson:

"I'm cold;

"I'm tired;

"I'm scared."

"I had never seen that part of Dana," Olson says. They were not hit again that night, and at first light Dana was up and joking again. When they went through the dead man's pack, he said, "The son of a bitch didn't have any fruit cocktail."

Smiser

The first time Dana took Louise to the field with him was on a routine visit to the 1st Air Cavalry Division's base camp. They had lunch with the enlisted men and laughed and joked with them as they ate the food just emptied from cans and cooked.

That night, they dined in near-elegance at the general's mess. The meal was still served in a tent, but there were cocktails before and wine served with the seven-course meal of fresh vegetables, steak, and ice cream. All of it was laid out on white linen tableclothes and served on nice dishes with real silverware and glass goblets. Being the only female, Louise was seated next to the general. Her job at the airbase in Seville had taught her that officers are not necessarily deserving of respect just because of their rank. And so, when the enlisted "waiter" served the general's ice cream before hers, she pointed out his bad manners. To her horror, the general berated the waiter and insisted she take his bowl of tutti-frutti.

After dinner, Louise and Dana talked with the men in the public information office. They were teasing Dana that every time he paid a visit the base got hit. Meanwhile, a newly arrived private stayed in the background, having no war stories to swap. Louise moved over and talked with the new man about back home. After Dana and Louise went to bed that night, the base was hit with rockets and mortars—one of them landing on top of the new guy Louise had befriended. The blast had splattered his body all over the inside of the press tent. Dana insisted that Louise go in and look at it because one day she would go back and tell people she had been in a war and he wanted her to know what she was talking about.

At the general's mess that morning, they had fresh eggs for

breakfast. "I hear one of your men got it last night," the general said to the PIO. "Too bad."

She was always "Smiser" to Dana, and so to the group, but she was just Louise to me. She in turn called me by the full name my mother gave me, something nobody had done since I left that little place near Asheville, North Carolina, which differed only in name and location from the small Kentucky town where she was born.

Louise had held onto her flat, nasal speech, while I had taken a course in college to get rid of my twang—trying for no reason I can understand now to imitate the sleep-inducing monotone of the instructor. It was something he called "General American."

She and I had a bond of language and sometimes we would laugh about how silly it had been in the fifties to ride around and around some hamburger and milkshake drive-in or to stay up all night listening to the latest rhythm and blues sounds on radio station WLAC, brought to us by Randy's and Ernie's record shops in Gallatin, Tennessee.

I could no more have considered Louise as one of the guys, as "Smiser," than I could have pictured my own sister Grace as one of the buddies getting decked out in combat costume to go off and photograph a war. There was absolutely nothing in her manner, makeup, or appearance that cast her in our chosen role of swashbuckling war correspondent. She says now she did enjoy the camaraderie if not the war. But the one reason that she was ever in Vietnam was that her husband's job happened to be there.

Louise Van Deren Smiser was born in Cynthiana, Kentucky —population 4,000—on July 25, 1939. Her father is a country doctor named Tod (called "Brud") Smiser and her mother was born Katherine ("Katie") Wigglesworth, the daughter of a local bourbon distiller. The father is a droll sort of man, typically conservative in his profession—resisting even longer than most of his comrades what he considers federal intervention (Medicare and Medicaid) into his private practice. The mother is a devout fundamentalist Baptist who tries to be understanding about her two daughters, the first born fifteen months before Louise. I have talked on the telephone with the mother, who worried that Louise smokes too much and was very troubled because she was briefly involved with "meditation." She is, however, especially proud that her daughters have both now gone back to the country to live—although she understands they could never live in Cynthiana—and that both of them still read a lot of books.

When Katie and Brud Smiser moved out to Shelter Row Farm (so called because the mother had always admired a "shelter row" of cedars planted for the cattle there), the girls were twelve and thirteen years old. The parents never allowed a television set in the house until the daughters were out on their own. Mrs. Smiser asked me, What was the use of living in the country if they were going to stay cooped up in the house watching television all day? Instead, they bought them horses to ride and whenever they would complain about not having a TV set, the mother would suggest they just find a good book to read. The only time she stood in the way of that was when *Catcher in the Rye* arrived as a Book of the Month Club selection. While Louise had read a lot of books before, this was her first real encounter with serious literature. After that, she was not just reading for light entertainment, as a substitute for television.

I think largely because of her appearance, Louise aroused a totally unwarranted pity from all those around her. All her life, she says, people would come up and say, "Don't be so sad," and there was no way she could explain that she just looked that way. She rarely, if ever, used makeup; and she kept her long brown hair pulled straight back and tied in a bun, granny-style, at the back of her head.

While she always appeared plain, she would often sit with such a peculiarly calm detachment (disinterest?) that she would appear strikingly beautiful. She really is two women—not just in appearance, but also in the way she thinks of herself. The photographer Richard Avedon posed her for several classic portraits in Saigon after Dana was captured. In all of these, she is the plain-faced country woman, staring somewhat fearfully into the camera like the woman in Grant Wood's "American Gothic." (Avedon has captured the despair of her life alone.) But there was also another side to her, known mainly to her and to Dana. This was not the country woman at all, but the free-spirited naked lady relishing every raw angle of her own body and every electric contact with the finely muscled body of that erratic runner who was Dana—the one and only true lover in her life. With him, Grant Wood's farm wife became a statuesque Modigliani nude.

Louise had been staying at home in Danang while Dana was in Hue that first week of the Tet Offensive. She was too scared to sleep. She would sit on the toilet seat in the little concrete outhouse during a rocket attack because Dana had told her it was safer in there. She would walk over to the press center in the daytime and then go back to her house by dark.

After five days, Dana came back and he and Louise got on the motor bike just at dusk and drove to their little house. Once there, Dana paced around, sat on the bed, and then jumped up and said, "Shit, I'm scared. We're gonna stay at the press center."

The two of them took an end cot in the row of five in the UPI room and this led to some delightful problems between them and two older reporters—one a veteran of Korea, the other of the Normandy invasion in World War II. To put it mildly, Louise made them nervous. She and Dana would sometimes have sex in the shower and word of this got out. They were always teasing and petting, throwing words and real objects back and forth. The World War II vet would sit there with his armchair pulled up to the doorway (in case any announcement should come from the communications shack) and he would try despearately to ignore the young couple.

Of course, once the rest of us found out that Louise made these older ones nervous, it became a running joke to see what could be done next to arouse their ire. Dana and Louise would sit on the terrace, talking too explicitly about sex while the Korean veteran squirmed and looked away.

Every time the World War II vet would leave his seat in the UPI room, Louise would shove it all the way back against the other wall. He would move it up to the door; then, Louise would come in and shove it back.

Any time they spotted him by himself, they went up and made conversation, just to see how uncomfortable he would become. One morning they sat down with the older guy at breakfast. He got up and went to the room; Louise got up and followed him, sitting on the bed just looking at him. He went out on the terrace; Louise went out on the terrace. He went back to the room; Louise went back to the room.

Finally, the two older veterans told the Marines in charge of the press center that this female had to be removed from the UPI room. But the Marines never told Louise.

Things Were More Clear-cut There

George Hamilton has his version of how and why Sean Flynn went back to Vietnam in 1968, after a year away from the war. Hamilton was vacationing in Beirut and Flynn had joined him there. The two were sharing a suite in the Phoenicia Hotel. They were the subjects of daily stories in the local press, the focus of all eyes when they went out.

One morning, Hamilton opened the door on a luscious Lebanese beauty who asked if the two of them would give blood to help publicize a Red Cross drive. Both of them gave and then Hamilton—as suggested—drank a Coke and ate some candy. Flynn didn't eat or drink anything, and once outside he threw up, Hamilton says.

They also befriended a local gangster who insisted on outfitting them with a changing bevy of beautiful models at his very elegant mountain hideaway. Both of them tired of this and they were flying back toward London when Flynn started talking about Vietnam.

Hamilton had been courting the President's daughter and meanwhile fighting a much-publicized battle to avoid the draft. Flynn told him he ought to go to Vietnam for this reason, if for no other. Flynn said he kept having to make excuses to all the GI's to explain that Hamilton was really an okay guy. Hamilton turned the questions on Flynn then, asking why he felt he had to go back, what was he getting out of the experience. Flynn answered that the drama of life was more clear-cut there and besides, "It's the most important thing happening in the world today." And that, as any journalist will tell you, is reason enough to go anywhere.

When the plane stopped in Geneva, Flynn said good-bye to his friend "and the next thing I heard about him, he was back in Vietnam."

It was in early March, 1968, when Flynn came back. Like so many other journalists I met at that time, he had surely resisted the temptation to return but finally had to give in as each day's newspapers and every day's telecasts included more and more incredible pictures from the Tet Offensive.

I first met Flynn at the Danang Press Center. I don't remember the precise moment or the situation and this is significant. A first encounter was almost singularly unremarkable—and memorable for that reason. A lot of people hated not Flynn, but the idea of Flynn. One—who was doing the same with his life—said to me, "Why is he toying with life?" Of course, he never knew Flynn and would never admit he would really have liked to be his friend. People had done the same to his father. He was just too handsome, too self-assured to be true. And so they envied him and that built into a snide sort of resentment of the Son of Captain Blood.

In fact, Flynn seemed shy and unstylishly polite and considerate. Far from being the shallow, arrogant son of the swashbuckler, he is a person of tremendous warmth—his calm good manners covering a well of strength.

I have never known anybody who has the sort of presence Flynn has. Especially in the journalism business, one meets hundreds of people just once and then forgets them. Few people ever forgot even a brief encounter with Flynn. Dozens of people have told me about seeing him only once.

It was, of course, an encounter with the Flynn legend. It was also a matter of being with a famous person, a real star. But it was something deeper than that. "Flynn really touched people," one friend said. There was something very disarming about this calm reflective person growing out of that legend.

Now, I think that calm was a very deliberate mask for an intensely restive soul. Flynn would stand there very quietly, but you always felt somehow that he was like a recently tamed animal waiting for an opening to leap. "He was the most gentle person I ever knew," a friend of his told me. "Yes," I said, "but I wonder what he was ever going to do with all those weapons."

Flynn just said something soft, like, "Hey, you wanta walk downtown and get stoned?" And I said sure. We walked a little way along the river, watching the boats, not saying much of anything. In earlier days, there had been bougainvillea trellises over nice benches about every forty feet along the waterfront. The few that remained were now blocked off by concertina rolls of barbed wire. Flynn and I mashed down the barbed wire and took a seat under the bare trellis.

We sat there smoking quietly for a long time. Flynn said something about the huge stacks of ammunition piled up near us. I said my pacifist friends in New York would surely be cursing me if they could see us sitting so close and not doing anything to destroy the war weapons. These quiet moments—so difficult to transcribe—are what stand out in my memories of Flynn. It was not so much in anything he ever said, but in all he did not say. It is the highest moment in a friendship, I think, when two people do not feel like they have to do or say anything.

After he came back in 1968, Flynn's most famous war venture involved a small action on another of those numbered hilltops just south of Danang. This one had been a "friendly" firebase, but had been overrun by the other guys. In three days of bombing, the Americans and Vietnamese had still not been able to retake the top of the hill.

Then, with Flynn and Dana Stone in attendance, the Special Forces advisers decided they were going to (their word) "charge." Stone was with one group and Flynn, another. The two were going to converge on the top, but they were close enough that Flynn and Stone could yell back and forth.

"There's an American hit over here," Flynn yelled to Stone when a young captain fell in front of him with what they considered minor wounds. I know this incidental fact because Flynn had a tape recorder going throughout the action and back at the press center he played it for us to hear.

The Vietnamese troops stopped in their tracks when the American captain dropped out of the charge. However, they continued firing—straight into the ranks of the other unit. With a grand sweep of his hand Flynn saved the day by shifting into one of Errol's movie roles and leading the charge himself. All of this was duly recorded by Dana Stone and his pictures of Flynn were published around the world.

Flynn was also lightly nicked by shrapnel in the stomach and that story accompanied the pictures. Later, Dana teased him about the wound and kept hitting him in the stomach to show it didn't hurt.

The reason Flynn kept playing the tape so many times back at the press center was that somewhere above the firing and his exchanges with Dana, there is another ghostly voice that says clearly and haltingly, "Get Out Of Vietnam." Flynn did not remember hearing it.

He had his cameras going the whole time, but this was one of many occasions when Flynn told CBS he didn't have anything worth using. This would be filed with his other pictures back in Paris—material for his own film (about death, he told some people) about the war. Flynn talked a lot about the film he would do. Sometimes he spoke of a documentary, other times he talked of a feature film set on the beach at Danang.

Because he moved so quietly and never said good-bye, it is difficult now to say with any certainty just when Flynn was in and out of the war. Apparently, he stayed for a few weeks in March and April, 1968, then went to Laos, where he traveled around with another photographer. I know Flynn was not in Saigon when Tim Page arrived in late April, 1968.

From my first day in vietnam until my last hours, I heard stories about "that fucking Page," "crazy goddam Page," or just "Page." His name alone evoked the wildest, wackiest escapades anybody could imagine doing in or out of a war. Never mind that a lot of these others resented—even hated—Page for surviving his recklessness, for taking more risks than they had. They felt he deserved to die. Page, they would say, was one of the "unlucky" ones. Not surprisingly, Page felt that because of his risks and scars, he had a special right to live: The world owed him a living.

I remember the night I first met him in the flesh. He had arrived in Vietnam without any money, without a proper visa, and with no promise of a job. The Vietnamese customs officials said he was not getting in the door. When we heard he was in the country, another photographer smiled and said, "Page loves Flynn and I knew he would be here as soon as he heard Flynn was back."

The call came into the UPI office and—although none of us even knew him except by reputation—we piled in a jeep and drove out to get a look. Page had also called friends at Time-Life and at CBS, so there was a sizable crowd inside the little immigration office. The two officials were refusing all entreaties by that time, stubbornly shaking their heads in silence. Page calmed everybody down and made an announcement. "All right," he said. "Everybody grab a bag and we'll just walk out and keep going." I obediently grabbed a bag. This was Page's real attraction—I would have followed him anywhere. But we didn't quite make it to the door before the guards shoved us back.

After a night at the airport, Page satisfied the immigration officials' demands and was once again accredited as a free-lance photographer. The timing of his arrival was fairly remarkable. The "mini Tet" attacks were staged the very next week. Page got in a good week's work, sold several pictures that were used in *Life,* and with five thousand dollars in his pocket he was his same old flamboyant self again. He moved into a room in the *Life* villa and—as only he could do—quickly redecorated it with a clutter of his own toys. The villa had a superb chef who had once worked for an ambassador and quite often Page would stage real banquets for his friends. When other *Life* reporters or photographers were entertaining their friends, Page and his friends would be smoking up his little room. The smoke poured out like vapors from a steambath when anybody opened the door.

My First Opium Trip

I wrote a friend:

Tried opium in Danang the other night: absolutely fantastic. Didn't sleep a wink all night and there was a heavy rain on the tin roof and it was trickling into every pore. I have never so enjoyed a rain.

Danang has been getting rockets right in the main part of town so there's a strict 6 P.M. curfew. But, hours after that, we were still eating a fabulous meal of froglegs and peppered crabs sauté and *cha gio* (little bitty egg rolls) and fried rice and champagne. It was our fourth bottle since Sean and Tim and I had devoted an afternoon already to smoking and drinking in my room and playing the tapes from Sean's latest wound—some grenade shrapnel barely tore the skin of his chest and leg.

We ate dinner in a little restaurant built on stilts over the river. Since we had kept them late, we volunteered to take the waitresses home, past all the nervous national policemen and Vietnamese soldiers at the roadblocks. After we took the girls home, we wound back around town until Tim said, "In here, in here." Sean swung the CBS jeep down a narrow little alley, opening into a compound of Buddhist families—with a temple lit up with candles at one end.

Tim jumped out into the pitch black with a couple of dogs yelping. He tried one place he knew, then Sean jumped out and I am left holding the brand new recorder playing soul sounds carefully selected with the Armed Forces radio spot announcements like: "How do you apologize to your buddy for shooting him?" or, "Let's talk about maintenance," or, "Tracers are fun, but let's talk about the waste."

Waiting in the jeep, I could see three or four guys fumbling with their little rifles over near the temple and I was really getting nervous. Then Sean and Tim came back for me. Sean—like a kindly old uncle—says for me to relax and I mumble something about getting back to the press center. The opium madame unlocks a rusty old gate and lets us in. Then she locks it behind us and opens another door. We

147

step into her one-room hootch furnished in bed, two chairs, table, two altars, and a chest.

She spoke a rich, deep French, cultivated as an officer's wife in Hue. He left the county in '61, she says, but she stayed on because she knew she wouldn't be able to smoke in Paris. She says the opium we will smoke comes from Saigon because it is very difficult to get anything out of Laos these days.

I don't know the process for getting it into the tiny little ink bottle, but it all begins with the ink bottle of liquid opium, two needles, a pipe, a lamp under a cut-crystal conelike glass lamp with a little round hole at the top. The pipe is a thick round thing, with an inch-round ivory endpiece for the mouth. Very slowly, meticulously, she dips the needles into the opium, then turns them around and around over the hole in the crystal lamp. They bubble up; she keeps dipping into the stuff and turning it over the flame. There is the sweet fragrance. Yes, you will have to know sometime yourself. Then she holds the pipe and carefully pushes the little ball of opium into the tiny hole in the wooden bowl. To smoke, you have to keep the little ball bubbling until it is all burned up. She holds the bowl over the flame and you breathe in; if you exhale, the pipe gets clogged up. She is very gentle with me and explains each step in detail. She makes tea after each pipe and I drink from a glass.

Conversation fills in the gaps and there is the low soul sound from Sean's tape machine. He's sitting there playing with the two strange cats.

She lies on her side of the bed, little thing of a bronze woman, dressed in white blouse and black pajama pants and bare feet. The bed has slats and a straw mat elaborately painted in red and yellow. She fixes two pillows on the other side where we lie taking turns. Three pipes, then up and rotate—until she prepares another pillow so we don't have to get up. We finish—eight pipes each for Tim and Sean, six for me, the initiate. We pay her the equivalent of $13 and she gives us still another pipe courtesy of the house.

Back at the press center, Tim and Sean go into the bar to "make the Marines nervous" and I wait out on the patio beside the river. I am sitting there lost in my reverie when the old opium itch starts somewhere on my legs and spreads upward until I am writhing and scratching in near ecstasy. I look up to see three Marines on the dock, standing up just gawking at me. They don't say anything, though, and I wonder if they will ever know such a pleasant thing as sharing an opium smoke with two friends like Tim and Sean on an evening in the war.

Snapshots

He was a stringbean character and we all made fun of his drawl and the sloppy way he dressed in fatigues that never matched. Above the United Press International patch on his shirt, he wore a Nazi emblem. He talked about the "goddam gooks" and "those fucking slopes." Only one thing he liked better'n taking pictures, he told Louise, and that was killing gooks. He had been a fine photographer in the U.S. Navy and that was also his job that day with UPI. But he had put down his cameras and taken up a rifle, counting off: one, two, three. . . . He said he would avenge the deaths of those correspondents killed the day before. One goddam gook for every one of those four who had probably never said a word to him. He was taking aim when Number Four got him. When they read his will they found he had left everything he owned and all his UPI life insurance money to a local wife and to some Vietnamese who were not gooks but friends.

We also found this inscription on the men's room wall of the Melody Bar next door: *God is a Chevy dealer in Phoenix and he's not getting involved in this stupid war.* Under that, in his unmistakable hand were these words:

Every war fought has been stupid; any war is stupid; why act as if Vietnam is the only stupid war we've ever fought? Dana Stone took pictures of the inscriptions, had several copies made, and passed them around to all who had known him: It was one war photographer's epitaph.

Aside from "Groovin on the Danger," my favorite among Flynn's collection of radio announcements was a military news report about an American troop plane being forced to land in North Korea. One of the soldiers on board said he looked out the window and saw the MIG's but he didn't think anything of it. He said, "I just thought it was some of our boys out there messin' around."

"Bombers" was a game invented by some UPI reporters and their Australian sidekicks. Each contestant had to stuff a coin in the crack of his ass and then waddle ten feet and drop it into a drinking glass on the floor. At the good-bye party for one "bomber," all the others dressed in tailored black pajamas with red and white bomber patches on the sleeves.

Graffiti from the San Francisco Bar on Tu Do Street in Saigon, July, 1968:

> These girls are very beautiful but be careful, man, they want money and that's all—but you can't have them, but take it easy one might go with you/YOU FOOL/You dumb bastard, get out of this place before you lose all your bread/OR YOUR HEAD/Dave was here 65–66–68/Is the Pussy here any good?/Worst I ever had was wonderful/This place is sorry/Phu Bai is All Right/For a country boy/Kilroy was here/LSD/Fresno, California the greatest/LOVE SEX/I hate God/God who?/God damn fucking legs/I cannot relate to this place/This is the year of the monkey/So fuck all the monkeys/It's all in the game/If you can't take a joke/Sorry Bout that/SNAKE 670/John Campbell, Kinston, N.C. 5-20-68/I hate God/GOD WHO?/If men's brains were big as their balls they wouldn't write on restroom walls/One of the Vietnamese girls in this bar is a guy, guess who?/Fuck all you chicken shit Saigon warriors, you are the sorriest legs I have ever seen/SORRY BOUT THAT/God is Airborne/So?/So you're so stupid you're in the Army.

When their bike kept getting mired up in the beach mud and sand, Louise had to get off and Dana pushed the bike in front on a narrow path between some refugee huts jammed between the road and the beach. A young girl in one hut cursed them and threw a rock that hit Louise in the back. Other youngsters heard the commotion and joined in the cursing, hurling cans and rocks at the two Americans. The path was just wide enough for the two of them or they might have been killed by twenty or thirty young Vietnamese grabbing and clawing at them and their bike. They kept hitting Louise, scratching her arms, tearing her shirt and pants. Dana finally beat them back and they sped off on the bike once they reached the road. It was the first time either of them had experienced this sort of violent hatred of the Americans. At the press center bar, they told a Marine officer about the incident. Exactly where was this place, he wanted to know. He would see to it that the American forces went in and straightened these people out. Louise and Dana stopped talking, got up, and left the bar.

Duke the dog was riding a bright red surfboard into China Beach near Danang the first time I saw him. Great pictures, I thought, great story. His keepers were three Marine combat veterans, wounded enough times to be guarding the general's beachhouse but not enough to be sent home. Duke was a killer scout dog who couldn't hack it, said these military spokesmen. There was a possibility he might be left to live out his days in disgrace in Vietnam. "I'm glad he's not vicious and a killer," said one gentle Marine from Vermont, "because I'm not either." The "peacenik dog" story was used by nearly every UPI client in the U.S.

Except for this dog story, I received a total of three letters in a year of writing about men killing other men. Duke's story brought hundreds of letters into the White House, the Congress (where an investigation was demanded), into the Marine commandant's office, and UPI's own headquarters in New York.

A little girl in Michigan collected enough money to pay Duke's way home. Jack Paar said he would pay the plane fare for the dog and the three Marines. A man in Pennsylvania said this was a crying shame that "an American dog" should be so abused. But the Marines sent out a letter saying it had been "a gentle hoax." Duke was no American dog. He was a native Vietnamese—the bastard pup of a local bitch and an American sentry dog. On hearing this, the little girl refunded the money and the Pennsylvania man withdrew his complaint.

But the U.S. Marine Corps in its confusion closed down the beachhouse (some letter writers were surprised to learn the general had one), gave the young Marines an early out, vaccinated Duke, and told one of the three: "You WILL take this goddamn dog home with you."

A spokesman for the sentry dog program in Saigon had explained to me that there is no way to "de-train" these killers and so, after their effective days in the war were over, they were killed in Vietnam. I have always considered this a parable of the way we told the war story. And so, one summer day when I was visiting in Southampton, new York, I called up one of the young Marines and asked about Duke. Did he still run on the beach?

Well, no, he used to run and play when he first got "home." But later, "He just got so violent with other people we couldn't take him to the beach anymore."

One morning at the press center, I opened the door onto a clear sunny day.

"Ahhhhh, sunshine!" I said.

"Air strikes," said a photographer friend.

"Napalm," said I.

"Women and children," said he.

Party Talk

The stories in this book might give the impression that we were either always stoned or in combat in Vietnam. I certainly don't mean to leave that impression; it is simply that these are the high points of my memory.

In between the parties and the action in the field there were many boring times . . . waiting at airports for flights that kept getting delayed, riding in cargo planes or helicopters where the noise was such you couldn't carry on a conversation. In one week in the war, I read eight different books—not out of interest so much as out of boredom.

But it was a very special time when we were all together. Generally, we were off pursuing different rumors or reports of real actions. During the course of a year, we smoked opium together only six or eight times, for example. There were many small gatherings at Dana and Louise Stone's house in Danang, but there was only one real party that I remember.

A Danish cameraman had wanted some party talk to go in a documentary film he talked about doing about Dana Stone, war photographer. So he brought along his new sound equipment and the following dialogue is taken from my copy of a tape he made that night. While Louise and Dana rarely ever smoked marijuana, they always kept it in their house for guests. It was the same with liquor. Except for a cold beer sometimes in the early morning, Dana never liked to drink.

We were so used to filming, photographing, and recording each other, we ignored the microphones after a bit, and we also ignored the warplanes taking off and landing at the near airbase, drowning out our voices on the tape.

The slow-turning fan rippled the "leaves" in a camouflage parachute from Khe Sanh that Dana had fitted into the ceiling. We lay on mats and pillows on the floor staring up as if into the branches of a tree. We passed around joint after joint. For roach clips, we used clamps and scissors from a North Vietnamese surgical kit Dana had liberated from a captured pack. The only light flickered from three or four candles dripping colorful wax over the splayed molten ends of exploded mortar shells which Dana had saved as combat souvenirs. On Dana's new stereo tape deck, Odetta was slowly singing: "Hey, Mister Tambourine Man," and Johnny Cash was singing "Folsom Prison Blues." Bob Dylan sang a romantic ballad of John Wesley Harding who had killed forty or more men by the time he was our age.

The tape is especially valuable to me because it refutes the memory of all those who characterize Flynn as a moody sort of shy fellow who couldn't take a joke. That was an especially evil thing to say about somebody in Vietnam, and I feel these excerpts from the party tape show he could also laugh at himself.

FLYNN: I was out there sweepin', you know, looting, and I picked up this canteen—
PAGE: Scoffin' up shit.
FLYNN: And this Marine comes up and says, "Careful o' that, it may have dope in it."
PAGE: YESS LAWD!
STONE: So he took the canteen and sold you the dope.
FLYNN: No, he was more concerned about the belt because he knew he could sell it for thirty-five dollars to the Navy guys back on the ship.
STONE: Yeah. That's what they keep sayin', but that's ridiculous. You ever try to sell anything to these guys?

STONE: You know that new camouflage?
PAGE: Aaaow, shit, man, it's STOLEN. NEW! Camouflage.
FLYNN: No, it's important to keep up with what's on the black market, man, because you can buy LURPS [prized field rations issued only to the "LURPS," long-range reconnaissance patrols] here sometimes if you look.

STONE: If you're lucky.

PAGE: Whaddaya want with a flight suit? Runnin' around looking like some teen-age super-savior?

FLYNN: Well, I don' know. What do you want anything for? Whaddare you looped for?

PAGE: What are you gonna do with a flight suit?

FLYNN: Fly.

LOUISE: I like 'em 'cause you can—

FLYNN: It's too bad they don't have—those NVA sneakers are really good. But they only got 'em in size six.

PAGE: You were not thinkin' anything, Flynn. Another story, Flynn. Flynn's storytelling. They get more bizarre each time you hear them.

PDY: Tell us again about the sign.

FLYNN: The what?

PDY: The dead gook by the sign.

FLYNN: I can't. I've told everybody.

STONE: Tell it differently. Like you generally do.

PAGE: Nice grass.

FLYNN: Good grass.

PDY: Yeah.

FLYNN: I see to get the musical effect I want I'm going to have to carry a speaker like that out into the field.

PAGE: What was that record you had in Paris? "Mind bender, car bender, remember November."

STONE: You wanta go with the Marines up there tomorrow?

FLYNN: It depends. If they're guarding the road, no. If they're fighting, yes.

STONE: You remember the day we were up that place and they were telling us about that convoy that got ambushed. Twenty GI's were killed.

FLYNN: That place where the cliffs overlook the road.

PDY: Well, the guy said we really had that all wrong. One of the guys was laughing and he said, "Yeah. We killed forty but we didn't see but two."

FLYNN: The Marines are getting pretty cool about that. The

grunts are really fatalistic. They know they're all gonna die.

PDY: You should of seen these two guys when I was waiting for a helicopter at Khe Sanh. These two guys had their faces just crouched in the dirt like in your picture.

STONE: Yeah! I got a few pictures of them. They had a few things to say about the way you got on a chopper, too, Perry Deane Young. You had a reserved seat on the Dong Ha bird and you just hopped on the first thing that came in.

PAGE: They're fucking so upset about their wounded being photographed too. This guy come up to me and said you can't take pictures of wounded. I said, Well, why not. I've been taking pictures of the fucking wounded for, you know, for—

FLYNN: For twenty years.

PAGE: He said there's no rational reason you can give me you wanta take pictures of the wounded. I said fuck you, I'm not gonna argue with you; I'm just gonna take my pictures. You wanta stop me, stop me, and I just walked away from him.

FLYNN: Ha! And took his picture.

PDY: You just said look this way son of a bitch.

STONE: During the siege up there, everybody wanted his picture taken.

FLYNN: They still do. Still pose like crazy.

FLYNN: You should of been out on this operation, man. You would have really dug it. Really weird things going. All these First Cav guys are special. They got a lot of spades and the inside of their MPC's or their APC's are really weird. They got weird photos in 'em—pictures of California, you know, really a lot of strange colors and everything. And I rode on this tank and this guy was weird. He had a scorpion on his helmet. I asked him what does the scorpion mean, and he said, "Ah, we all put this shit on our helmets."

PAGE: Listen at him. He started talking about the Australians and he's now burbling about—

FLYNN: No, I'm talking about this operation. I said he woulda liked this operation. They had a lot of colorful guys out there.

What Did We Do?

MEMORANDUM FOR THE PRESS *Saigon, 29 January 1968*
Subj: Security
  *1. All concerned will recall that when a correspondent is accredited
by MACV he signs a statement stating that he will abide by the
"Ground rules" and, if he does not, he realizes that he is subject to
having his accreditation suspended or cancelled. . . .*

To hear some correspondents tell it now, we either won or helped
to end the Vietnam war, depending on the speaker's politics. The
question remains as to what we really did do during the war; and,
more importantly, what effect did it have.

It was the first television war and I think the TV guys suffered
most. I also think their work will measure last in any accounting of
Vietnam reportage. This is largely due to mechanical reasons. While
correspondents can do so much stand-up commentary from the
palace gate in Saigon, they must also provide as much action footage
as is possible. To do this, a crew of three men must travel to a place,
then hope something happens within range of their cameras.

A number of the "talker guys" among the television correspondents in Vietnam would overdramatize their films. In a situation of no
danger at all, you would come on a correspondent crouched down
behind a wall or in a trench as he described the fierce action he had
just survived. Apparently it never occurs to the viewer that in order
to get the film of that man crouched down, some cameraman must
be out there somewhere standing up.

The very best television footage was therefore not the action
reports of firefights, but the sort of long-range, in-depth studies such
as Jack Laurence's *Charlie Company.*

Because so many people saw so much of the war on television, I think they came to believe they were seeing it all. But, just as in the riots in America, the very presence of cameras caused things to happen. I have seen it several times where a network crew would arrive after an action. The commander—anxious to get his own picture on the screen—would restage his side of the fighting. One of the worst correspondents tried to "forge" his own appearance in a film brought back from the Laotian border by a Vietnamese cameraman. He did the voice-over and stand-up commentary back at the Danang Press Center, saying he was "somewhere on the Laotian border." He happened to be dealing with one of the best cameramen in the business. The cameraman refused to go along with the plan; the correspondent called him lazy. Whereupon, the cameraman loaded his camera, shot the lying sequence—and then destroyed the film.

The correspondents—television men, writers, and photographers—were no more intelligent or sensitive than a similar group of people in any other profession. The TV people, I believe, were the most insensitive because they were dealing in a medium that—for all of us—had started out as make-believe. The correspondent was just another actor, and most of them dressed and primped for the parts.

I think the television people did not shock Americans nearly so much as they bored them with their seemingly endless reports of places, names, and statistics that had no meaning to most of the viewers.

The most boring reports of all, however, came from the medium I was a part of. There were many kinds of writers in Vietnam. There were reporters for daily newspapers, reporters for the wire services, and some magazine writers. The magazine writers, of course, had no deadlines. They could spend days and weeks in the field, get to know the men and their commanders, get some feeling for what it was like to be a part of the war day after day. The very best writing about the war has come from these people.

Most of the daily newspaper reporters did not have to file every day. The New York *Times* functioned largely as a wire service did—its reporters were responsible for everything that happened and they had to write the lead "war story" every day, even though the *Times* could have used the same story from the wires.

I was told that the impulse from the teletype machines in the UPI office took one minute to go from Saigon to New York. Anyhow, the machines were wired directly to those in New York and they never stopped. Twenty-four hours a day the war reports were going into the UPI headquarters, where they were rewritten and sent back out to UPI television, radio, and newspaper clients around the world. The television reports took a little longer. The Saigon bureaus of the networks would reserve time on the satellite broadcast from Tokyo to New York. There were special military flights the networks could send their film on. And it was possible for a TV correspondent to be in some action near Khe Sanh in the morning and (because of the thirteen-hour time difference) have it broadcast from New York on that evening's news.

Of all the news services in Vietnam, UPI had the worst reputation. One bureau chief had "needled" (exaggerated) stories to such an extent that UPI's name never quite recovered. However, the staff was quite competent when I worked there and it functioned much as a UPI staff functions in any city in the world. And this is my major complaint against UPI and all services in the war. With very few exceptions, our reportage in Vietnam was the same handout (press release) journalism practiced in Des Moines.

People would criticize UPI and its reporting to me and I would always come back with this: "The thing that should concern you is not the difference in our reports, but in the way that they are all the same."

To explain how the process worked, I will take one story that was sent out on the wires of the New York *Times*, UPI, Agence France Presse, the Associated Press, and Reuters on the afternoon of March 16, 1968. The *Times* provided maps with their story which took up two full columns in the newspaper. Except for a variance in adjectives, details, and length, the stories of all these agencies were essentially the same: For the simple reason that they had all come from the very same unquestioned source.

The story I'm talking about is the story of My Lai. The truth of that story did not come out for more than a year after most of a village of women, children, and old men had been massacred by an American unit near the central coastal town of Quang Ngai.

Lieutenant William Calley had told a lie. He said that "one

hundred twenty-eight North Vietnamese regulars" had been killed by his unit during a day-long fight. His lie was routinely passed on up the chain of command of information officers—company, brigade, division, and finally to the Military Assistance Command Office of Information (MACOI) in Saigon.

MACOI provided two sets of mimeographed releases to the agencies in Saigon. One set was sent out in the mornings, the other was handed out at the daily afternoon briefing, "the Five O'Clock Follies," as it came to be called. At least 90 percent of all the wire service copy from Saigon came direct from these releases.

The day of My Lai, UPI's deskman in Saigon was able to get through by telephone to the Americal division headquarters and get a few more details for the "night lead Viet." The New York *Times* story differed from UPI's only in that it lacked these details.

This was the original My Lai report as UPI sent it out worldwide:

> SAIGON (UPI)—U.S. infantrymen landed from helicopters under cover of an artillery barrage today and killed 128 Viet Cong in a raid on a Communist-held village near Quang Ngai on South Vietnam's northern coast.
>
> Elements of the 11th Light Infantry Brigade dismounted from helicopters around My Lai village just after dawn and fought scattered bands of Communists until about 2 P.M, a spokesman at the Americal Division headquarters in Chu Lai reported.

I am haunted more by that story and all it represents than by anything I ever saw in the field. While the Vietnam war has gained the reputation as being the most accessible war in history, it was, in fact, routine to cover up anything that might have harmed the cause of the American military.

During the very last days of the Five O'Clock Follies in Saigon, it was the American briefer's job to tell the reporters during the full-scale bombing of North Vietnam at Christmastime, 1972, that no information would be forthcoming from U.S. spokesmen in Vietnam. He called it "protection of information." The phrase, he said, "Just come out of my ass up there on stage." But his superiors in the Pentagon liked it and wired their congratulations on his use of it. The briefing, at its close, had become what it always was—not a forum for disclosing information, but a ruse for withholding information.

Because of the pressures from their own headquarters and because of the scattered actions that never lasted more than a few hours, the news agencies really had no choice but to accept these reports from the military spokesman. In most cases, a government wire service could have done the same job just as well.

When I persisted in asking the last briefer in Saigon about My Lai and how he would have handled that story—if he had known that the original report was a lie—he quipped, "Well, these things happen. . . . You wouldn't expect Raskolnikov to go on the stand and say he killed the old lady and her friend?"

One morning in the war, I was at Phu Bai when I heard that Viet Cong sappers had infiltrated the 101st Airborne Division's base camp nearby. I went over and interviewed the survivors. A young information officer escorted me—he wanted to be a reporter one day and he seemed especially interested in the way I worked. A full squad of sappers—their bodies painted green, wearing only black shorts and flat charges of TNT taped to their bellies—had got under the wire. There was about the same number of American and Viet Cong bodies left after the fighting. I typed out my story, called it in as the young lieutenant watched and listened. He insisted on riding back to the airstrip with me because he had some questions. He had written up the division's own "war story" that morning and called it into MACOI in Saigon. He had been ordered to report that no sappers had got inside the base and that no Americans had been killed. He asked me where UPI would have obtained that story if I hadn't been there. I explained that UPI would have relied on the MACOI report based on his report. In fact, it was the lead item in the release that day. I doubt very seriously if he had ever lied before that morning in Vietnam—doing his duty. It was just another day in the war story, and so was My Lai.

The still photographers, meanwhile, never suffered the suspicion endured by the TV guys and the writer guys. If a photographer crouched behind a wall, he knew he wouldn't get his pictures. He could not photograph a briefer's lies.

There was no way you could argue with a picture, they would say. There was also no way some rewrite man in New York could chop it up and rearrange it. (This was not exactly true, but generally it was.)

For all these reasons, I think the lasting documents about the war in Vietnam are the still photographs taken by a number of very young and very courageous (or reckless) photographers. Their work provides an unprecedented illumination of the real stupidity of war—whether they intended to do that or not.

It was as if—after years of romance—the cameras were suddenly focused not on the taut thighs of the brave matador, but on the gory mess of blood on the bull's back. In 1972, there were simultaneous exhibits in New York of the Vietnam pictures of David Douglas Duncan and of a group of younger photographers either missing or killed in the war. The striking difference in the two exhibits was that the older Duncan had not focused on the fear the American GI's felt or on the obscenity of death (of mud and shit and blood and guts all mixed in ugly colors). The younger photographers all knew this was what war was about. And finally in Vietnam, with all past pretense of glory stripped away, they could show it for what it was.

As to what effect they had, I am not at all certain. And if there was no effect from such an overwhelming display of ugliness, why did they do it? Was it possible, as one reviewer of the exhibits asked, that these young photographers were just pandering to the same lust for violence that brought Americans out to the new movies? I don't know the answer.

I do know this: At a certain point in history, Americans (most Americans) were revolted by what they knew about Vietnam. And I do not think they learned nearly so much about it on the television news (and certainly not from the newspaper stories) as they did from these incredible still pictures taken by Flynn and Stone and the others. As early as 1965, my own mother wrote about the "horrible pictures" of what our boys were doing in Vietnam; she has yet to mention anything she ever read about the war.

Another Side of Flynn

In late 1968, Flynn went through an outward and visible transformation that many people attributed to a deep inner change. The Green Beret swashbuckler suddenly became a pious student of Oriental art and religion. It is a fact that the Flynn I described in earlier pages as being gripped by a fascination with death weapons had reached the point where he begged these same Green Berets not to fire their weapons.

But I think it would be presumptuous to read so much into the change. In fact, I wonder if men do change as they get older or if—with time and experience—they simply learn better control (or repression) of those parts which are unpleasant to others and themselves, and better ways of expressing the parts which are acceptable and rewarding.

With Flynn, the transformation might be explained as simply as this: He had done the combat thing and become bored with it. Now he was ready to try something else.

He had a willing teacher in the person of young John Steinbeck IV, who had dropped out of high school and joined the Army, served a tour in Vietnam, returned to the States where he got busted for possession of marijuana. He then wrote a book about pot smoking among GI's in Vietnam and returned to Vietnam in late 1968 as a free-lance correspondent accredited to Dispatch News. By the time he met Flynn one afternoon on the terrace of the Continental Hotel, Steinbeck says he was "two years into psychedelics."

Through his father—who had been a war columnist for *Newsday*—and through Dispatch, John had cultivated an interest in the Vietnamese religions and he had read some of the classics of Buddhism and Hinduism, as well as the *I Ching.* This was unusual. The story, in our time, was focused almost entirely on the Americans in Vietnam. And for most of us the Vietnamese might as well not have been there. Only five or six American correspondents ever bothered to learn to speak Vietnamese. I never even learned the words for "hello," "good-bye," or "thank you." John and his girlfriend, Crystal Eastin, generally preferred the company of the Vietnamese. They even spoke the language. Crystal had been in Southeast Asia since 1966 with the International Voluntary Service in Laos.

A lot of people in our circle of friends did not especially like John Steinbeck's young son. He had an abrasive young man's personality, an arrogance bolstered by the insecurity he felt with the famous name. He and Flynn had this unspoken bond between them. John has told me that Flynn "saved me decades of learning to live with a name that is only partly your own."

John says that Flynn was "always afraid of that silent witness. He was very worried about being a bad person in the eyes of God." Flynn didn't know any of the texts, but he would listen as Steinbeck explained his fascination with war in spiritual terms. "Flynn wanted very much to be absolved of his thrill in a bloodletting situation," he says.

"I had a lot to teach him spiritually," says Steinbeck. Flynn's spirituality, John felt, was "sublimated with a dance with war—a love affair, an innocent cosmic dance. He dug me because I could keep reminding him of that when he was feeling guilty or perverted."

Steinbeck says he would quote from the *Bhagavad Gita:* "If the killer thinks he slays, or the slain thinks he's slain, neither understands." The spirit "takes on new bodies like man takes on new clothes," he said.

Flynn had a .51-caliber slug which he kept on his desk as a sort of talisman. John's brother Tom (though older, he always followed John—dropping out of high school, joining the Army, going to

Vietnam, drugs, working in television) made a nice wooden box to
hold the talisman and John wrote a poem for it and for Flynn:

War has a life, the evolution of strife.
And in peace, it knows its beginning.
So, when the killer knows what eternally is so.
There is killing without any sinning.

One morning in Danang, Flynn and Steinbeck and one other
correspondent decided to take a trip down to the caves in Marble
Mountain south of the city. Up some high steep stone steps there
was a huge carved meditating Buddha. Situated directly under a
shaft of light that came through a small hole in the mountain, this
statue was considered one of the most sacred shrines in Vietnam.

They were still a mile from the mountain when a black Marine
guard stopped their jeep and said an operation was going on in the
area and they had to go back. Flynn and Steinbeck flashed their
press cards and speeded past before the guard could protest.

At the base of the mountain, they encountered a tough-talking
Special Forces captain and three sergeants with a platoon of Nung
mercenaries. They immediately radioed back to their headquarters
for an Army public information officer to be sent out to get rid of
these press people. The sweet-talking PIO arrived and assured them
the caves would not be damaged and asked if they couldn't just
postpone their visit until the next day.

About halfway up the mountain, they could see the body of a
young American lieutenant hanging on a crag where it had fallen.
The lieutenant had led a charge earlier that morning after snipers
had fired on the super-secret Special Forces "CDN" compound
nearby. This unit directed assassination squads and also conducted
forays into North Vietnam, among other duties.

While the PIO was trying to placate Flynn and Steinbeck, a truck
roared up with a load of line charges of C-4 explosive. The PIO said
he didn't know what they were going to do with it, but it was
obvious the captain meant to blow up the caves. Flynn sent the
other reporter back to the press center to get reinforcements.

Everytime Flynn and Steinbeck would aim their cameras at the
mountain, the captain would aim his automatic rifle back at them.

The captain said, "I lost a man up there and you fucking press jockeys can't stop me from going after him."

As the Nungs were carrying down the lieutenant's body, the captain moved the truck in front of the cameras and had his men hold up their field jackets to block the view. He told one sergeant to "get out three cans of CS gas and use it if these guys move."

By this time, the captain's colonel had heard about Flynn and he came rushing down to meet him. It was the officer with whom Flynn had been in the 1966 operation into the Ashau Valley. He was delighted to see his old friend. He ordered the captain to pack up the explosives and leave the area. The officer invited Flynn and Steinbeck to dinner. And that is how one sacred place in Vietnam was not destroyed.

The Boys' Club

The apartment we shared fit all our romantic notions about the city itself. There was an iron gate between a dress shop and the Bluebird Bar right on Tu Do Street, just down from the main square, the National Assembly, the Continental and Caravelle hotels. The gate opened onto a narrow alleyway back to a carved wooden stairway that wound up four floors. Our second-floor apartment had been converted from a bordello, they said. The top two floors were still lined with girls in cubicles who would laugh and squeal out their front windows when we came home after curfew and had to throw beer cans to wake up the old concierge to unlock the gate.

It was part of our romance that this was the apartment Graham Greene described in *The Quiet American.* It was only much later that a real character in the book took John Steinbeck IV to another building further down the old Rue Catinat and said this—not our place—was the apartment in the book.

Some very straight employees at the American Embassy had lived in the apartment before us. The place was actually two apartments, about the size of a four-room house in America. The floors were made of foot-square brick tiles and there were slow-turning fans up in the high ceilings.

Two young Englishmen—Nik Wheeler and Derek Maitland- —were the first of our group to live there, starting in early 1968. Nik was a UPI photographer who had done some amateur acting in London but ever since he dropped out of college, he had rambled about the Middle, Near, and Far East—never with very much money, but always with style. When he rented a cheap flat in

Athens, it had—of course—a view of the Acropolis; his place in Beirut overlooked an ancient mosque and the bay.

Nik was the most handsome one among us, and he enjoyed a succession of very attractive women, ending up married to a beautiful Vietnamese woman named Rosemarie who had left Vietnam at age eleven, but returned after a very fine education in Paris. Maitland was a writer of fiction and I have always enjoyed the fact that he, an Englishman, used the title, *The Only War We've Got,* because it was that—not just for us Americans but also for the Europeans needing the same experience. There were always more than 400 accredited correspondents in Saigon and always more than half of that number were "third country nationals."

Maitland only stayed in Vietnam a few months getting material for his novel, then Wheeler asked Dana Stone about a new roommate. He said his only requirements were somebody who liked to "screw, drink, and smoke." Stone introduced him to Flynn, who promptly moved in. When the last two of the American office workers moved out in September, 1968, Tim Page and I moved in and set about creating a real New York psychedelic pad in the heart of Saigon.

The idea for such a place was not original with us. In 1966–1967 Page, Flynn, Stone, Corpora, and numerous others had also shared a whole house near the Presidential Palace. They called it "Frankie's House," for the houseboy who had a seemingly endless supply of girls to service them. I know Page was trying to recreate the mood of that place—although he and others have told me it was never as close a group as we had. For one thing, they were busier in those days. By the time we got together in our place, the peace talks had begun in Paris, the violence in America had pushed the Vietnam story to the back pages, and all of us talked about where to go next. Both places had, however, functioned as a way station for various reporters moving back and forth from Saigon to Danang to the field. It was a rare moment when a group of five or six was there at one time—and always an occasion for a party.

In our place, there was a ten-foot high wardrobe which we moved around as a room divider. We pushed our beds into an L in one corner next to the kitchen and we threw various pillows and pads around on the floor in the other half for a living room. To the maid's horror, we shoved an old buffet front against the wall under the big windows. Then we bought some barstools so we could sit behind it, drinking and smoking and watching all the action on the street.

Page and I borrowed the UPI mini-moke, went to the market, and came back with a small jungle of tropical trees which we arranged around the living room. He fitted his expensive stereo equipment into two sides. And soon a set of dayglo posters arrived from a friend of mine in New York. With a strobe light aimed at that wall, Jimi Hendrix would burst into flaming colors behind our heads. We also liberated two enormous spotlights from the U.S. Army.

We kept a set of binoculars on the bar and we had a number of characters on the street whom we kept track of. Mainly, we watched three stoned cyclo drivers who didn't seem to worry about the lack of customers. Like us, they would just sit there grinning. We had a variety of bamboo pipes, as well as some small hash pipes. We kept several crocks and gourds full of grass as a proper host would keep bowls of fruit and nuts on tables for guests in America. Page had two antique opium pipes—complete with the crystal lamps and needles.

We inherited a gentleman's gentleman opium man from a French planter. He was "Mister Long" and he brought us leather pillows made in Hanoi. For a nice fee, he would cross his legs and solemnly prepare the pipes for us to suck in the sweet acrid smoke. The only time I ever saw him smile was when we borrowed sound equipment to record our smoking—erotic moans and groans, sucking in the sweet smoke in one long breath, expiring like after sex. The only time I ever saw Mister Long sad was the night he came by to mourn after he read about Page's last wound.

"Tu Do Street," or "The Tu Do Street House," as we called our apartment, came to have a reputation that far exceeded anything we ever did there. For one thing, we were always making trips and a lot of times, the place just sat empty. People who never ventured inside would speculate on our carryings on when, in fact, we were most often just sitting up there stoned, staring out the windows or—especially Flynn—just lying in bed reading a book or staring up at the fan.

One girl called the place, "The Boys' Club," another said it was "Grand Central Station" because so many people had sleeping privileges there.

Page assembled a hideous collection of plastic Buddhas—his answer to those pretentious correspondents who made off with various treasures of the Oriental religions. He also bought a toy electric racetrack with two cars that could be manipulated from two sets of controls. The racetrack took up most of the living room floor until one of the cars broke and Page lost interest.

On the bar, there was a tambourine Page had bought for Flynn. Occasionally, he would bang it rather listlessly in time to the acid rock music on the stereo. Page wrote, "If Flynn was Your Muvver" with a magic marker on the tambourine and several other places in the apartment. One afternoon, sitting quite stoned at the bar-window, we lettered the entire wall around the window with graffiti. Page wrote: YOU WATCH ME WATCH YOU; Flynn wrote: PLAYEZ VOUS DE GOLF OUI JE L'AIME. I wrote: WHO LIVES HERE. Page also wrote: HUMMING CLOON IS WATCHING YOU, a slogan from Frankie's house with the drawing that always accompanied the World War II slogan, Kilroy was here.

I had just spent some time on the aircraft carriers at Yankee Station in the Gulf of Tonkin. I copied down an original poem by one of our fighter pilots, starting: "I am an American fighter pilot doing my duty." Another pilot let me copy some entries in his diary and I dutifully transcribed one of those onto our wall: TOOTER GOT SHOT DOWN TODAY. THE MOVIE WAS LOUSY TONIGHT AND I CAN'T SLEEP AGAIN.

It was a peculiarly democratic gathering of people in our apartment. For an opium smoke one night, I looked around and tried to imagine what it would be if our fathers were there instead of us. There was no way in hell any of them would ever have known each other, but here we were—the son of Errol Flynn, the actor; of John Steinbeck, the writer; of Bob Stone, postmaster in North Pomfret, Vermont; of an English accountant; of a North Carolina mountain farmer.

The police never bothered our little clubhouse. Once, I did come home to find the opposite corners covered by three or four "white mice," the Americans' name for the little Vietnamese policemen in white and gray uniforms. Their weapons were trained on our windows, but they never asked any questions and never came to our door. Apparently, they were just waiting for the next move from inside. Flynn, Page, and Steinbeck had built a catapult and launched a purple smoke grenade out the window. But the contraption didn't work right and it landed below the window—spewing purple smoke all over people on the sidewalk.

The Vietnamese Were Also There

It was always a disquieting realization in Vietnam to know that being tall, blond, and green-eyed, I was among a small number of people who lived above suspicion. To be a native Vietnamese—short and dark—was to be suspected by both sides.

If the Americans caught a Vietnamese man, woman, or child without identification papers, that was reason enough to arrest and interrogate him or her. Only the Viet Cong—whom every American civilian and soldier begrudgingly admired—was respected enough to be called "Charlie" or, after the Tet Offensive, "Sir Charles." All others were "dinks" or "gooks" or "slopes."

There were, however, a number of Vietnamese men who had obtained jobs with the American news agencies. Some of the best photographers and cameramen, in fact, were native Vietnamese. While the other correspondents moved around like lords of the land—ignoring curfews, demanding priority on all flights—the Vitenamese had to be especially careful and stop at all checkpoints and roadblocks, or else they would be shot on sight.

Every time a press bus was stopped at a Vietnamese Army checkpoint, the guards would not even look at the papers of the "roundeyes," but all Vietnamese newsmen were ordered off the bus and interrogated.

One of the hardest-working Vietnamese photographers for the Associated Press was named Phuoc. He was wounded several times in pursuit of his stories. And, having got the job after selling ice cream on the streets of Saigon, he was intensely loyal. Once, Dana Stone was with Phuoc in the field and some American GI's were giving him a rough time. Dana stopped them, explaining that Phuoc

172

was working for the "Hanoi Herald," which only caused more serious problems: the GI's believed him.

Another time, after the Army had taken over the Danang Press Center, the Americans ordered Phuoc to get in a lineup of Vietnamese employees who were being questioned about some missing silverware. One of his co-workers intervened, saying, in effect, He's no Vietnamese, he's an AP photographer.

Once when Phuoc was wounded, however, an American pilot went out of his way to get him back to a base hospital where he could be properly treated. Most of the GI's really liked him. "He was like a puppy dog," another AP man said. "The Americans loved to have this kid along."

Later, I discovered that this kid was thirty- four years old. It is not a footnote of no consequence. This was the very best attitude (of Big Brother and Little Buddy) which I ever observed between the Americans and Vietnamese. Even their generals were a foot shorter than we were. The Vietnamese men were almost as thin and graceful as the women.

I just don't think the Americans ever took them seriously, ever trusted them as grown-ups capable of making their own decisions. It affected decisions from the highest diplomatic levels on down to the most personal contact between privates of the two armies. More than anything else, I think this attitude caused "Vietnam" to become the humiliating debacle it was for all of us involved.

The way we talked to them: Hey, baby/You number one/I want you/I want beer/Ba-mi-ba ("33"or Ba Muoi Ba beer)/Bia Hop (canned beer)/Hai Bia Hop (two canned beers)/Ti Ti (as in "ti ti grass")/Beaucoup (as in "beaucoup grass")/Fini (as in "fini grass" or "fini you")/Same Same (Same).

The way they talked to us: Hey you, GI/You want girl?/You want boom boom?/You number one/You number welve/You number welve towsan/You buy me chop chop?/You buy me tea?/You buy me?

Datelines we never learned to pronounce: Khe Sanh/Cam Lo/Cua

Viet/Dong Ha/Quang Tri/Tan An/An Nhon/Quang Dien/Phu
Vang/Gio Linh/Hue/Nam Dong/Danang/Hoa Vang/Mieu Bong/Hoi
An/An Hoa/Que Son/Thang Binh/Tam Ky/Chu Lai/Quang Ngai/
Song My/My Lai/Phu Vinh/Truong Xuan/Phu Cat/Qui Nhon/Binh
Thanh/Tuy An/My Phu/Tuy Hoa/Nha Trang/Cam Lam/Cam
Ranh/Ban Me Thuot/Gia Nghia/Kontum/Dak To/Phuoc Binh/An
Loc/Duc Lap/Dak Song/Phuoc Vinh/Phu Cuong/Moc Hoa/Gia
Dinh/My Tho/Go Cong/Vinh Long/Ca Mau/Ha Tien/Phu Quoc.

Confronted with the language, Tim Page would just call them all:
"Men Foong. . . ."

The way the U.S. Military Assistance Command Vietnam talked
to itself: MACV / MACOI / JUSPAO / APO / ARVN / VNAF /
THIRD MarDiv / Three MAF / PIO / PAO / CIB / OpCon / Conex /
CommSymp / CORDS / ROK's / Cax / MIA / WIA / KIA / CIA /
USAID / USIS / USIA / MPC / DMZ / VC / NVA / WBLC / LST /
LCU / BDA / ETA / ETD / DEROS / FRAC / SRAC / TRAC / DRAC /
RMK-BRJ / Pan AM / Chase Manhattan / Mutual Funds.

Our First Good-byes

In April of 1968, the Associated Press offered Dana Stone a salary of $700 a month, plus a $300 living allowance, plus $10 a day for expenses, plus the usual vacations and $l00,000 in life insurance. UPI had never given him a living allowance because his "home" was in Danang, so his new salary, with the allowances, was almost twice what he had made with UPI. Some of his friends pushed him to demand even more money, but Dana really didn't see the need.

He and Louise took off on a two-week vacation from the war, flying first to Hong Kong, then back by ship to Bangkok. Dana wrote a friend: "Louise and I are taking a vaction since you people have your own war going in the States and won't use my pictures from Vietnam."

The ship they took was called the *MS/Halldor.* It had seven Norwegian officers. The captain had been in the Orient for forty-four years, another officer for twenty-two, and another for eighteen years. Except for a brief exchange the first night they boarded, they never saw any of the officers again, which meant they had the dining room to themselves at mealtime.

For the voyage, Dana took along a sheaf of writing paper and wrote to almost every one of his old friends. Many of these letters he never finished, but he saved them like a diary for himself. He wrote in two or three of them: "No one to talk to except Louise and I've already told her all I know so I'm reduced to writing lies to all my old friends. Being a passenger is considerably duller than working on a ship and the idea of paying to ride a ship worst of all. But my friends will think I'm having fun."

Once they arrived in Bangkok, he was glad the vacation was over. "I'm tired of vacationing and am afraid I might miss something in Vietnam," he wrote.

They arrived back just in time for the May Offensive or "mini Tet" as the correspondents called it. There was some fierce street fighting in Danang, which he photographed, and then the lull began. That summer and fall were generally uneventful in Vietnam—especially after the excitement of Tet in Saigon, the siege at Khe Sanh, the battle in Hue. In fact, it is difficult for me to realize now that Dana worked for the AP as long as he did, from May 1 through December 1, because so little happened in that time.

We spent many happy afternoons in the sun out front of old Tai's pink house on China Beach across the river from Danang. Tai had come down from Hanoi. She was a tough and wiry character, as mean and conniving as she was fun and lively. Tai could get you anything from drugs to girls to the very best of booze from a stock (valued at more than $10,000 when they found it) of supplies she had got illegally from the American commissary.

Flynn would swim back and forth in the calm waters of the South China Sea. Sometimes he would sit there, not talking, beside little Minh, Tai's grandchild. Minh adored Flynn and he would jabber to him as if he were actually conversing.

Several times, Flynn talked about what a great film could be done about "Minh's house," showing all the Americans (military and civilian) in and out of the front and back doors, the correspondents out front, old Tai and her daughter (married to a Vietnamese naval officer), and little Minh, who had somehow come through it all unscarred.

One afternoon, Flynn and Stone and some others arrived on the beach and were just relaxing as usual when some Vietnamese fishermen started sniping at them from their boats. The correspondents later found out an American helicopter had swooped low over the beach, a door gunner had dropped out two grenades, and a little boy was killed. The Vietnamese army quickly moved in, rounded up the Vietnamese fishermen, and searched them for their weapons.

Dana and I had set December 1 as the day we would quit our jobs, but I had been plotting my escape from UPI almost from the first time the mail brought back a clipping of one of "my" stories.

Everything I wrote in Vietnam was routinely rewritten by deskmen in UPI's New York office, and after the first few clippings I simply had no heart for what I was doing. I knew that no matter how good it was when I put it in my end of the machines, it would come out the other end reading like everything else on the UPI wires. It also became apparent that quality or originality were not expected or appreciated by my superiors. In fact, the more the stories stuck to the place names and numbers handed out by the lying military briefers, the happeir UPI was in New York. Those stories were so much easier to transcribe. And the clients never questioned them.

By November, I had saved up enough money for some travels around Southeast Asia. I also found out that UPI had to pay my way back to the States and I got the most expensive ticket (with fifteen stops) I could plan.

Dana and Louise had already flown to Singapore where they ordered a Volkswagen camper for their trip to some imagined logging camp in northern Sweden. Just on an impulse, Flynn had boarded the plane with them. They sat around the pool at an elegant English hotel there, the girls coming up to meet the famous American star. Flynn responded graciously to the girls, and with good humor to Dana and Louise. Then Dana came back to Saigon to finish out a month with the AP and left Louise in Singapore.

The last week of November, Dana and I were both in Saigon. Mainly, I remember how determined he was to get out of Vietnam alive. He was taking no more chances. It was an attitude he shared with the GI's. They seemed to feel it wouldn't be so bad to be killed when you still had most of your tour to serve. But to be a short-timer and get killed with only a few more days left, that was the worst fate of all. Anyhow, Dana was incredulous when I told him that UPI was sending me up to the central highlands the last day I worked for the company. "You mean you're getting on a goddamn helicopter?" he asked.

One night that same week, he and I decided we would investigate all the ships docked in Saigon to see if we couldn't get a ride down to Singapore. It was a beautiful moment in our relationship—Tom Sawyer and Huck Finn shuffling along the docks, talking to the seamen, talking to each other about all the places we had been, all the new ports we would visit.

Finally, we found a great antique. It was a yacht commissioned by King George VI (the plaque was still in place in the wardroom). It had been redesigned as a torpedo boat in World War II and was now doing service as a cargo hauler for some American war profiteer. We rambled around the decks until a Filipino steward came and told us the captain would like to see us.

The captain's cabin was straight out of our most elegant fantasies of life at sea. It had a built-in canopy bed, built-in desk, and two couches—all made of thick mahogany. The years of abuse had only enhanced the beauty of the room in our eyes. The captain himself was another relic. A sad, sagging fellow with no beard, not much hair on his head, and no special costume to go with the setting. But he kept us entranced with tales of his younger days as the chief pilot for the port of Rangoon. He talked with deep resentment of some mysterious accident which he had been blamed for and which had cost him his career, left him beholden to this corrupt American. But no, he couldn't take us to Singapore. It was illegal and there was no way we could get in the port once we got there.

We walked back to the apartment, delighted with the experience. And one morning we said our good-byes, with promises to meet up in Singapore or somewhere on the road to Europe.

I had decided to stay on another month in Vietnam and do some sightseeing. I flew up to Hue and spent two full days touring the city with a very articulate Vietnamese historian as my guide. He explained that the "ancient imperial capital," as the Americans always called it, was actually built in 1801. We also visited three of the emperors' tombs a few miles outside the city. I paid especial homage to the spirit of the anti-Westerner Minh Mang, who now resides in a fantastic park that features replicas of the palace buildings and a large lagoon built around the mountain in which his body was buried.

Back in Danang, I said good-bye to my friends at the press center. Whatever its devious purpose, the Danang Press Center was central to all our best memories of the year 1968. It was the way station for all our hairiest combat adventures and the only place in the country where large numbers of correspondents ate, slept, got drunk or stoned and became friends and enemies at such close range.

The press center had been converted from a seedy old French hotel on the banks of the river at the edge of Danang. It was a cluster of low, barracklike buildings around a restaurant, bar, and a separate communications shack. A window in the fully stocked bar afforded a view of the patio, a wooden dock, the river, and the opposite shore. There were fresh Stateside movies on the patio nearly every night. The restaurant featured a changing menu with a small selection of wines to go with the flown-in Kansas City steaks. None of us realized how large the profits from the press center were until the Marines paid cash for four Toyota vehicles.

After some early bad publicity, the Marines had provided the press center and staffed it with a full command of two colonels and staff and various enlisted men who worked as drivers, mechanics, and "escorts" for the correspondents. It was a successful ploy and I firmly believe that it was a major reason the Marine Corps didn't suffer as it should have from the war—considering the fiascos of Khe Sanh, Con Thien, and other places where their lack of training and equipment were as much to blame for the casualties as the enemy. We spent more time with the Marines because they made it easier for us. The writers and photographers may have thought they were depicting the horrors and stupidity of the war, but the Marines saw it as recognition, anyhow. And no Congressman could dare question their appropriations when such splendid color photographs were showing the sacrifices of the Corps.

There were often as many as fifty to seventy-five correspondents camped out at the press center. The news agencies and the networks maintained regular "bureaus" at the press center, with permanent rooms reserved. They were mainly boozers, but they tolerated the few of us who were early pot smokers and, by the end of 1968, most of the older ones had at least tried marijuana, if not opium. I remember several nights when correspondents just back from the field would relieve their tensions first by getting drunk and then by gathering in somebody's room to recount their stories and sing bawdy songs as men have sung in every war.

It was this sort of farewell I bade to the old press center. It was two days before Christmas, and a group of us had gone to the Bob Hope show on a hillside covered by several thousand Marines. Rosey Grier gave the black power fist and every black man in the audience stood up proud. One of the Golddiggers flashed the peace sign and a roar went up from the GI's flashing it back.

There was an obnoxious right-wing radioman in our little group from the press center. He bragged about a letter from Pan American which promised him $1,000 if he could get the airline's name mentioned in two wire service stories. He was always drunk and insulting everybody with his talk of killing Commies and winning the war. He fell off his seat once and two Marines kicked him on down while the rest of us laughed. He reached up for the door to the press van and another reporter inside kicked him in the face and knocked him back in a ditch.

Later that night when the radio guy was drunker still, he bought several bottles of whiskey and invited all the Marines back to his room. I went along with the group, mainly to be with a young corporal who was refreshingly honest and uncynical in that setting. We were all singing Christmas songs in bitter parody of the season. The radioman decided he would record the scene. He started talking into his machine about the danger we were in, but that our boys in the trenches could still pause for a moment of the Christmas spirit. Then he passed the microphone for each boy to give his name, rank, and hometown . . . which each did, in turn, ending with a resounding curse: "Fuck Vietnam. Fuck Christmas. Fuck you."

Two real heavies in the room—a barrel-shaped major and his equal in a correspondent—started belly-bouncing back and forth across the room like sumo wrestlers. They hit a small table and the radioman jumped up to tell them to be careful. Triggered by his concern, the major led the rest of us on a rampage. We jumped up and down on the beds until we had broken them and everything else standing in the room.

The young corporal whom I liked and I slipped out of the noise and sat out back beside the river. We shared a joint and sat there not saying anything. The quiet contrast was a fitting end to my days at the Danang Press Center.

From Saigon, I wrote a friend: "No job, still here. Ain't that strange. The obscenity of it all is closing in now, though—228 killed last week while their leaders argue in Paris about whether the table shall be round or square. It's really very difficult to leave this place—rather, to leave the friends I have here."

An Island of Peace

As a farewell excursion, I decided to accompany our group on a trip to visit the "Coconut Monk" on the Island of the Phoenix in the Mekong River about sixty miles south of Saigon. The group included Carl Robinson, an AP photo editor, John Steinbeck IV, Crystal, Sean Flynn, Tim Page, Nik Wheeler, Rosemarie, and me.

For the trip, we rented an old Chevrolet station wagon that had somehow made its way to the Orient to live out its days delivering fish. We kept the air thick with incense and pot smoke to keep down the smell. At the river town of My Tho, we hired two longboats outfitted with lawnmower motors hooked to a long shaft extended over the side to a tiny propeller in the water.

There had been very few Western visitors to the island except for John and Crystal, and they were considered near-godlike celebrities. We were welcomed like Kipling characters a hundred years out of time as we stepped ashore to the bows and curtsies of the natives. We accepted their tribute in our best stoned graciousness and were shown a place of honor overlooking the fantastic complex.

The Island of the Phoenix looked like a Disney version of "Gods Around the World"—rather, it looked like a child's fantasy of heaven run wild with brilliant colors and lights and tons and tons of USAID concrete and yellow-painted oil drums. In one open courtyard, there were enormous pink and blue dragon columns rising up twenty or thirty feet to honest-to-god smalltown American mercury streetlights. This courtyard was used for prayers by a rotation of all the monks continuing the peace prayers twenty-four hours a day.

At one end of the courtyard there was a green-painted magic

mountain, with a grotto underneath and a winding trail around it up to the pinnacle where the Dao Dua (Tsow You-uh) meditated. His name was a pun meaning holy man or "Coconut Monk" which was what the Americans called him. He had taken a vow of silence in 1949, pledging never to talk until peace came to Vietnam. He had also meditated from the top of a tree and in a tower near Saigon. He had another perch atop a metal tower in the river in front of the island.

Behind the mountain a tall billboard depicted Jesus and Buddha arm in arm. There was also an altar with three photographs (two from *Time* and *Newsweek*) of Ho Chi Minh, President Thieu, and the Dao Dua. Fresh coconuts always rested on the altar as symbols for each man. On stilts above the water there was a concrete topographic map of both Vietnams that stretched perhaps thirty feet. All the countries involved in the war were represented by flags on the map—including Spain, which had a medical team in the highlands, and West Germany, which had a hospital ship in Danang.

In one area of the island, the men were busy building an eight-sided peace table which the Coconut Monk had decided was the solution (according to the *I Ching*) to the arguments in Paris at that time. Everybody on the island was busy working on his or her assigned projects. Above it all was the incessant clang of the gongs. Hammered out of artillery shell casings, they hung on little stands. A bigger gong was sounded every few minutes from a high platform at the back of the prayer courtyard.

At the right moment, our group was escorted up the mountain and presented to the holy man. He was a wiry little elfin creature. (He forbade meat, weapons, and alcohol on the island.) He grinned and grinned at each one of us—gesturing with his hands, a language which his own interpreter passed on. He insisted on posing for pictures with each of us.

Apparently, the Coconut Monk saw us as visible evidence his dream had been realized. Here were representatives of the mighty Western press; he was building the peace table and soon the delegates from the warring countries would arrive on his island for the talks.

That night, the Dao Dua dreamed that one of us would die if all of us didn't have newly-made clothes just like the monks wore by daybreak. So, very late that night, we were measured for hats and loose-fitting pajama tops and bottoms in sackcloth brown. Those members of the community charged with making clothes stayed up all night finishing our new outfits. We were thoroughly stoned and grinning in the new costumes as we lined up on either side of the old man in front of several hundred of the religious kneeling in the open courtyard the next morning.

It was a truly historic moment on the island and the Coconut Monk had written a proclamation. It was read by one of the younger monks, a simple statement that we had all lived together in peace, so why did our countries have to be at war? Though the island itself was off-limits to the American and Vietnamese military, we could see and hear the American planes bombing beyond both shores of the river.

The monks flew the flags of all the combatants and there was even a memorial service on the island later, when Ho Chi Minh died. The reverence of so many hundred men and women was truly awesome to me. At one point in the prayer ceremony, I slipped away from the group and found Nik Wheeler's girlfriend, later his wife, Rosemarie, sobbing uncontrollably—all the sophistication of her Paris upbringing breaking down to disclose the little Vietnamese girl she had come back to her homeland to find. "You people," she said, "you come here and you get stoned and you laugh and it doesn't mean anything to you. But I am still one of them. That woman in the trance just now, do you know what she was saying? She was praying to God like she was a child and he was her father. She was asking him over and over, 'Why, why, why must we have this awful war; why, why, why did my children and my husband have to die?'"

None of us talked very much on the trip back to Tu Do Street. At a checkpoint just outside the city, we were stopped. No questions were asked of the Americans, but Rosemarie was ordered out of the car. She produced her French passport, spoke to them in French, and after some minutes, we were allowed to pass.

The next day, the last day of 1968, I said good-bye to the group, good-bye to Vietnam. I had to catch a plane, so I missed the group's "demonstration" at the American Embassy.

It began with an acid trip in which John Steinbeck IV saw the various members of the group in the major roles of "Monkey," a

legend of how Buddhism was brought to China. His flute turned
green, so he decided he was the Monkey Sage; the Coconut Monk
was the Jade Emperor; Carl Robinson was Turtle; Flynn was the
Sandy Priest, because he loved to run on China Beach. In the midst
of John's trip, an emissary of the Dao Dua knocked on his door to
tell him the holy man wanted to see him and Crystal. John sent back
little gifts which told his story and the Coconut Monk was delighted.
They met in the upstairs of a little tea shop in Cholon where the Dao
Dua's saffron Packard was parked out front. They decided they
should take their peace prayers directly to the American ambassador.

Flynn wore both top and bottom of his new monk's costume; Page
only wore the top. Both of them carried cameras—moving and
still—as they joined Steinbeck, Crystal, and a small delegation from
the island. On a tray for the ambassador, the Dao Dua carried a toy
plastic truck, some bananas and coconuts from the island, a
Buddhist begging bowl carved from a coconut, and a letter
addressed to the President of the United States of America. The
letter asked only this: Why couldn't the President come to the island
and bring peace to Vietnam?

The straggly little group made its way across Saigon, along the
wide sidewalk up to the gleaming white fortress that the embassy
became—with machine gunners at four corners of an exterior wall
and at each corner of the roof. The Marine guards quickly locked
the big iron gates and trained their weapons on these strange
visitors. A high-ranking CIA man saw them and yelled orders that
the group was not to be admitted. A young Army clerk with ten
weeks' training in the language was brought out. He pronounced the
words in Vietnamese as if he were vomiting: "The government of
the United States cannot accept these gifts."

Who's Gonna Miss Us?

And so, on New Year's Eve, 1968, I arrived in Hong Kong in time to get as drunk as the British soldiers cavorting in the fountain in front of the Peninsula Hotel at the stroke of midnight.

That night was the first time I had heard Mary Hopkin's "Those Were the Days." I kept playing it over and over—trying not to think that the days ahead might never measure up to those in Vietnam. "Those were the days, my friend, those were the days. . . .We'd fight and never lose, for we were young and sure to have our way." Another song that fit my mood was Scott MacKenzie's "What's the difference if we don't come back? Who's gonna miss us in a year or so? What's the difference if we go?"

I went by freighter from Hong Kong to Singapore, then down to Indonesia where I stayed awhile in Jakarta and then took the train across Java.

I wrote a friend on February 14, 1969: "I was in Khe Sanh a year ago this day. Now, the boy has lowered the big bamboo curtain so that the rain does not splatter me as I type on the little terrace of my six dollar (meals included) room in the Hotel Garuda near the railroad station in Jogjakarta. I came here by train, 12 hours through the most beautiful countryside you could ever concoct out of some romantic tale of the South Pacific."

From Bali, I wrote another friend, March 8, 1969: "Truly a magical place, in spite of all the tourists. Went to a fantastic parade for a royal cremation . . . great happy occasion here with much laughter and dances and cockfights. Rented a motor scooter and ducked in and out of the line of march singing my own little song:

"Come to the cre-ma-tion." Beautifully gracious people—I like to think of them as the Vietnamese without the war—and they are only mildly interested in the American tourists. They see nothing in us they want to become."

Friendships

In late 1968, Sean Flynn and Carl Robinson became close friends, sharing in some new quieter ventures which we had never had time for. Carl was the son of missionary parents, who brought him up in the Congo. He attended special schools (which he recalls with a shudder) for the white children. At first, because of his background as a U.S. government employee, a lot of us thought that Carl was the spook (spy) among us. But, as we got to know him, we came to realize that he was the most sensitive one among us, whose concern for the Vietnamese people went back to 1964, when he first visited the place on vacation from college.

Robinson worked with USAID in Vietnam from July, 1964, through June, 1965. He returned to college and graduated *cum laude* with an honors thesis on the Geneva Agreements of 1954 and U.S. policy in Vietnam. he returned to Vietnam in July, 1966, again with USAID in the province of Go Cong. He got more and more disgusted with the U.S. aid program and finally quit in early 1968, after releasing a denunciation of the program. He then became a photo editor for the Associated Press and married a woman named Kim Dung (pronounced "yung") whom he had first glimpsed as a willowy schoolgirl in Go Cong. He was working with Dana Stone after he took the AP job and Dana and Louise would visit him when they were in Saigon.

Robinson first met Flynn in late 1968 at our apartment. He wrote me the following about their friendship:

> There was much loud music—Stones and Hendrix—super-joints and mumbling conversations going on here and there. Flynn was

187

holding forth in a chair of his part of the house. We nod hello, no handshakes, or have-you-two-met-befores. I presume we both knew each other.

Me, I was that spooky guy who worked as a photo editor over at AP, not much into Saigon's social circles. I try to make conversation. "Ah, yes, you and Dana were good friends—used to go out on operations up north." A mumbled reply, nothing, nods of the head. I leave. What a stuckup bastard that guy Flynn is.

Later, I find that is often a first impression of Flynn, arrogance. The dude has nothing to say, he's sizing you up. If he has nothing to say, he says nothing, small talk is a waste. More basically, it's probably a defense mechanism—too many people rubbing up to be pals with this "son-of." It's better to turn them off quick. And later, I find, it's also a touch of shyness—shyness more than arrogance.

So, a month or so later, I'm on R&R and end up at Siem Reap, in Cambodia. The Auberge sucks, I go downtown to Siem Reap and move into a Chinese hotel. Sean's eating dinner at a Chinese restaurant. I sit down, still that strained conversation, there's nothing much to say. He started talking about his days around Angkor—hiring a bicycle for 50 cents a day, toting his sounds and stash to off-the-road temples, exploring all day.

"I've been sighting these temples with a compass," he says, "and they're all lined up east-west and north-south." That's the sort of things he likes, he doesn't talk about his pictures, the double exposures, etc.

The next couple of days we see each other more frequently and when it was time to return to Phnom Penh, I ask Flynn to join us in the car. He'd come up by bus or taxi. It was the beginning of our friendship. We stop for lunch at Kompong Thom, he rolls a super-joint for the last leg of the trip. The cassette goes on and Jimi Hendrix sees us back to Phnom Penh. Incredible countryside—yellow-green paddies, dotted with palm trees, bright blue sky, purple mountains. Back in Phnom Penh, we have dinner and then move down to Madame Chung's.

In many ways, the lamp became part of our friendship—we shared the "opium understanding." a mystique of incomparable relaxation, conversations and impressions, and friendships.

Back in Saigon, I became a regular at the old Tu Do house. A midday break from the office or a place to go after work. Also the morning at the Pagode where we'd talk or watch the girls stroll by.

Sean talked about leaving. He was always going to leave. He'd finished his footage, he said, and he wanted to go back and see his girl in Paris. But, it was always a dream, maybe I'll get some non-war stuff, he said. He missed Dana and said, "I used to give him a lot of shit when we worked together up north, but now I see he's a real friend.'' The companionship they shared was the war and I think it was Dana's leaving that got him off of that. He talked of the operations he'd been on but didn't seem to want to go out anymore. It's better to do that in company, I guess. Also, in late 1968 there wasn't much of a war left.

Page, Flynn, and I used to frequent a nearby dive on Nguyen Thiep Street called the ''Casino.'' We used to watch the street through binoculars for hours and then venture out. The old bartender used to pass cigarettes coated in opium across to us at the bar while we sipped high-powered rum and Cokes.

It's hard to describe Sean's relationship with women—certainly they were more interested in him than he in them. We talked of the Western view of friendships and our often puritanical views which inhibited more open friendships, the friendships forged by an experience like Vietnam—in French *camaraderie* or comrade-ships—and outside the American realm of kicking each other in the ass to get to the top of the heap.

One night, he said reflectively, ''Someday, we are going to go a long way to see each other again''—a mourning, perhaps, that the *camaraderie* forged by Vietnam comes rarely and binds men together forever. It is something very out of the American view of things and, unfortunately, comprehensible to Americans only in that puritanical view of one's ''proper'' role.

In his view of women, Sean looked more to something illusive—a pedestal, perhaps—something to nourish dreams. A girl in the Casino became ''the Cham princess,'' a bastard offshoot of a long-dead civilization, and perhaps because of this view, he never got anywhere with her. The dream was shattered when she took off early one night with a band of Filipinos.

He could also talk fondly of a seventeen-year-old Cambodian who'd roll him pipes in Phnom Penh, massage him to sleep, and cuddle up next to him. I take it that in earlier days he had been more active with the girls in Vietnam. He talked of how clap and the fear of clap was such a moderating influence—a legitimate fear, certainly. But, in all, he wasn't a ''hustler''—he kissed off a girl from Mimi's after a couple times ''because she was stealing too much of my money,'' he said. His view was more distant.

Another small item from the Casino: A very effeminate young man hung out at the Casino. I never did figure out his ''function'' there. He fell in love with Sean and really led himself on. The attention, beyond a non-hostile attitude, was never reciprocated and after Sean disappeared he told Steinbeck and I how heartbroken he was. He still asks.

Sean eventually moved his motorcycle down from Danang and we started motorcycle trips, something else we shared. This was part of his different view of Vietnam, taking off south toward the Delta, an area he had never known very well. The war there is less evident, and for me, it was the area I knew best.

On one trip, we went down to Go Cong (with my wife, Kim Dung) and then on to Chau Doc province near the Cambodian border. Kim Dung can be very yes-and-no about my friends but with Sean she felt something different. Perhaps it was the conversations that went beyond the "Oh, how are you?" They used to talk about customs, superstitions, what girls from different provinces were like—e.g., the girls from Kien Hoa are beautiful, the girls from Vinh Long are crafty as hell—food, and other things. And she went along on this trip which was really a resupply mission.

We ended up buying a couple of kilos of Hoa Hao red in some border town. It was a different scene for Sean—staying in local hotels, eating in small restaurants, and wandering around morning markets. On the way back to Saigon, we were sirened over by some MP's who demanded to know why we weren't wearing helmets. I did most of the talking, Sean just stood there. When I asked him why he didn't say anything, he said, "I don't talk to MP's."

This was a prelude to a later trip—in March of 1969—through Laos to Luang Prabang. Sean was a good guy to travel with—he had his shit together, the cameras and sounds.

Robinson left Flynn in Luang Prabang and Flynn said he planned to move on up to Ban Houei Sai—along roads even the CIA was afraid to travel.

Flynn wrote several friends about his adventures in Laos. He was fascinated by all the tribes and their elaborate costumes and jewelry. He feared that they might all be "McLuhanized" if he or some other photographer didn't work fast.

But, he said, he wouldn't be there long enough for that. He was missing the war and he wanted to go by boat on the Mekong from Ban Houei Sai to Luang Prabang. He canceled the trip, however, when he heard that some of the boatmen were getting shot up.

In spite of this spoken caution, Flynn was scaring at least one friend in Laos with his stories of places he was going. Why did he do it? the friend asked. Flynn grinned and quoted that line from the AFVN disc jockey: "Just groovin' on the danger."

By the next month, Flynn had reached Vientiane by the time I arrived there on a flight from Bangkok. Another friend had told me about Flynn's plan to travel by road through Cambodia to Saigon and I hoped he would let me tag along. But I wrote a friend in the States that "we are both such loners," he probably wouldn't.

Flynn was sitting there at the little downstairs bar by himself when I walked into the old Constellation Hotel in Vientiane and checked in with the bartender. I was all smiles and ready for a back-slapping welcome. Flynn glanced up from the bar, said, "Howya doin', boy?" and calmly asked where I'd been, where was I going.

We smoked some grass that night, drank beers in a trashy bar in the first floor of the big old wooden Lido Hotel, a real firetrap inhabited by bargirls and their Air America customers. I talked mainly about my trip to Bali. I told Flynn I had never seen any place like it in all Southeast Asia. It was even better than Katmandu, I said. The people and the land were still unspoiled by war or tourists.

As we talked that night in Vientiane, Tim Page was being wheeled into the operating room at the main neurosurgery ward of the Army hospital at Long Binh, just north of Saigon. He had been sent out on a routine assignment for *Time*—merely to get a good aerial shot of the "market" on the South Vietnam-Cambodia border. He got his pictures (though *Time* never used them) and was flying back when the helicopter pilot got an emergency medevac call.

The chopper landed and a sergeant jumped out to help carry the wounded. Page was close behind him. (The last picture on the film in his camera showed a stack of mutilated bodies, but Page was never able to recall where he had snapped it. The sergeant tripped a booby trap made of a 105 shell. The blast of hot splinters of jagged metal ripped through the sergeant's body. Although he lived, he lost both his legs. Other parts of the shell tore through Page's stomach and chest. One fragment entered his forehead above the right eye, traversed the motor center, and lodged in the rear skull.

Remarkably, Page walked back to the helicopter without help and he was still conscious when *Time*'s bureau chief, Marsh Clark, walked into the room where he was being prepared for the operation. The surgeon said it was doubtful Page would survive the operation, but he marveled at his will to live. Page was bitching at Marsh about the assignment: "Goodamn fucking *Time*," he said. "I'm never going on another combat assignment for you people." He also worried about his film, whether his cameras were all right, whether *Time* would buy his pictures after all this. His head shaved and marked for the cutting, Page was wheeled into the operating room. Hours later, when he was waking up in the recovery room, his first words to Clark were about Flynn. Could he please send a telegram to let Flynn know he had been wounded?

The telegram—sent through emergency embassy channels—arrived the next afternoon: VOTRE AMI EST GRAVEMENT BLESSÉ ET PEUT-ÊTRE MOURIR. . . . I don't know when Flynn had received the telegram or how many times he had read it before I knocked on his door. He just said come in, and sat there in quiet despair, holding the telegram in both hands. "Page got hit," he said, adding that it was really serious, he might die. He said all this with no real emotion, it seemed. Then he got up and said, "Let's go for a walk."

As he locked his door and turned to go down the stairs he said—in the actor's voice—"Well, you just have to make new friends." I don't think he meant that for a second; it was the studied response to a sentimental scene, the words a tough man would be expected to say.

There was no direct telephone facility to Saigon, so we sat in the lobby of the hotel while various friends made calls to their Bangkok offices to catch the latest news about Page from Saigon. In between calls, I remember that one of the others talked about the kinds of people who covered the war: Page was one of the "unlucky" ones.

Later that night, Flynn and I went to an opium den he knew in some stilted shacks behind the hotel. The place was full of children, he said, so we stopped and bought a bag of balloons to blow up for them. We moved along a catwalk in and around the flimsy hootches until we came to the right door. The wife and kids were shooed off the sleeping platform and we lay on either side of the opium man. We didn't talk much, which was unusual, and we smoked pipe after pipe. We were trying to use opium as our elders would have used alcohol—to forget. But the opium only made our memories more vivid and Page was very much with us. There he was, alive and laughing, as the opium took effect; there he was in the hospital in Saigon: perhaps dying.

I think I smoked twelve or thirteen pipes, when three or four would have been enough to send me reeling. My mind was racing backward in a jumble of real memories and fantasy. Then, the old man started gesturing for us to leave. He said it was after curfew and the police would soon be checking his house. He would be in serious trouble if they found us there.

We got on Flynn's motorcycle and headed in the direction of a Vietnamese restaurant he knew about in Dong Palane, a section of bars and whorehouses down a muddy row about a half-mile from the hotel. Flynn guided the thing as expertly as he would have straight, but I was reeling on the back . . . holding onto the seat behind me, swaying precariously.

The blue gate had already been pulled down over the front of the restaurant and locked tightly against the ground. Flynn pounded on the metal gate and an old woman waddled out and unlocked it. He walked on in and ordered a bowl of soup. But I was in no condition for food. In fact, I had to go outside and throw up whatever food was in my stomach. Then I asked the woman for a chunk of ice. I went out front and oblivious to some local bystanders lay on the ground and rubbed the ice all over my body. It may not sound like an erotic experience, but it was.

Flynn, meanwhile, ate his soup and talked in somber tones about his friend who was *"peut-être mourir."* From the restaurant we walked a few doors down to an after-hours bar, full of rich American civilians and the most expensive of the bargirls. The girls surrounded Flynn and he began telling one of them about his friend who was *"peut-être mourir."*

"But Flynn," I said, "why do you keep saying that? We don't know Page is dying." At that, Flynn whirled around from the bar and fled out the door and up the muddy road into the darkness. I ran behind and finally caught him by the arm. He was crying and was painfully embarrassed to be seen doing it. He sobbed, trying to gain control of his emotions. I tried to console him. "Listen, man, it's all right to cry." I jabbered on and on about how it would be worse if he didn't feel anything enough to ever cry. "Yes," Flynn said strongly. "But a man shouldn't."

Since I am writing this book and Flynn isn't here to speak for himself, I could leave that scene as I have just written it. However, the words alone leave the wrong impression—once again, left with a sentence or two it seems the swashbuckler's son is playing the same role. But that is not accurate. Flynn was deeply upset by the news about Page; and he was also troubled because he couldn't just read that telegram and cry like a normal person.

We got back on his bike and drove up the road to the house of an American girl he had known. The porch light was on, but nobody answered our knocking. I sat on the edge of the porch and Flynn stood in front of me. We raved back and forth for hours, it seems. If I were somehow able to transcribe that conversation, it would not make sense. The seeming logic of the moment was actually blurred by the opium. And, again, it would be dishonest of me to reproduce a coherent dialogue (with mine the voice of reason) when in truth I can't remember it that well.

I do remember saying "bullshit" several times as Flynn tried to explain what it was to be the son of Errol Flynn; what it was to be raised in Palm Beach. He told me he had never met a "real" person until he got to Duke University. He knew all that stuff about being a man was bullshit, but I also had to understand how its importance had been drilled into his head from the time he was a child. He did tell me he had started keeping a journal. For the first time, he was writing out everything about his father, about his childhood, from the time at age four or five when he fired a pistol through a desk at his father. I asked if he could actually remember that far back (I can't) and Flynn said he could not, but his father had told him about it later on.

I have no memory of how we got off that porch and back to the hotel, but I followed Flynn into his room once we got there. He squatted, cross-legged, on the middle of his bed and slowly peeled an orange. He didn't want to talk about Page, about crying, about anything anymore; and he simply didn't respond to my sentences. Quietly, he offered me pieces of the orange. I ate one piece and then went on up to bed.

The next morning we booked seats on a flight back to Saigon. The old friends gathered around us in the kitchen of that old apartment on Tu Do Street. Nik and Rosemarie Wheeler had taken over Flynn's side; Tim Page and Linda Webb (an English girl who got sidetracked from a hitchhiking tour of the world) had taken over the side where I had lived. A Danish friend came by and soon had us laughing on the floor with his imitations of the patients around Page in the neurosurgery ward. He did perfect imitations of every moan and groan and twitch of Page and all the others.

The next morning we went out to the hospital—a complex of low prefab metal buildings. The ward was jammed from end to end—a long sterile room with two rows of beds. I walked in between the rows of men—some conscious and staring blankly, some moaning in unconsciousness, others dead asleep. We came unexpectedly on Page and nothing could have prepared me for the way he looked. His long black hair had been shaved off and there was a pie-shaped outline where his head had been sewed back after the surgeon had sawed out a chunk of skull and stuffed the brains back in. His face was badly bruised. The image flashed before me of the time when I had nearly fainted when my daddy took me to the slaughterhouse to watch our calf being lined up to be killed behind others already skinned and cleaned farther down the line. I grabbed at the footrailing of Page's bed to keep from falling, said a quick hello, and then dashed for the nearest doorway. Flynn stood there in a white linen Pakistani wedding shirt he knew Page would like and calmly presented him with a very special old stone Buddha he had found in a cave in Laos. If this were what Flynn meant about being a man, I admired it especially at that moment. And I still do.

Apparently, I had successfully blocked out everything but the good memories of Saigon. I had forgotten how messy the place was for one thing; I had also forgotten the omnipresence of American force. Two MP's stopped me, demanding I go back and get my passport to prove I was not an AWOL GI. More important than the city itself, there was Page laid out like a side of beef. I decided I had seen enough of Vietnam, enough of war, and I booked a seat on a direct flight (twelve hours across Russia) from Bangkok to Copenhagen.

Before I left, I tried to console Page's girl. She had stayed right beside him day and night, massaging his paralyzed left side, obeying his every silly command. But no, she said, I had no reason to pity her or Page. "You people," she said, "you come here when you don't have to and this is the chance you take. . . . But I just look at

all those other young men around him. They're just out of high
school and they didn't even want to be here. Now, their lives are
ruined.''

In Copenhagen, an older Danish friend—a very scholarly student
of literature and history—met me at the airport. We had met in the
Virgin Islands. I was young and tan, living a carefree untroubled life
then. Or so it seemed to him. We had been together only minutes
after I arrived from the war when he said something about the
politics of it. I reacted violently. "Well"—he smiled—"has my
young man come back with some opinions of his own?"

From his library, I wrote this letter to a friend in New York:

I fled the East after a real bad scene in Saigon. Sean and I were in
Vientiane when a telegram came saying Tim Page was gravely
wounded. We then had a wild, beautifully-sad night of absolutely
mindless wandering, stoned out of our heads on opium, mourning for
the pain our friend was feeling at that moment. We went back to
Saigon. Sean—steady rock that he is—was wonderful. He stood there
and talked with Tim as if nothing were wrong. I came within two
seconds of fainting at the foot of his bed. Luckily, he couldn't see that
far and I made it to a doorway. If you know how much I have seen,
you can perhaps realize what an awful sight it was—something much
more obscene about seeing these boys shaved and dressed in sterile
bandages, their wounds more permanent.

The awful part is that Sean and I had spent the previous night's high
arguing about just such an accident. I was saying that he and all other
friends should get the hell out and he was saying, honestly, "Where
do you go from here?" I know exactly what he meant. But, for me
there was no longer any question. Where I go may not be so exotic
and I may never have such an interesting circle of friends. But,
whatever it is, it's got to be better than Vietnam. Anyhow, all that is
halfway around the world from me now.

Questions We Never Asked

They never knew. That is where any discussion of my homosexuality must begin in this context. For a complication of reasons, my friends in the war never asked and I never told them that I preferred sex with my own kind.

In many ways, it was none of theirs or anybody's concern. But to leave sex out of any book about war would be almost as dishonest as ignoring the subject in a book about marriage.

I would always ask the military men—after watching one of a hundred kinds of "dirty" movies they all had in their lockers—if they ever thought of sex during combat. No, they would always answer, never during combat. There was something there which obscured the deeper sex drives. Maybe, also, it was another outlet for the very same feelings. Anyhow, back at the base camps, they would say, "I nearly go crazy thinking about sex."

Now I know that Dana Stone would never have cared who or what I had sex with. Louise tells me he never really knew for sure and she knows it would not have mattered to him if he had. He was so curious about all kinds of people that he had very early developed a rare tolerance of others' sexual proclivities. He knew there are not just one or two or even three, but many kinds of people, many kinds of love.

Once, in a steam bath in Saigon, I made a pass at an Army friend of Dana's. He promptly reported the incident to my friend and Stone said, "So what?" Louise said it hadn't struck Dana as unusual or important and he never mentioned it to me. That I would

197

reach out my hand to another man did not mean that I was irredeemably cursed in a silly societal category.

It would have mattered to the the others, however. I am certain Flynn would have been polite about it, but he would have eased away from any close acquaintance with me—and he would never have shared an apartment with an acknowledged homosexual. While a psychiatrist might find certain sexual inclinations in my striving so hard to be a member of this group, friend and brother, member of the team, the fact remains that I had absolutely no physical attraction toward Flynn. I have talked with several people about this and it is an incredible thing to explain to people who know only the legend and never met the real Flynn. The women in our group tell me the same—he was warm and gentle, nice to be with, but more like a brother.

At this point in my life, so many years after the war, I am certainly not ashamed of my sexual preference. But this comes after many long years of guilt and confusion (when acknowledgment would have cost me my job). This new attitude also comes at a time when the society I move in really does not care how I have sex.

In fact, I grew out of the sissy child and into just as strong and masculine a person as any of my brothers. I have never seen any reason to affect feminine gestures. I think my homosexuality is a traditional masculine expression. It is not a denigration of being a man or a mockery of being a woman. Like Thomas Mann's and Visconti's Aschenbach and the real Gustav Mahler, I cringe at a glimpse of me (in society's eyes) as a foolishly painted "lady."

This maturity comes after the war, however. Although I led a fairly active sex life in Vietnam, I always knew that real disclosure would have cost me my job, all my acquaintances, and most of my friends. The military would have discredited me on the spot and forced me out of the country.

There was surprisingly little physical contact among my friends in the war—except for Dana's poking and jabbing. Maybe the others felt the same fears I was feeling. Anyhow, I knew the most innocent contact (even jostling in the barracks) might be misinterpreted.

The peculiar thing I know now is that at the same time I was living in terror my friends and employer might find out, I was coming to the realization that it didn't matter. Rather, I finally had to face up to

the fact that homosexual was something I had always been, always
would be; and I would either be open and honest about it or live the
rest of my life in a lie. As far as I'm concerned there was never any
choice involved in that, it was just a matter of when I would say to
all my friends: If you don't know, there is something I want you to
know about me.

Maybe I was even pushing disclosure by the way I lived in Saigon.
Several times I brought GI's back to our apartment—although that
in itself was not at all unusual since all correspondents cultivated
"sources" in the field. But there was also a real gay bar on the top
floor of the hotel in the next block down from our apartment. When
I was in Saigon, I went there every night and could often be seen
going and coming with various civilians who were more open about
being homosexual.

I think the war had a lot to do with my decision about the way I
would live the rest of my life. However, I have many friends who
shared that experience and still feel they must keep their sexual
preference secret. Maybe my decision came about as simply as this:
I had made the team, I finally had men friends whom I admired and
who also liked me. And, once I had gotten there, I found that it
didn't really feel any different. At some point in the Vietnam
experience, I decided that none of those old games were worth the
effort. From then on, I would be myself. In the ensuing years, I lost
no real friends and very few acquaintances through my disclosures.

On reflection, it seems incredible that my friends wouldn't have
noticed something different about me. Didn't they see that I never
once brought a girl back to the apartment, never once followed up
the bargirls' chatter? But in the war, the focus was elsewhere.
Because of the urgency of the moment, all kinds of eccentric
behavior were tolerated. In a real way, the war allowed either for
the full expression or the complete repression of sex. I am
suggesting here only that I was not the only one who didn't go with
the girls.

And so, none of the friends ever asked the question. I never
volunteered the answer.

Here I should explain about the young Marine I mentioned at the
Danang Press Center. He was not just an acquaintance. And that
night after the Christmas party, we didn't just sit by the river quietly

smoking. He was very muscular and masculine and he wore tight-fitting fatigues to accent the lines. He was also very warm and gentle. After one joint, we crawled into a bunker on the riverbank. And there we made love. It is the proper word: It is a lovely memory to me, measuring up to any heterosexual romance described by Hemingway or Mailer.

Just before I left Saigon, one day in the UPI office, a Japanese photographer came back from a visit to the 1st Air Cavalry Division. He was missing a large growth on his face and he carried a Christmas card addressed to me. A young doctor assigned to the division had seen the growth and performed the simple operation on the photographer. "By the way," he asked, "do you know a reporter named Perry Young?" He had been an anonymous sex partner in New York. I never knew he was a doctor and certainly did not know he was subject to the draft. He would just call up every week or so and come to my apartment and spend the night, until I told him I was off to Vietnam.

The young doctor arrived in Saigon, sweaty and dirty from so long a time in the field. We got a cheap hotel room where he showered and we lay there in each other's arms for the afternoon—talking, remembering the times in New York. He changed into civilian clothes and we wandered around town. I took him back to the apartment, introduced him to Flynn and Page, Nik and Rosemarie. I was delighted that my friends really liked him. When I left Saigon for Hong Kong, my gay friend stayed on another day in our apartment. In a way, it was none of the others' business that he and I went off every afternoon and had sex in a hotel room. Now, I wonder why it ever mattered. But, I know it did.

There was one very handsome young Navy lieutenant with whom I would talk in Saigon. Once, he loaned me a book which I returned to him one night just before he was leaving. His buddies had taken him out for a round of drinks and he pulled me down to the seat in the booth beside him. As the others teased and laughed in the usual fashion, the lieutenant first made knee contact with me under the table and then rested his hand on my leg. We went to that same hotel I always used. He said this was his first time. It was something he had had fantasies about many times, even though he was married. So I moved very slowly and made it a free and memorable experience. The book on the nightstand beside us was Norman Mailer's *Why Are We In Vietnam?*

And Suddenly We Are a Long Way from Vietnam

The Volkswagen people in Singapore told Dana and Louise that it would be at least two months before their camper arrived, so they decided to make one last tour of Southeast Asia. They planned to hitch all the way up the west coast of Malaysia into northern Thailand, cross over into Laos, and then travel down the Mekong River into Cambodia and back across Thailand, back down the east coast of Malaysia to Singapore. It was several thousand miles in all, but that's exactly what they did.

It was a hot Sunday afternoon in the dry season when they hired a flatboat to get them across the Mekong from Thailand to Ban Houei Sai, a busy market town in northern Laos. There were no guards and the little customs office was closed, so they just walked on in.

They went to the USAID office to get some information. A bullish old woman started raving at the sight of them. Didn't they know they were supposed to register at the U.S. Embassy in Vientiane before they started walking around Laos?

"Since when does the U.S. own Laos?" Dana snapped, sending the old woman into yet another tirade.

They walked around the town, taking pictures and staring at the various tribal costumes—some all-white, some all-black, some brightly colored, all with heavy silver or gold necklaces and bracelets. Louise, with her bare legs hanging out of a short skirt, was far more a curiosity to them than they were to her and Dana.

Their plan to take a boat down the river to Vientiane was extremely unwise, a number of people told them. They were quite willing to go anyhow, but none of the boatmen would carry them for fear it would compromise their neutral flags with the Pathet Lao troops along the shores. Louise and Dana flew out of Ban Houei Sai on a Royal Air Lao cargo plane— the only Western passengers on it, and the only passengers who didn't hide their heads under pieces of cloth as the plane took off.

After a few days in Vientiane, they set off walking on a road they were certain led south toward Cambodia. But the road became more and more narrow until finally they had to admit it was a cow path. Of course it never bothered Dana that they were on the wrong road—at least they were going someplace. Once, he even stopped and helped a farmer thresh his rice.

They turned back and a friendly truckdriver stopped and gave them a ride to the right road. They made it across on the last ferry over a tributary of the Mekong. There were no more cars then and no reasons to stand there hitchhiking, so they accepted a Laotian man's gestured invitation to come drink with him and his buddies. As their luck would have it, they had landed in a logging town and the two were right in their element. They laughed at the thought of a reverse situation in which two Laotians stumbled into Sawyer's Bar.

The owner of the little bar and restaurant fixed them dinner and gave them a bed in his house for the night. The next morning, he smiled and thanked them, but he refused to accept any money for his hospitality.

They got some short rides, but mainly they walked and walked until finally they came to a simple pole gate across the road. They figured this just had to be Cambodia. There was a little guard shack by the gate, with one entry the day before and another six weeks before that. They waited for the keeper to come back from lunch, thinking they should make a legal entry into Cambodia.

Once inside the gate, they realized they had walked for hours without seeing any cars on the road. Their hopes rose once when they heard a motorbike spluttering toward them. But just before it reached the hill in front of them, the noise stopped, then faded off into the distance. Apparently the bike had wrecked and the driver had gone off to get help for his injured passenger. They found a boy lying by the road with a deep gash across his thigh. Once again, there was no language but gestures. The boy seemed to sense that Dana could help him. Dana cleaned out the dirt the boy had packed into the wound to stop the bleeding. Then he put penicillin ointment in the gash and bound it with a sterile battle dressing saved from the war. They carried the boy to the nearest house and left him chattering to the people, presumably about the nice foreigners who had helped him.

After long hours of walking, Dana and Louise began to hear the unearthly roar of a great falls, that a better map would have shown them was inside the border of Laos. They came to a village of about thirty houses located just above the falls and were welcomed into the celebration of a house-raising.

Some of the people escorted them down to the river to bathe and they got invitations from all sides to spend the night. Men, women, and children were getting more and more drunk. There was one old man who stayed fairly sober, and he gestured that they would be safer to come stay in his house about a mile outside the village.

The "house" was nothing more than a pallet tied to stilts, but the man grandly offered them a haystack to sleep on. He built a fire and roasted some tapioca root for his guests. It was charred on the outside, raw on the inside, and they couldn't eat it. They gave him some of their Army C-ration bread and cheese and he spat it back out. The man insisted he was Laotian, but they said that was impossible since they had to be in Cambodia. (After all that walking.)

Among them, they didn't know enough French words to carry on a real conversation, so they pronounced names of countries back and forth. The man pointed to a torch he had made from rice straw dipped in pitch. *"Batterie du Laos,"* he said, laughing.

The old man wouldn't accept any money the next morning as they left, but Dana did give him a razor blade. They set off walking once again, thoroughly confused about which country they were in. After some time, they arrived at a checkpoint which, this time for sure, was inside the border of Cambodia. A Cambodian man at the checkpoint said they had just walked through a sort of "no-man's land" considered too dangerous for regular traffic. He said the roads near the borders were used only by the poor farmers who lived there. If the danger were not prohibitive for all others, the documents required to pass through were.

After another long walk, a rickety old car emerged out of nowhere and Dana and Louise climbed in with nine Cambodians and rode thirty miles to the town of Stung Treng, where they hired a car for another ride down river to the town of Kratie. (Just a year and a half later, there were several reliable reports that the captured journalists had been taken into this same area where Louise and Dana had been treated with such genial hospitality.)

At Kratie, they boarded a riverboat for the trip to Phnom Penh. The day was Christmas Eve, 1968. They bought some barbecued chickens and other treats for a real feast they spread out on their blankets on the deck of the ship. It was all too exciting for either of them to sleep that night. They stayed up and watched the traffic on and off the boat when it stopped at every little village. Once they watched as fifteen water buffalo were loaded up the ramp onto the deck. The animals didn't fight back, they just stood there wonderfully calm, refusing to move.

They reached the city of Phnom Penh on Christmas morning. Louise had never been there before and it seemed a wonderful contrast to what she had seen in Vietnam. There were the white, gold, and red palace and museum buildings, the well-kept parks and gardens, the people all friendly and trusting. Nobody was yelling, "Hey you, GI," as they did in Vietnam, Laos, and Thailand——wherever the Americans had moved in.

One morning they were getting ready to ride from Phnom Penh up to Siem Reap, the town nearest Angkor Wat, when Dana realized he had lost his wallet. They returned and found a Cambodian man who had been looking for them. Much to their amazement, he had the wallet and all the money was still intact.

They spent a week in Siem Reap, bicycling around the ruins of the magnificent Hindu temples. Then they took a bus on over to Thailand and slowly made their way back down the east coast of Malaysia to Singapore.

I was in Singapore by then and I wrote a friend:

> Dana and Louise Stone, great couple I knew in Vietnam, invited me to share their Volkswagen camper on a trip out of Kathmandu south to the Taj Mahal, then into Afghanistan. I have several friends here

now. One guy played guitar with a group I used to pal around with in the war; plays every night on a converted junk—discotheque in the hold with the bridge and deck forming a quiet place to sit and drink and watch the boats go by. Met a crazy Swedish girl there. She wears a witch's hat and velvet robes; drinks opium tea, is having a party tonight.

On the junk are two white rabbits, a four-foot-tall emu, a baby kangaroo, and Louise, a dear little baby gibbon. The Bunny Ball '69 is Saturday night and it's just what it sounds like. My favorite place here is Bugis Street, looks like Contrescarpe in the daytime, jam-packed with British and American servicemen and tourists, seamen of every nationality, and a variety of 50 transvestites, 20 real old whores, a wretched old man who sings opera for 30 cents and can sell you opium, marijuana, hashish, morphine, young girl, young boy, whatever, and show his blue-bruised legs where he has been injecting three times a day for 16 years. Anyhow, your boy overseas takes home something different every night.

I returned to Singapore from Bali in mid-March. A wire service friend mentioned that Dana and Louise were still in town and he gave me their hotel number. After only a few sentences of hello, where have you been, Dana took charge and said I was paying too much for a room and I should just move into the room beside theirs. It was clean enough, cost only a dollar a day, and we would be together again.

The three of us had quite a circle of friends in Singapore and we had some delightful times—roaming the town, staying up late on Bugis (pronounced "Boogey") Street. Louise and Dana's room looked just like their place in Danang. There was the familiar camouflage parachute from Khe Sanh, the poncho liners or "camouflage comforters" as one veteran called them, and there was the incredible jumble of field equipment which Dana always carried with him. Much of it he had liberated from the Army or Marine Corps of the United States: you never knew when you might need some C rations or a fresh battle dressing.

Their Volkswagen bus arrived and we went down to inspect it. Dana opened up the top bunk that pushed up the roof and said I could stay in there if I would meet them in Katmandu or Athens and ride through Europe with them.

Two other friends and I escorted them and all their gear to the docks that day and went up to the upper deck where their cabin was. It was an old deck-passenger ship and there were 2,000 Indians sleeping on the lower deck, going home to Madras. Louise says she was more than a little nervous when *Lord Jim* turned out to be the movie shown on deck one night.

Seven months later, when I returned to New York, there was a letter waiting for me that Dana had written from Kabul.

so we went on to nepal, trekked for 8 weeks (to the base camp on Everest and back) and returned to Kathmandu and of course you weren't there—strange, you were always so dependable too! We sometimes think of you as we use our british army surplus tea pot and I remember the day we bought it and how we hurried home along Jalan Besar, then to go buy Bata shoes that you lost hours later. In India we looked at lepers and elephants, saw bodies burned beside a river and went north where they have pine forests and apple orchards at 7000 ft. In Pakistan, Kashmir, all the wags wore guns and we drove to a glacier and watched them load log trucks by hand—here we see camels, russian trucks and no trees and I wish it were '67 and in I Corps with options of DMZ or China Beach.

so you write us at the Embassy in Athens telling what you have done that we can all be proud of—we saw Corpora in Kathmandu and Heller in New Delhi and heard that Phuoc and Page had been hurt bad but now in this town we no longer even get the asian editions of Time & Newsweek and suddenly we are a long way from Vietnam

He also wrote his parents from Kabul: "so yesterday I met a man whose son was somewhere between here and London but the father had no idea where because the son hadn't written and I realized how much a post card with only longitude and latitude might mean—but I guess you are used to not knowing"

The ostensible reason for their overland trip was to get to some logging camps in northern Sweden that Dana had heard about. Here, he had heard, they still floated the logs down rivers to the sea—something which is now impossible in most countries because of dams across the rivers. But, after the long trip (ten months), when he and Louise got to northern Sweden, none of the towns looked like they expected. None of them were as primitive or remote as Sawyer's Bar had been. They were clean and civilized and even had electricity. The only job Dana could get—because of his size—was marking trees which looked like saplings compared to the giant redwoods he had handled in California.

And so, at the end of another road, they stopped and discussed where they should go next. Should they go back to sea? Or should they go back to Vietnam?

The Dani Fight Because
They Want to

Flynn was more shaken by Page's last brush with death than he had ever been by anything that happened to him. The doctor had said that Page might be paralyzed in his left side for the rest of his life. Staring down at the stitches, bruises, and bandages, and at Page's face twisted almost beyond recognition, none of us could imagine a more hideous end to our adventures.

Page gave Flynn specific instructions about crating up all his plastic Buddhas, the toy racetrack, the cameras, and the prints from New York which I had given him. After Flynn packed Page's belongings, he wrote out his own will and left it with Carl Robinson:

> unWILLingly
> if me so bad, medivac-acked immediately [or within a 1000 cybernetic years] send goods to me: [his address in Paris deleted]
> if cool-aid, celestialy unredeemable: [his mother's address in Palm Beach deleted]
> have goods crated by same did brother Page's—him good. Ask Dang at Time office, or Marsh Clark, boss. felios SF May 3, 1969

Most of the rest of us had either gone or were in the process of leaving, so Carl Robinson and Flynn renewed their friendship. It was "the old Cafe Pagode in the morning and evening after-work smokes. The pipe was still an old favorite—the old man ('Good Humor Man,' as he was known) would come by pretty regularly. Sean didn't seem to want to do too much—had an assignment now and then for *Time* or CBS, but really, things were in a bad lull," Carl wrote me.

During this period, Flynn would always time his arrival at the

Atterbea Restaurant at least two hours after the regular lunch crowd had left. It was at these odd hours that Marsh Clark, the *Time* bureau chief, and his wife, Pippa, would see him. Flynn would also come by their house. I think they represented that stable kind of good life which he admired even to the point of wanting it for himself. Pippa would ask Flynn all the questions—about his father, his movies, why he was in the war—which everybody else was afraid to ask. And, perhaps because she was serious in her questioning, Flynn would answer her as seriously as he could.

When it was announced that President Nixon would visit Indonesia in July, 1969, Clark asked Flynn if he wanted to photograph the event for *Time*. Flynn said sure, got on a plane, and met up with a lot of old friends from the war. Joe Galloway, a big friendly fellow from Texas, was the UPI correspondent in Jakarta and Flynn stayed with him most of the time.

The *Time* reporter assigned to Nixon's visit was David Greenway, the only true "gentleman" I ever met among the press corps in Vietnam. I never knew that much about Greenway in the war except that he was respected as a man of elegant taste and unusual daring. He had been wounded in the battle in Hue. Even his combat fatigues were neatly tailored and freshly pressed. He smoked small cigars and flicked the ashes with the proper emphasis. He spoke with a light Oxonian accent, but with more wit than hauteur. When I met his sister at a party in New York, I stopped her in mid-sentence and said, "But you don't have an English accent?" David had gotten his as a Rhodes Scholar. He came from an old Boston family and was also closely related to the Carnegie fortune.

Greenway already had an assignment from *Time* to go to New Guinea and write about the tribesmen in the mountains who were soon to be given the vote. He arranged for Flynn to go along and take some pictures, although they were not used with the article.

After they finally cleared all the paper hassles in Jakarta, they still had to get up to Port Moresby and then fly on a small plane into a tiny airstrip in the mountains, where they got out and walked for several miles. Greenway recalls the moment of euphoria they shared when they had passed the last civilized village. Flynn took off his hat and threw it up in the air with a wide grin and a silent whoop.

Aside from the long gourd penis shields that curve up to their heads, the Dani are also famous for a long tradition of "ritual wars." Although the missionaries claim there hasn't been one in ten years, I'm sure this was among the reasons Flynn was interested in the trip. We had the book *Gardens of War* in our Saigon apartment and I know Flynn was familiar with the authors' observation: "The Dani fight because they want to and because it is necessary. They do not enter into battle in order to put an end to fighting. They do not envisage the end of fighting any more than the end of gardening or of ghosts. Nor do they fight in order to annex land or to dominate people. The Dani are warriors because they have wanted to be since boyhood, not because they are persuaded by political arguments or their own sentimental or patriotic feelings. . . ."

In the village they visited, the men lived in round thatched mud houses and the women and children all lived in one long house. The two honored guests were put in a round grass hut away from the others. They were shivering in the cold when they heard some of the tribesmen yelling in another hut. They crawled in around a fire in front of the chief. They had brought gifts of tobacco and salt and presented them to the chief. The tribesmen were fascinated by Flynn's cameras and he showed them how they worked.

The chief couldn't understand why Flynn and Greenway didn't understand his languages, and he kept getting frustrated and angry as he tried to communicate. Finally, he started gesturing—slicing his finger across his throat. Flynn and Greenway thought he meant them and they grabbed each other and said, "Not us." The chief caught their meaning and laughed and laughed. Then, he brought in a pig which they were going to roast in celebration of their visit. But they couldn't build much of a fire or the neighboring villagers would smell it and demand a share. So they browned the pieces of meat a bit, then presented the rare pork to their guests, who nearly choked trying to chew it.

"How would it be to stone the Stone Age men?" Flynn asked Greenway. But the respected *Time* correspondent told him to wait until after he was gone. The primitive tribesmen had no cloth or metal. Flynn and Greenway found a fine ancient stone ax which they bought and sent back to Marsh Clark in Saigon.

They stayed in the village several nights. Alone in their hut, Flynn would tell Greenway about his life. He had followed his father (that "young man of New Guinea") full circle at this point and he asked David if he knew that his father had once lived in New Guinea, that he had once killed a man there. Flynn said his father and Ernest Hemingway had argued about shooting and his dad always explained that this early experience was why he had no taste for hunting anything. Another night, Flynn told him about killing the man-eating tiger in Pakistan.

Then it was time for Greenway to go back to civilization. Flynn walked back down to the missionary plane with him, then stayed on for another month. He walked around to the various villages with a Catholic priest who became his friend. (Greenway said the Protestant missionaries—even among primitives in a jungle—were remarkably narrow and bigoted; they talked then about the shame of Teddy Kennedy's accident at Chappaquiddick.)

Later, in Bali, Greenway met up with Flynn and he asked him if he ever stoned the Stone Age men. Well, yes, Flynn said. It seems the priest had been trying to build a chapel in the village for a long time, but every time he decided on a spot, the chief and his advisers would say that the moon crossed that point or that the ghosts didn't approve. So, one night, the priest and Flynn sat down with the chief and his elders. Flynn passed around his pipe. The tribesmen soon agreed on a spot and the priest started building his chapel the next day.

Flynn returned to Jakarta and soon became enamored (the old-fashioned word fits) of a very beautiful young Indonesian girl, the daughter of a prominent lawyer. She was named for a Hindu goddess and that was exactly how Flynn regarded her. For many months after it happened, the journalistic gossip mill produced the wildest rumors about him and her and a fight he had with a pimp who insulted her.

Flynn told the story to every friend he saw afterward—it was full of the complexity of the man and not without a touch of humor. He loved to tell it on himself. The girl was in the eleventh grade and Flynn would meet her at the school, carry her books home for her. Their relationship—from all reports—was an old-fashioned court-ship. But one time Flynn did hire a Mercedes taxi and driver to take them for a long ride into the mountains.

The problem arose when the driver turned out to be a pimp. He assumed that Lacsmi must be a whore if she were riding around with an American. So, some time later, he called up and told one of her family servants to tell Lacsmi to be ready in a nice dress to go and make it with a rich Chinese man. Lacsmi reported all this to Flynn and he exploded. At the appointed hour, the Mercedes pulled up in front of Lacsmi's house and Flynn stepped out of the bushes swinging a baseball bat. He smashed in the car's headlights and windshield, then attacked the driver. The Chinese customer meanwhile had fled. Flynn was put in jail in Jakarta for several days. No news stories were printed about the episode, but friends around the world heard about it and telegraphed offers of help. Flynn somehow cleared himself of the charges and resumed an idyllic life on the island of Bali.

He stayed with an American friend in a cottage on the beach there. He ran and swam, stuck to a vegetable and fruit diet, did yoga exercises toward the sunset. He wrote friends in Saigon that maybe it was best they didn't visit him there, because they would never want to leave. He said he had finally found his place of contentment. He would buy some land on Bali, build a little house there, and live out his days in peace.

Joe Galloway's front porch in Jakarta was a special place for a whole group of us who had been in the war. We would sit there and smoke, watching the passing parade of pushcart peddlers, remembering in silence the times we had shared in Vietnam. One day, Joe and Sean were discussing their favorite trees. Sean liked the African baobab; Joe favored the flame tree of Southeast Asia.

Then, on Christmas Eve, 1969, Joe was sitting on the porch when Flynn rounded the corner in a pedal cab, holding a sapling flame tree between his legs. They planted the tree in front of the porch and Sean said the man he bought it from said it would bloom in one year.

In March, 1970, Sean came by to say good-bye to Joe. He said he was going to Saigon and close down his apartment there, going to Paris and close down that apartment, going to Palm Beach for a final visit with his mother, then he was returning to the island of Bali to live out his days in tranquility. He pointed to the flame tree and promised he would be back to see its first blooms.

Two years after Sean was captured, Joe wrote me that the tree had spread over twenty-five feet, but had yet to produce a single blossom. "So long as it grows without a bloom we remain firmly convinced that Sean is alive," he said. Then, in November, 1972, he wrote: "I must report to you that this week Sean's flame tree began putting out the first flowers since it was planted almost exactly three years ago. . . ."

Cambodia

Louise says it was pure chance that sent Dana Stone back to the war in November, 1969. She says he did it only because they couldn't get jobs on a ship at the time. But, being a television cameraman was something he had thought about from his earliest days as a photographer. In a tape to his parents in late 1967, he said he had applied for a job as a cameraman, but "I fouled up trying to do it.

"Goddamn these TV people," he said. "Some of these TV cameramen come over here and these guys get about five hundred dollars a week plus that much in expenses. Nah, they get more than that in expenses. Then they get a cost of living and they get R &R every six weeks. It's really a good deal. And it's hard work. TV guys (cameramen) don't get bylines either. . . . Some of the still photographers over here pick up a movie camera. . . . Ah, but it's another thing. You gotta have beginnings and endings and you gotta tell stories. Still work is so much easier. All you do is catch little glimpses."

Stone also never liked the idea of traveling with a crew of three. "Quite often," he said, "the TV guy, the talker guy, the correspondent, is some fat old guy, doesn't wanta walk, doesn't wanta stay out in the field or anything."

With his usual persistence, Dana was able to get free-lance camera work with CBS almost as soon as he arrived back in Saigon. By the time Louise could get their belongings from Germany back to Cynthiana, Kentucky, CBS had already used film shot by Dana and given him a credit line—unusual recognition, especially for a new man not even on their staff.

He was missing Louise, however, and with the drudgery of learning a new job, Dana got discouraged. He was also living in our old Tu Do Street appartment with Flynn in Bali, Page gone, and only Nik Wheeler left among the old friends. And he would leave in February. At this time, Stone wrote a friend:

> I've decided to become rich and famous as a TV cameraman and am free-lancing for CBS becoming neither. It's harder than I thought and I'd quit if I hadn't made so much noise about doing it. The fun has gone out of the war, there is no doubt in anyone's mind that it's a bad war and who wants to be the last man killed for Ky and Thieu anyway. . . .
>
> Before we came back I thought of catching another Swedish freighter, Smiser liked her ship pretty well and she would have liked to go to sea again. But we didn't and now we want a baby so I don't guess we ever will. It's nice to have the ships to fall back on when things are dull or messy and it's sad to think I won't go to sea again. . . .

But, after Louise arrived in January, they started fixing up the apartment and Dana got more and more interested in his work. His old friend, Keith Kay, and Jack Laurence had come back to do a documentary about a company in the war. Laurence, the "talker guy," was not only not fat, he was built very much like Dana and he is perhaps the most talented young television correspondent in the business.

Dana was brought along to do some of the camera work for the film. Laurence recalls:

> We were flying up to Tay Ninh in a brigade commander's C&C ship (minus the colonel) after flying down to ship film that afternoon. Keith and Jimmy Clevenger had taken the chopper crew out to dinner and they got drunk. The pilot was so uncertain about being able to fly, he wouldn't let us get aboard until he had taken it up alone for a few minutes. The crew chief and one of the door gunners were so smashed they had to be tied into their seats. Jimmy put a bottle of Chivas Regal on top of the massive radio in the back seat, left the top off, and people just took a swig when they were thirsty. Dana was impressed by the zaniness of it. "This is something you read about in war novels."

The segments of film they were shooting each day of this one company were first broadcast on daily news programs of CBS, then they were pieced together to make *Charlie Company,* one of the finest television documentaries done about the Vietnam war.

Dana had become very serious about his work and one of the finest sequences in *Charlie Company* is a simple piece he shot which shows the drudgery of being a foot soldier. The film Dana shot was so good it was shown—without narration—first on the Cronkite news show and then as part of the documentary. It was not a question of being in the right place and focusing the cameras: this involved the true artistry of the profession, of sizing up a scene, then getting it onto film. This was the classic argument about war photographers and cameramen. Some people would say that war photography was more a matter of being in the right spot than it was skill. But, Dana Stone was one of the few who (to use the photographers' own idiom) could "go back and make it as a regular photographer."

Dana enjoyed the work on *Charlie Company* more than anything he had done as a television cameraman. But, he was called back to Saigon and told that CBS wanted him to go into Cambodia. Prince Norodom Sihanouk had been overthrown in a U.S.-backed military coup, and no one knew what would be happening in Cambodia—but it was sure to be an important story for several weeks.

While he appreciated the chance to get in on a major new story, Dana really wanted to stay with Laurence and Kay—and with Flynn, who had just arrived back in Saigon. But, he was a more professional man by now. For the first time, he and Louise talked in more permanent terms. He would become a good cameraman, they would have a baby, and maybe someday even a house of their own. He talked with Louise about his career with CBS, about what it would mean if he refused to go to Cambodia, and finally he took a plane to Phnom Penh.

Flynn had just come back to clear out his possessions and pay off his part of the rent on the Saigon place. Carl Robinson said he only saw Flynn once or twice during this time. "After Indonesia, he seemed afraid to venture out into Saigon's streets," he says.

One night in the apartment, Laurence tried to talk Flynn into going back to the field with him to do some camera work on *Charlie Company.* Laurence recalls that Flynn seemed to have changed:

"His hair was much longer; he was very quiet and thoughtful. I was struck by the length of the nail on his left hand little finger, an inch, in the tradition of the Mandarin leisure class."

They sat in the apartment with Flynn rolling one super-joint after another—passing them around, smoking them himself. "He was skeptical," Laurence says. "Didn't want to cover war anymore; hadn't any need for the bread. He passed around the joints on a worn copy of Mao's red book, smiling."

Finally, Flynn agreed to go with Laurence and Kay back up to Tay Ninh. The first night they stopped in at an enlisted men's club for hot dogs and beer. "The men were very hip," Laurence says, and "there was a sign painted on the wall, 'Snow White was a Head,' and 'Draft Beer, Not Students.' It was late at night and a lot of the people were stoned. They formed a small, curious circle around Sean, who looked like another grunt except that his hair was surprisingly long.

" 'Hey, man,' someone said to Flynn, 'How'd you manage to grow all that *hair?*'

" 'Oh,' said Sean, 'I've got this real cool CO, dig, and he just lets us do anything we want.'

"There was a chorus of 'Far out,' and 'No shit,' and 'Dig it.'

"Flynn was having fun blowing their minds."

They kept trying to get a chopper on out to Charlie Company, but they kept getting stuck. Once, Laurence says, they were waiting beside some crates full of a new kind of quick-fuse hand grenade. When everybody ducked from the dust of a chopper landing, Laurence watched Flynn slip one into his pocket. Flynn said the Marines had once experimented with these same grenades but had never put them into use because they were so dangerous. "You pull the pin," Flynn said, "and it goes off behind your ear."

Later, another friend woke up very early one morning and saw Flynn sitting on the floor of the apartment with this grenade completely disassembled.

Flynn never did make it to Charlie Company. He talked about the situation in Cambodia. The newspaper stories implied that Phnom Penh ("Nompers," as we called it) was about to fall to the Communists. Flynn envisioned tank fights in the city streets and he wanted to be there with Stone when it happened.

Laurence woke up before dawn the last morning he ever saw Flynn, who was sitting there with a flashlight reading the lead story in *Stars and Stripes:* NVA ADVANCE ON PHNOM PENH.

Robinson says: "I never did have a chance to say any sort of good-byes" to Flynn. "I went by the Tu Do House one day and they said he'd left for Cambodia. . . ."

That's What Made It a Good Story

After so many years, the war in Vietnam had become messy, routine and—this worst of all—back-page news. The reporters there were delighted with the front-page developments in Cambodia. It was like being reassigned from the squalid ghettos in Watts to a disturbance in Disneyland.

Although reporters had been officially barred from Cambodia under Sihanouk, it was easy enough to lie about your job (one TV man always went in as a "fertilizer distributor") and even the prince didn't seem to mind. He had managed a delicate balance with his Communist detractors by publicly keeping the Americans out. As a result, his tiny kingdom was the only spot in Indochina that had not been ravaged by the war and American business interests.

Sihanouk had created a national festival for Jackie Kennedy's visit to Angkor Wat; and when his people captured a boatload of U.S. Navy men, he treated the prisoners as if they, too, were visiting royalty.

Even the overthrow of Sihanouk had been preceded by a confused incident that showed some flair. With remarkably bad timing, two young American seamen had seized an ammunitions ship, the *Columbia Eagle,* bound for Vietnam and forced it into the Cambodian port town, then called Sihanoukville. Shortly thereafter, the town's name was changed after the generals had taken over the government while Sihanouk was out of the country. The new government didn't know what to do with the American prisoners— the rightists blamed the Communists, the Communists said the CIA had brought the ammunition in for the coup.

It was known that the right-wing general who became Prime

Minister had a magician on his staff of advisers. It was also said that the royal family descended from a cucumber farmer who acceded to the throne after he killed a prowler (the king himself) in the royal cucumber patch. Reporters were also told stories about armies of the dead, about evidence of cannibalism and ancient torture rites, but over all this there was a certain geniality in Cambodia that had never existed in Vietnam. After all, Cambodia had not had a war in recent history.

The town of Phnom Penh was every reporter's favorite place in the Orient. Without the American presence (and the million noisy Hondas of Saigon), it had retained all the charm of a decadent colonial outpost. The decay that had set in since most of the French had left only added to its charm.

The Hotel Royale (renamed "Le Phnom") was straight out of the works of Maugham and Conrad. There was a nice terrace restaurant opening onto a courtyard around a swimming pool behind the hotel. Every day at lunch, reporters could mingle with the remaining Frenchmen and their lovely daughters. There was a cute little gray poodle that would run and then leap into the water and paddle back to everybody's laughter and applause.

The hotel fronted on a pathetic old boulevard, wide enough for two highways, the few buildings along it dwarfed by the magnificence of the plan. An old concrete fountain hadn't worked in years; the trees lining its sides shriveled up in the dry season. At the end of this street, near the banks of the Mekong, there was a high hill that went straight up like a child's sand mountain. On this hill *("phnom")* a certain Mrs. Penh had found two Buddhas from Angkor in a tree trunk. And that was sign enough that there should be a town around the hill. Weird old men squatted along the paths crisscrossing below the old gray stupa that crowned the hilltop. They dispensed magic and read futures—in cards, faces, palms— —while the monks offered quiet meditation on the hilltop.

Dana Stone had checked into a room in the hotel as soon after the coup as CBS could get him in on a flight. He had been there a week when Sean Flynn arrived to share the room with him.

Neither of them had thought about how long they would be there—expecting the city to fall by another coup any day, just as a succession of reporters has predicted almost every day since the coup several years ago now. Dana missed his wife and he sent letters to her by others flying back to Saigon. He asked Louise to come on over and bring him and Flynn various pieces of equipment and clothing they had left behind.

Most of the Saigon press corps had been transplanted at the Royale. The terrace by the pool replaced Saigon's Continental Hotel terrace as the afternoon meeting place. Early in the morning, a reporter could rent a chauffered Mercedes, get a box lunch and some wine from the hotel restaurant, then venture out into the very picturesque countryside. In peacetime, one could have driven the length or width of Cambodia in four hours. By midafternoon most days, the reporters would each have brought back exclusive stories and they could all relax and laugh around the pool. Whenever I ask anyone who was there about those early days, they always smile at the pleasant memories: "It was like, well, it was like a carnival in many ways."

The dangers which seem so apparent on reflection were not at all obvious to them then. With none of the warning signals they had learned in Vietnam, the reporters roamed about as carefree visitors in a pleasure garden. One morning, three of them set off in a gray Peugeot to a market town on the Vietnamese border. One reporter had heard that the North Vietnamese soldiers were openly buying cattle at the public market there.

After so many years of looking at the map from the other side, of quoting only American generals and politicians about those fabled "Cambodian sanctuaries," every reporter was anxious to visit the area and see what—if anything—was going on there. Bill Cunningham and a cameraman from the Canadian Broadcasting Corporation went along on this trip to the market town. They reached the border town without incident; they stood watching American planes bombing inside Vietnam. They talked with a local police chief who said, yes, the Communists controlled both sides of the road that had brought them there. But, he was almost casual as he talked about "the enemy," and there was no sense of danger.

The three reporters and their driver left the town and stopped at a grassy place beside the road where they spread out their picnic. They shared the food with some Cambodian children who came up to watch. Cunningham ate, drank some wine, then he crawled in the back seat and went to sleep. The next thing he heard was the other reporter in the front seat saying, "Who the hell are those guys?" As far as he could see along both sides of the road, there were men and women in fresh fatigues and camouflage hats. Some older men in black pajamas stopped the car, pointed their rifles and pistols at the three Westerners, and told them to get out. Cunningham said in French that they were all Canadian journalists. One of the Vietnamese men held a pistol at the back of his head and said (the driver translated later): "Let's kill them—let's kill them."

The three journalists were taken over to a shady place off the road, still with weapons pointed at them from all sides. One of the uniformed soldiers came up then; he seemed to be in charge and he spoke French. He explained the troops were "forces loyal to Sihanouk. With Sihanouk, there was no war, now there is a war."

Cunningham says the troops were obviously North Vietnamese. Their Chinese equipment seemed new and they had just moved into the area. The men in black pajamas—apparently Viet Cong guides for the new troops—were very nervous, wanting to shoot the Westerners and move on. The uniformed man would not allow them to take pictures, but after he searched their car, he shook hands very warmly and told them to return to Phnom Penh.

Their stories were the talk of the press corps for days. Louise remembers that Dana chided one of them for not taking advantage of the situation, not figuring out a way to come back with pictures and more of a story. But with this incident, it seemed for the first time that reporters in Cambodia just might be able to watch the war from the other side—and live to tell about it.

Flynn got his chance that same week, on Friday, April 3, 1970. He and *Time* correspondent Burt Pines, along with a Frenchman serving as interpreter, rented a beat-up old Peugeot and drove down to the towns along the border.

They went right into the "Parrot's Beak," as American correspondents in Saigon had always called that corner of Cambodia jutting into Vietnam. There were two major stories there which American correspondents had speculated about for years, but which none had ever documented with eyewitness reports. These were:

Whether the Communist troops did—as American politicians and military men swore—have "sanctuaries" in Cambodia; and whether the Americans had been bombing in Cambodia in spite of their denials.

Pines' specialty had always been European affairs, but he had finally come to Vietnam because, he said, "It was history in the making." A Hemingway aficionado, he says he would not have wanted to be the same age in the 1930's and have missed the Spanish Civil War. Actually, he was roughly the same age as Flynn, Stone and others in our group, but he was much more office-type than outdoor adventurer.

He says they were thankful they hadn't been able to get one of the newer black Mercedes with a chauffeur that morning. Later, they would count this among the reasons that had either kept them from being killed or captured.

In the town of Svay Rieng, they talked with the district chief who told them, Yes, the Communists had been staging small attacks in the border towns and villages. In his report published the next week in *Time*, Pines said that "200 to 300 Vietnamese Communists launched a brief night attack against the district headquarters town of Chi Phou, but were held off by Cambodian troops. At the same time, other Communist units attacked a small village near Chi Phou, and a third force burned down the community hall of the village of Bavet. . . . Last week's series of attacks may have been intended as a warning of what lies ahead. . . ."

Pines, Flynn, and their interpreter drove to the village and then to the town of Chi Pou (as most correspondents spell it). Here, they inspected the damage done in the attack and then were getting ready to leave when they saw American planes flying right over them, bombing an area nearby—well inside Cambodia. "It was fantastically exciting" to be witnessing such a story, Pines says. Flynn started taking pictures and the three Westerners soon attracted a crowd of about thirty Cambodian children and adults. They had not yet encountered Americans on the ground, so the villagers were friendly and not one asked for "chop chop."

They got back in their car and were driving out of the town when they saw a crowd of people standing quietly at the edge of the village, which ended abruptly at some rice paddies. "They were yelling at us, trying to stop us," Pines recalls. "Eventually, we figured out they were saying 'VC.' "

About fifty yards straight in front of them, they saw a Communist patrol crossing the road. They were obviously used to moving in the area because they had not posted guards and none of them even looked toward the village. Flynn and Pines crouched down in the car hoping none of the Cambodians would give them away. The French interpreter kept muttering, "Why have you people brought me here?" There were three squads of eight or nine men in this patrol.

As soon as the patrol had crossed the road, Pines started up the car and was just beginning to move up the road when Flynn hit his elbow and said, "Look over there." It was yet another patrol. Pines slammed on the brakes and jerked the car into reverse. Once again, they hunkered down in the car and again, nobody in the patrol looked their way. After this one had disappeared, Pines pushed the accelerator to the floor and they sped out of the village, safely up the road.

"You can't imagine the high we were on," he says now. "Here we were in the Parrot's Beak; we had always looked at the map from the other side. It was just fantastic: we saw American planes and Communist troops."

During the long drive back, Flynn and Pines talked about the close call, about what could have happened if their timing had been just a minute off. Flynn said maybe if he came back down to the area, he could get some film of what they had seen. (His pictures were not used because there was no way to prove the planes shown were in Cambodia.)

They talked in philosophical terms about why they were there. Pines asked Flynn why he had ever come back from Bali. Flynn said it was mainly an accident of timing—he had accompanied a friend to Singapore and decided to come on up and close out his Saigon apartment. He told Pines about the beautiful Indonesian girl he was in love with; about the good life he had found in Bali.

"He seemed a beautifully tranquil person and I think Bali had spoken to him." Flynn worried, however, that in two years the tourists would have spoiled the island's tranquility. Pines asked what did Flynn expect. He quoted from the conversation in Hemingway's *For Whom the Bell Tolls*. When young Maria says

Yes, the earth moved, Pilar says, One has only three such times in a lifetime. Two years was long enough, Pines said.

Back in Phnom Penh that night, Flynn, Stone, and another friend had dinner at the Venise, a little French restaurant in town. Afterwards they went to Madame Chung's, the most famous opium parlor in Southeast Asia. (Her funeral cortege the next year looked like that of a Chief of State.) The place looked like an ordinary house at the edge of town, but once inside, you took off all your Western clothes, put on a sarong, and lay down on mats to smoke while young girls (or old crones) massaged your body.

Stone sat there for a few minutes, but he said he didn't want to take his clothes off, didn't want to smoke opium. He had tried the stuff once and got so sick he never had any interest in smoking it again. Being left out surely increased his longing for his wife, whom he hadn't seen in more than a week.

Flynn and the other friend lay back and smoked and talked. Flynn told him about the plan for him and Dana to ride motorcycles down to the border towns and stay overnight. The friend remembers saying, " 'Well, for Christ's sake, be careful. . . .''But, at the time, it didn't seem so crazy.''

The next morning, Saturday, April 4, Louise arrived in Phnom Penh. Sean and Dana had been out inspecting two motorcycles they planned to rent for the trip. Louise and Dana took over the room, went out and bought several kinds of cheese and some wine which they ate and drank beside the pool that afternoon. They had a late dinner in a French restaurant, then came back in the back gates to the hotel. The lights were off around the pool so they slipped out of their clothes and into the sun-warmed water. In all their years of lovemaking, they had never made it in the water. So they played and teased and made love, two little kids as much in love as they had ever been years younger in California.

Flynn woke them up very early the next morning. Dana teased him about the girl he had been with. "How much did she charge this time?" Stone asked. "Not as much as she did the night before," Flynn said.

They planned to be gone four or five days, but they didn't want to pack so much that they would be taken for journalists, soldiers, or CIA men. Sean wore cut-off shorts and rubber flip-flop sandals;

Dana wore dungarees and desert boots. Both of them wore T-shirts and floppy cloth jungle hats. Louise had forgotten Dana's favorite hat in Saigon, so she gave him her reversible one. It was green on one side, bright yellow on the other. She had taken it out of an American pilot's survival kit. Dana put on the hat, looked in the mirror, and said, "Nothing's going to happen to me, I'm so ugly."

Dressed as if for a beach outing, the two got on their rented motorcycles behind the hotel. Louise kissed Dana, whispered a good-bye remark about the pool, and waved as the two rode out through the hotel gates, turned left, and disappeared.

Nobody knows where they went that Sunday or where they stayed that night. Considering the towns were only a two-hour ride from the hotel, they could have gone several places in one day. The next day, Monday, April 6, they joined a press tour of the town of Chi Pou.

Woody Dickerman—a reporter in Vietnam since 1966, first for the New York *Herald Tribune,* then for *Newsday*—was on this same tour. He says the press cars lined up between some antique French armored cars driven by Cambodian soldiers. The purpose of the trip was to show that the government had retaken the town of Chi Pou—where the guerrillas by this time had blown up the police station, burned down a barracks, and broadcast warnings to the people.

"It was quite a festive occasion," Dickerman recalls, "full of that stupidity and humor Cambodia had in the early days." When the caravan arrived at the town—many of the press cars in front of their "escorts"—the reporters were greeted amiably. No shots were fired and the town went about its business while the press people toured the damaged buildings.

Word spread among the group that there was a guerrilla roadblock across Route 1 about two miles outside the town toward the Vietnam border. Flynn and Stone rode out in that direction, but they couldn't get close enough to get any pictures. They could see a burned-out car where the roadblock was supposed to be. The correspondents then assumed that this belonged to some Japanese and French correspondents who had been in the area the day before but had failed to return to Phnom Penh.

Bitching about their failure to get any decent pictures, Flynn and

Stone rejoined the press group for a casual press conference. The reporters got only vague answers from the Cambodian military spokesman about whether the army was going to move out and do something about the roadblock. After a while, the Cambodians, as Dickerman expresses it, "Said, 'Okay boys, thanks for coming, the show is over. Why don't you go back to Phnom Penh.'" Most of the reporters did just that.

Dickerman and Dan Southerland (then with the *Christian Science Monitor*) felt there might be some action out toward the roadblock, so they stopped in at a little cafe and waited awhile. Flynn and Stone were already in the place drinking tea. Dickerman says he could overhear a lively discussion between the two in which Flynn was arguing that they should do it, while Stone was resisting, being more cautious and practical.

At one point, Flynn grabbed Stone's motorcycle keys and tossed them out the window into a puddle. Then, Flynn got up and rode off by himself. Stone muttered something about "That Flynn's off to scoop me" as he followed in quick pursuit.

Bill Cunningham also met the two of them stopped on the road out to the roadblock. He remembers hearing Stone say something about having a wife back at the hotel and that he had been too long in the war to end up getting captured. Flynn said, "I know it's dangerous. But that's what makes it a good story."

The Cambodian soldiers were moving out of town and after a half hour or so, Dickerman and Southerland got in their car and followed them. About a mile outside town, they stopped at a command post. The officer in charge told them the troops were not going to retake the roadblock; he said they were just sweeping the area and then they would withdraw.

Dickerman says the scene was deceptively peaceful. In Vietnam, you could always sense the danger by the mood of the civilians. But here, the civilians were at work and play as usual.

"It was a bright, very pretty sunny day," Dickerman says . "The peasants were out working in their fields, waving and smiling for photographs." Up at the site of the roadblock, he could see Flynn and Stone on their bikes beside the burned-out car. There were a number of Cambodian army armored vehicles and troops spread out in the paddies on both sides of the road. It seemed to be completely secure, so Dickerman set off walking toward Flynn and Stone, leaving Southerland to interview the officer at the command post.

He had gone about two-thirds of the way when the Cambodian armored vehicles started moving back past him. It was a casual retreat, however, and the soldiers all waved and smiled for pictures as they moved past Dickerman. "I said, 'Well, what the hell, I'll walk up and say hello to Sean and Dana.' "

There was some distance still for him to go and he called out and waved to Flynn and Stone. He kept taking pictures of people along the road; meanwhile, the Cambodian army had disappeared. He was just sauntering along in the sunshine when his hired Mercedes roared up beside him. The driver was yelling frantically for him to get in the car. "Viet Cong! Viet Cong!" the driver shouted, gesturing in every direction. Dickerman says he still didn't sense the danger, but this was his only ride back to Phnom Penh, so he waved good-bye to Flynn and Stone, got in the car, and rode off in the safer direction.

Apparently, there was one last group who saw Flynn and Stone that day. These were members of a French television crew who were also headed up the road when Flynn yelled back at them. One of them turned on his camera as Flynn rode toward them, crying, "Pathet Lao! Pathet Lao!" Nobody can figure out why Flynn would yell that instead of "Viet Cong" or "Khmer Rouge." But there is a last glimpse of Flynn gesturing, then turning around and riding back down the road. Stone is not shown in the film. When the French crew returned to Paris, they told their story in a movie magazine: THEY OWE THEIR LIVES TO SEAN, SON OF ERROL FLYNN.

That night, the Communist forces took control of Chi Pou and the area around it. Flynn and Stone never returned to Phnom Penh.

Two of the Guards Rode Bright Red Motorcycles

That night when Louise came in from eating dinner in town, she passed by a huddle of reporters in the hotel lobby. They were talking among themselves. She didn't stop and talk, but went on up to her room and went to bed early.

They were talking about whether they should tell her Flynn and Stone were believed to have been captured that afternoon. The wire services had already reported this, but Louise did not realize the seriousness of their situation for more than twenty-four hours. The next morning, when she went out to sit by the pool, everybody around her was talking about it, but nobody was aware she didn't know.

That morning after their capture, she had been awakened by a CBS reporter calling to ask if she wanted to go down to the area where Sean and Dana had been. He said only that there had been some action in the area and they were concerned about Flynn and Stone. But, of course, Louise was not worried. Every time Dana had been out in the field it had been dangerous; there had been some action where he was or he wouldn't have been there. She could only assume he would be coming back as he always had. Also, there was the chance he and Flynn had got their film and then just crossed over the border and taken it back to Saigon—where it would have to be shipped from anyhow.

An NBC cameraman named Dieter Bellendorf spent a lot of time talking with her beside the pool that day. He didn't seem so worried; he said they had probably taken pictures of one action, then gone on to some other place. On April 8, Bellendorf himself rode down that same road—and never came back.

Late in the afternoon, the CBS reporters came back and said it was impossible to get anywhere near the area where Sean and Dana had last been seen. Louise was still not convinced they could be in any real danger. Then, Henry Kamm and Gloria Emerson of the New York *Times* came back from a similar attempt to get near the place and had a long talk with Louise.

They told her there was at least the possibility Flynn and Stone had been captured. If so, Louise should take some definite action to let the Communists know they were not CIA men, but American correspondents. Louise immediately started making the rounds. She wrote letters—saying that Dana and Sean were civilians, noncombatants, journalists—and she got them through to the North Vietnamese and National Liberation Front (which still had liaison offices in Phnom Penh) and to the Bulgarians, Poles, Russians, Arabs, "everybody I could think of" who might get through to the guerrilla soldiers.

The letters pointed out that the work of Flynn and Stone had surely helped the Communist side. She always mentioned the peace prize Dana had won and his award from the Soviet news agency.

At least ten correspondents—Japanese, French, and American —disappeared within that same week. In the weeks and months that followed, several correspondents were captured and released. Most of them were treated well by their captors, none had any definite information about the others. To this day, there are still twenty-two journalists missing in Cambodia.

Louise made contact with every prominent person in the city who had been friendly to Sihanouk. One of his Western speechwriters met with her, but he was so fearful for his own safety he said he could not help. The first person she had tried to reach was Wilfred Burchett—an Australian journalist who had reported on the Korean conflict and the Vietnam war from the Communist side—but he had already left his house in Phnom Penh. (Later, Louise met Burchett in Paris and he was very helpful in approaching his contacts in Peking and Hanoi about the missing journalists.)

She then flew to Hong Kong where she could call her parents and Dana's parents and where she could get in touch with a number of friends in New York who would help get support from the various peace organizations in America. All these groups were willing to carry letters in and out of Hanoi about the journalists. David Greenway met with Noam Chomsky in Vientiane and gave him a letter to carry to the North Vietnamese in Hanoi. In Paris, the reporters covering the peace talks were finally pressured into asking a question of the North Vietnamese delegate about the journalists. The North Vietnamese replied—as they did to Burchett and all the peace groups—that they held no civilian journalists among their prisoners, but that they could not speak for the Cambodian National Front.

By the time Louise got back to Phnom Penh, various civilian journalists and military personnel had been to the Chi Pou area (the American invasion occurred during this time) and they reported no Caucasian bodies had been found there and there were more and more reports from villagers that some Western civilians had been seen in the hands of the guerrillas.

Crystal and John Steinbeck had heard about the capture while they were staying in an ashram in northern India. They rushed to Cambodia, thinking they would host a big party when Flynn and Stone came walking out—with the great pictures and story of their time behind the lines. The days became weeks and then months. In May Crystal and John moved to Saigon and into the Tu Do Street apartment with Louise. Their baby girl, Blake, was born while they were living there in October.

They were especially good at keeping Louise's spirits up—they would never let her become the war widow, but would always keep a sense of humor about the situation. Crystal was bureau chief for Dispatch News and for as long as she lived there, the apartment was the Saigon office for that young news agency.

Louise began an extensive correspondence with Sihanouk. She immediately drew an analogy between his situation and hers. His family was under house arrest by the right-wing Cambodians; her husband was being held by the Communists. Every time anything happened to his children or his mother, she would write him a letter. She was never able to talk with the mother, but she did talk with her physician, an old friend of Sihanouk's. Louise had volunteered to carry letters from the mother out of Phnom Penh to mail to Sihanouk. But the doctor talked it over with her and the mother decided she would not see Louise; she would not be writing any letters.

Sihanouk seemed genuinely troubled by Louise's letters. He told her he was doing everything he could to find out what had happened to her husband and the other missing journalists. But, he always mentioned that communication was difficult—and not made any easier by the American bombing raids. He always thanked her for the news of "my poor family." But, finally he had to tell her he had no information, he was out of touch with the guerrilla forces himself, and she should address her letters from then on to the Prime Minister of FUNK in Cambodia. A lesser official of FUNK merely acknowledged receipt of her letter and never answered the questions it contained.

In late June, Louise flew to Vientiane where she talked with North Vietnamese representatives in their embassy there. She then flew to India, where Madame Binh—foreign minister of the Provisional Revolutionary Government of South Vietnam—was visiting. She left letters to Dana and Sean with the North Vietnamese in Vientiane and with Madame Binh's secretary.

In one letter to Dana, she said, "If you have been given a choice and you have decided to stay in Cambodia a while longer, I will understand. Although I miss you dreadfully and want you at home, I realize that this experience is one of the greatest in your life and you may wish to prolong it."

Meanwhile, a committee of distinguished journalists was formed—with Walter Cronkite of CBS as chairman—to represent the profession in dealing with the Communists in an effort to free the journalists. Zalin Grant, a former Army intelligence officer who spoke Vietnamese and had worked with *Time* and then the *New Republic* was sent to Cambodia a month after Flynn and Stone were captured.

With his contacts, Grant was able to interview captured prisoners, defectors, villagers, and refugees from the Chi Pou area. He kept getting corroboration of the story that as many as six to ten civilian journalists had been seen being led off, then being transported in a truck.

American intelligence had intercepted a Communist communiqué regarding the journalists already captured, saying that in the future journalists should be well treated, taken to a safe area, and turned over to the Khmer Rouge. Grant also interviewed a North Vietnamese defector who said he had worked at a prisoner of war camp where American military men were being held inside Cambodia. Although he had not seen them, he had been told that about ten American journalists were being held in another camp.

After the cease-fire in early 1973, Grant returned to Southeast Asia to interview various Vietnamese soldiers who had been released from Communist prisons in Cambodia. He reported, "One ARVN returnee said he saw aproximately six Caucasians in eastern Cambodia on 1 May 1972 who were specifically identified to him by a North Vietnamese guard as foreign journalists. Three more returnees reported that on or about 6 March 1973 they were told by a North Vietnamese guard near Mimot in eastern Cambodia that foreign journalists were being held in the area."

A Cambodian who had been held by the Communists told Grant he had actually seen the ten journalists in the same camp where he was held as a prisoner. He said the camp consisted of tin-roofed stucco buildings surrounded by barbed wire. There were eight guard bunkers. He said about 200 Cambodian guerrillas were stationed at the camp, apparently a regional headquarters. He said the Oriental prisoners were not allowed to talk with the Westerners. The journalists wore black or blue civilian clothing and sandals. Several had mustaches and beards and long hair. He said they were all fed rice soup at 7 A.M. rice with meat (every three or four days) at 10:30 A.M. and rice occasionally with vegetables at 5 P.M. He said that none of the Westerners appeared to be sick and medical care was available in the camp.

The Cambodian said he was told repeatedly by camp guards and other prisoners that the Caucasians were journalists. He was also told some of them had been captured in Svay Rieng Province and others near Angkor Wat.

The most detailed description of the missing journalists came from a Communist soldier who defected and was then presented at a press conference in Phnom Penh. He did not volunteer any information, but when a reporter asked about the missing journalists, he said he had seen them.

Louise heard about this and flew to Phnom Penh where she tried to get permission to interview the defector. By then, he was in Saigon. She kept trying to get past an American colonel at the Central Military Intelligence Center and he kept telling her the defector had not seen her husband. Meanwhile, a friend of hers who worked at the center started sneaking out the transcripts of the defector's interrogation. She was also planting detailed questions about the journalists.

By the time she wrote to General Abrams—who ordered the CMIC officials to let her interview the man—Louise had almost all the information she needed. But with two interpreters of her own, she got the following from him: The date was May 31 (Flynn's twenty-ninth birthday), 1970. The defector said: "It was about dusk when they brought them to the house, and we were stationed around there and we came to see what was going on. When we asked the Cong An (security guards) they told us these were journalists captured in April on Highway 1."

He said that one of the journalists "had a light yellow-brown mustache and long sideburns. His hair was long, down t o his collar. He was very big but his stomach was not very big. I heard he was American." He also mentioned that two of the guards rode bright red motorcycles.

Then one day, late in August, Louise heard that a Dutch adventurer had been released with a group of French correspondents captured in Cambodia. He claimed to have information about Dana but would not talk with any reporters.

When Louise finally located him in Bangkok, he told her, "Your husband is alive." The Dutchman's name was Johannes Duynisfeld, a disheveled character variously described as a student, seaman, adventurer, who said he had traveled with Regis DeBray in Bolivia. He was a hulking, ugly fellow with a full red beard and a balding head with a ring of gnarled hair down to his shoulders.

Louise had no choice but to listen to his story and hope it was true. Duynisfeld said he had been kept in a field hospital where Dana was for three weeks. It was a small mobile medical unit that moved every few days.

He described Dana's wounds and said he had to be carried on a litter. Dana would try to sit up, he said, and his captors would make him lie back down.

Louise asked Duynisfeld if he had ever seen Dana naked——because he has an unusual tatoo which she has asked me not to describe here because it is the one positive way of identifying him.

Duynisfeld said, No, Dana was always wearing shorts. Then, he said that Dana had "big feets." He showed Louise what he meant—very wide, very short feet. He described Dana's feet perfectly—a detail he could not have picked up in a bar. He said the guards had laughed and said Dana had "Vietnamese feet."

After this, Louise was willing to go along with Duynisfield's game of intrigue. He had various contacts—in Bangkok, Vientiane, and Phnom Penh—who he said could arrange for him to go back across the lines, find Stone and two other journalists, and bring them out to safety. Louise, meanwhile, checked with doctors about the wounds he described and found that they were probably not fatal. As a gesture of good faith, she bought a big stock of medical supplies that she gave to Duynisfeld to give the guerrilla medics.

Duynisfeld gave Louise a letter to send to Sihanouk in case he was not back in three weeks. He gave her two other letters—addressed to his parents and to a friend—to mail in case he never returned. Louise gave him $20 in French francs (all he asked for) and watched him ride off on a bicycle for the other side of the war.

There were three other characters of intrigue who entered Louise's life at this time. One was a deserter from the American army in Thailand; the other two were the young men who had seized that shipload of ammunition the day before the coup. They had lived one day as heroes and spent the time after as prisoners. They had been kept in squalid quarters in a prison ship until an American peace group came through in September and protested their treatment. Then, the three were moved into a government guest house, a real palace with no furniture except for three cots and a small table for the prisoners.

Louise found out where the three were staying and she went by to take them some books to read and to wish them well. They seemed to be in a peculiar legal situation in which they could not be extradited for trial in America, but neither could they get on a plane for Russia. As long as their guards were in sight, they could move about rather freely. Louise would take them out to dinner or have them over for a swim at the hotel.

One was an unstable fellow who later turned himself in at the American Embassy, was sent home, tried, convicted, and given a ten-year sentence. The other two had to talk behind his back, lest he reveal their plans. But once Louise mentioned the possibility, they started discussing the practicality of escaping their guards, defecting to the Communists.

Just three weeks after she met them, they left their guards to go to the restroom in a downtown restaurant. They jumped out the back window, stole a car and made their get-away.

For three months—September, October, November—Louise waited in Phnom Penh for Duynifeld to come back if not with Flynn and Stone, at least with some information about what had happened to them. She mailed the letter to Sihanouk and resumed her wait.

She then moved back to the apartment in Saigon with Crystal and John Steinbeck. (Nik and Rosemarie Wheeler and their baby, Adam Sebastian Nikolas, had moved to Beirut even before Flynn visited Saigon in March, 1970).

Among the many Vietnamese friends of Crystal and John and Dispatch News in Saigon was a distinguished old man who had once been a government official. While he was vehemently opposed to the Thieu-Ky government, he was careful not to say anything that could get him in trouble. He would talk to the young Dispatch writers and to Louise about the various Vietnamese religions and customs.

He showed them how to read a person's personality and future in their face. He said Louise should always keep the mole at her hairline covered up—not that it showed anything bad about her, just that it revealed too much of her personality. Louise brought out photographs of Sean and Dana and asked the man to read their faces. He found mostly good signs in Sean's face. The fact that his eyebrows met was an especially good sign. He couldn't see that 1970 held any special dangers for Flynn. But, when he looked at Dana's face, he said it was a very bad year for him, "but if he can live through this year. . . ."

Louise showed him a picture of Duynisfeld and asked if he were an honest man. The old man looked at the photograph very carefully and then he said, "But this man is dead."

Two days later, Louise heard that Duynisfeld had been killed while traveling with a unit of guerrilla soldiers fighting the South Vietnamese inside Cambodia. Phuoc, a Vietnamese photographer for the AP, was with an officer when the report came in that a Dutchman had been killed and that he had a diary in his gear. Phuoc told them a Dutch photographer named Hugh Van Ess worked for the AP and he would translate the diary.

Van Ess spent hours translating. It was clearly the writing of an uneducated man, he said, and much of it was just rough notes. Louise persuaded the AP writer not to use the most damaging entry, which said that Duynisfeld had been told his second day with the guerrillas that all the journalists had been killed. A North Vietnamese officer had said that the journalists were being held in a village post office when the buiding was destroyed by American bombs. Duynisfeld also noted that he didn't believe this officer because when he questioned him, the man would not give him additional information about the journalists.

It turned out there were a number of contradictions in this diary and in two earlier diaries Duynisfeld had kept. He makes no mention of the missing journalists (whom he supposedly saw as a captive) in his diaries prior to the time he met Louise. After he went back, there is only the single entry concerning journalists and then he talks about his secret "mission."

Louise continued to live in our old apartment with John and Crystal and John's brother, Tom, and his wife, Adra. Almost a year after the capture, all of them decided it was time for them to leave Vietnam. They went first to Laos—a sort of peaceful halfway place between the war and home.

The apartment in Saigon was left to an American who worked for a Vietnamese commercial movie company; and to a young college student who had argued so fiercely with his millionaire father about the war that the father had paid his way to Vietnam "to see for yourself." Eventually, the apartment passed back into Vietnamese hands.

Louise went to Paris where she met various people interested in the plight of the missing correspondents. Pierre Doublet, foreign editor of *L'Express*, had been told in late 1971 by a National Liberation Front official that his half-brother, Gilles Caron, had been held by the NLF until May of 1970 when presumably he was turned over to the North Vietnamese.

After six months in Europe, Louise came home to Kentucky. She arrived a matter of days after I had my dream-conversation with Flynn. I called her up and told her about it. She wanted to know every small detail. She accepted it and seemed greatly relieved to hear some words—even if indirectly and through a dream—indicating her husband might still be alive. She had been having trouble getting anybody to write about the missing journalists, so she came to New York and stayed in my apartment to help me with an article about them for *Harper's Magazine.*

She positioned herself on the big mattress on the floor of my front room. Except for a meeting every week or so with Cronkite and the journalists' committee, she never left that room. She rarely ate, and when she drank coffee she never used cream because "I always figured we might be out someplace where I couldn't get it and I just didn't want to get used to it."

For two months she stayed in my apartment and for two months we talked of nothing but her missing husband. No matter how remote the conversation, she would always relate it back to something Dana had said or something they had once done together. Their relationship was of such intensity that it seemed she is still preoccupied with thoughts of him, even though they were half a world apart and he is now listed among the missing. She lives almost as intensely with his memory as she did with him in reality. She is remarkably faithful, not just to the man, but to the crazy complex spirit of the man. Especially, she has never lost his sense of humor and when she tells one of his stories, she tells it as wryly as he would.

Louise helped the committee prepare a pamphlet about the missing journalists and Cronkite carried copies of it with him on President Nixon's trip to China. She was given the enlarged photographs used in the pamphlet and she proudly placed them on the mantel in my apartment. The lineup of somber faces looked like men facing a firing squad. Dana seemed to be staring us down as we talked about him. For once, he was not smiling.

Louise's Life

She waits now in a picturesque old farmhouse, a nice long walk up the donkey path from the whitewashed mountain village of Alhaurin El Grande, thirty miles inland from Malaga, Spain. The house has five big rooms, each floor dropping down a foot, falling with the landscape. There is a flower garden of geraniums and rosebushes in front of the terrace where Louise has planted sweet peas, wisteria, and jasmine over a rough pole arbor. Surrounding the house are long rows of oranges, olives, and figs, terraced fields of potatoes, garlic, and onions. Old Miguel who lives down the hill fusses if she buys too much at the market.

She has learned to live with her memories and with her hope—without drugs, without alcohol, without friends or family. "It's been good for me," she says. Every room of her house is decorated with paintings she has done since she moved to Spain in early 1973. There are two that she based on Dana's photographs: the little Vietnamese boy with the bandaged head; a group of Vietnamese women wailing in mourning.

In the dining room, there is an orange-and-copper-colored portrait on black, the mask of Apollo. She has painted (from a photograph he never liked) the smug young face of Dana Stone; and he always seems to be looking down on her sleeping or reading on a leather couch in the next room.

Last year, her sister wanted her to come along on a two-week trip to France. Louise said no, she just could not be out of touch that long. (She has a special arrangement whereby the telegraph office calls up the nearest neighbor with a phone and they relay the message to Louise.) "But Louise," a friend told her, "if anything happens now it's not going to be all that quick."

"I know, I know," she said. "It has nothing to do with the reality of the situation; but this is the way my head is now."

After I finished the rough draft of this book, I visited her and stayed for a month in a room that had been the stable. Every night I would walk down the path to the bars in the village. It was one of the happiest times in my life. I made friends with a group of young men in the village and we sang flamenco songs, clapped, and laughed as I tried to learn the language. One night, a group of us was very stoned and drunk. One old fellow said, "Everybody in Alhaurin is a little strange, but we are very friendly people." I rushed home to tell Louise the line. She lay there on her couch, reading another book (she reads several a week) and listening to the BBC radio station. Much as she would have liked to share in my good times in the village, she has made her decision. Until she knows something about Dana, she will wait. She will tend her flowers, read, and listen to the radio.

There were many questions I couldn't ask about such a life, and one night I came back up the path to find that Louise (always ahead of my questions) had typed out the following:

My first reaction after I realized that Dana and Sean were actually captured was constant hope. I felt that any minute they might turn up, as other journalists were doing who had been captured. I lived in a state of perpetual expectation—any telephone message or telegram might mean they were back. This lasted about five months and then I began to calm down a bit.

I was living with John and Crystal then in Saigon. They were a great moral support for me in those times. Sometimes—with them there to take any messages, but always after curfew—I would drink myself into oblivion. This problem became serious later when I returned to the States in 1972. I needed help and I went to a psychiatrist. Now I haven't had a drink in over a year.

When John and Crystal came to live with me in the Tu Do Street apartment they really saved my life. To many others, I was now a "special" case, not the same ol' Smiser. John and Crystal were my same old friends and they understood my attempts at humor in my situation. They also gave me something to think about besides myself.

I learned many things about myself during the first year after Dana's capture. I learned how to be a pushy little bitch. I also found that—when the occasion demanded it—I could be the vapid beehived American Housewife, makeup and all.

By the early summer of 1971, I realized that my usefulness in Southeast Asia was about over. It was going to take more than I could ever do to get any information about the missing journalists. My parents wrote to me that they were making a trip to the Greek Isles and would I join them. I met them in Greece and then went on to Paris. Some friends there asked me to meet them in Spain and then I had to face the questions:

What could I do? Where was I to go? I had no home; there was nowhere I could think of that I wanted to live. Actually, I didn't want to live at all. I wanted to go to sleep and wake up when it was all over. I wanted Dana. I wanted to quit fighting and pushing and persuading and playing games. I wanted Dana there to say, "Why don't we try Australia, or maybe go see what it's like in South America?"

But, he wasn't there to do it and I couldn't enjoy doing anything like that on my own. So I went to Spain in September and returned to the States in November, 1971.

I didn't want to live in the States. I remember going to a football game at the University of Kentucky with my parents. There were all the people dressed up in their expensive clothes, with their thermos bottles of coffee and bourbon and their portable cushion seats with backs. They were all screaming, "Get that bastard. Kill him. Atta way. Hit him, hard." Then a man in front of us had a heart attack and was carted off while a woman beside me (who didn't know him) stopped screaming "Kill" and cried hysterically. This was America and I knew I couldn't live there.

Everybody who talked to me put me in a category with the POW wives. I finally gave up trying to explain that Dana was a non-combatant, a civilian. He wasn't there to kill but to take pictures.

I went to New York in January, 1972 and eventually John and Crystal and I were back together in a small apartment in the Village. That summer was very discouraging. The war was still going on. Nixon was bombing again and obviously going to win the election. I did some work for McGovern and I marched in the peace marches. At a demonstration outside the Senate in Washington, I was arrested, jailed, tried by jury, and given a choice of 30 days or a fine of $150. I paid my $150.

Just before the election, I allowed myself to be tricked again. I believed that there really might be some kind of settlement that would bring peace to all of Southeast Asia and maybe then I would receive some official news about Dana. When Nixon resumed the bombing at Christmas time, there I was hanging on a hope that didn't exist. I got a Christmas card from the Nixons that year and I think I went slightly insane at the sight.

My only consolation when I begin to feel sorry for myself is to remember all the times in history when men have left their wives and the wives must sit patiently and wait for their return with little hope of hearing any news until their return five, fifteen years later. Nearly every woman I met in Southeast Asia had somebody missing in the war.

People who say, "Make a new life for yourself" don't understand. No matter how much I would like to be able to cast the problem aside, the problem follows me. The fact that my happiness depends on international events which I cannot control is something I must live with.

I cannot see myself giving up hope. There has been too much positive information that at least some of the journalists are still alive. I still get a gripping of the heart when I receive a letter or a telegram. I just wish now we had had a child. At first, I was glad we didn't because it gave me the freedom to jump at a moment's notice. But now, it would be a part of Dana to hold onto and a responsibility to occupy myself with.

At first, in 1970, it was very difficult for me to eat anything that Dana especially liked. He wasn't getting any. Gradually, I overcame that sort of thing. But again, when I start feeling sorry for myself I remind myself that I am free, well fed, and know I am loved by parents and friends. Dana may have none of these things. There is no reason for him to think I or his parents and friends consider him alive. At the time of his capture he had been covering the war in Vietnam where journalists were killed, not captured.

I want to reach through space and grab his mind and tell him he is loved. And I am waiting for him.

One Final Question

After four years of longing, I finally had the money (from the publisher of this book) and an excuse (an ending to the story) to go back. Like the narrator of Lawrence Durrell's *Clea*, looking back on his city of memory, I knew I hated the place but it now "held out something different for me—a new evaluation of the experience which had marked me. I must return to it once more in order to be able to leave it forever, to shed it."

"Going back" also meant a visit to Tim Page and his wife, who were living in a small apartment up the hill from Whiskey A Go Go and Filthy McNasty's on Sunset Strip in Los Angeles.

I had not seen Page since he had married an American girl he met in Rome or since he had lost the job *Time* gave him after he left the rehabilitation hospital in New York. When I visited him in that hospital, one of his wardmates said he was up on the roof. I found him there smoking a joint with a teen-age boy—who was paralyzed from the waist down and confined to a wheelchair. Page had stormed out of his physical therapy sessions one day, tired of those silly exercises. And he had never gone through the psychiatric counseling recommended for anybody in his condition. His left arm was locked in a right angle and his left leg was permanently twisted and stiff. For the rest of his life, Page would have to take a handful of pills in the morning to prevent spasms.

Whenever I had called him after he moved to Los Angeles, he had sounded as depressed as I had ever heard him—out of work, out of money, no dope, no hope. After months of trying to help him, *Time* had tired of Page's shenanigans. He had failed to produce any pictures on so many occasions, they had stopped giving him assignments. Gossip in New York had it that Page was physically incapable of taking pictures again. His wife had left him in Europe, but he had followed her to her brother and sister-in-law's place in Seattle. They lived for a time in her mother's house trailer in Olympia, Washington.

His wife had left him another time, I had been told, because she was "sick of hearing about Vietnam." That line had endeared her to me and I was looking forward to a pleasant meeting with her.

But, when Page met me at the bus station and drove me home in a rickety old Volkswagen, he hinted that Jan might not be so friendly. When we walked into their apartment, she wouldn't even speak to me. She snarled something about "Page's friends." I said I could stay with another friend down the hill and fled.

The next day when I came back, Jan welcomed me as if we had been dear friends for life. She had borrowed a bed for me and was fixing a real feast for dinner—roast leg of lamb, rice pilaf with a favorite Mediterranean sauce made of yogurt, cucumbers and garlic. We laughed about our first encounter and I assured her, "Believe me, I understand. . . . ." She explained that Page's friends were in and out all the time and talked of nothing but Vietnam, but if she tried to have her friends over Page would always insult them.

At that time, she said, Page had not worked in months. When I started getting up and doing some articles for a friend who was then editor of *LA* magazine, Page started going along with me. Another photographer had been assigned by the magazine, but it was great fun to be working with Page again, and we laughed a lot about the old days. The younger photographer was in awe of the legendary Page. And Page was almost humble as he dispensed advice. The magazine bought several of Page's pictures to use with my stories. There was obviously no physical reason why he couldn't do as good a job as he had ever done before. He was never one to run, even before his last wound.

One night, a fellow in Page's rap group came by with four friends who wanted to talk about hiring Page as a consultant on a movie they planned to do about a prison camp in Vietnam. It was the sort of ineffectual talk one encounters in Los Angeles—no hope of any real production coming out of the discussions. But, Page was delighted at the recognition and talked for hours on end in minute detail about how it really was in the war.

He flipped on his own projector and started showing the ghastly images of war he had snapped. The four would-be movie men sat on the floor watching the horrible pictures in silence. The stereo meanwhile was playing a tape recording of "Stickball" (by "P. Vert and D. Ment" on "B-Zarr" records). It began rather softly with organ sounds from the mass and innocent sounds from every boy's childhood, "Can Johnny come out and play?"

Then, as Page pushed the button onto another Vietnam atrocity, the sound from Stickball blared: "Then you stick two pencils in her ears and say, 'Whip some skull on me, BITCH . . . Suck! Suck! Suck! . . . Cause the world is built on sucking. . . .'"

Page sat there grinning at the scene, his shirt unbuttoned to show the scars down to his navel. He was all of twenty-eight years old, but his hair was streaked with gray and his body was a middle-aged man's. Another member of his group had accurately depicted all this in one pastel portrait of Page that hung on the wall, and in two charcoal drawings Page had tacked onto the lampshades.

His rap group was something that really surprised and pleased me about Page. He had never seemed the sort who could endure any kind of honest criticism of himself. But he said it was the best thing that had ever happened to him. All the others were active, interesting men and they really talked to him straight. Among other things, they had told him that he seemed to think the world owed him a living.

The last night Page went to that group, he came in very late and went straight to bed without saying anything to me or Jan. The next morning he was irritable and distracted. Like a hurt little boy, he tried to keep up a good front, but he kept choking up in mid-sentence. Late in the afternoon, we had drinks at a bar with a friend of mine. We belted down several straight scotches and Page's talk became more and more animated. On the way home, he told me the members of the group had asked him to leave; they had told him they couldn't help him anymore—that he needed professional help.

Buoyed by frustration and scotch, Page swung through the door and slumped into a chair facing Jan. He was ready for a fight and so was she. Suddenly, the two of them were arguing violently about nothing that made any sense to me.

I started to leave; Jan called me back. She said it would be just like it had been with her mother. The mother was crippled with multiple sclerosis, but Page had beaten her rather badly. The policemen who answered the call were veterans of the war; they started rapping about the good old days with the Special Forces in Cai Cai, Vietnam and took no action against Page.

"Your fucking family," Page screamed at her. At one point he lunged at her with a glass. I grabbed his hand and removed the glass with little effort. I think he didn't really want to hit her. She was a very strong woman who could have defended herself very well—especially considering Page's condition. But she just scrunched up like a child waiting to be hit in a corner of the couch.

Jan went into the bedroom, slipped out a back door, and was gone for the night. Page and I sat there talking about what he felt was the end of the road for him. He couldn't get work; he couldn't even get along with his wife. "I just can't go on," he kept saying. I told him there was no reason why he couldn't be working every day. I said he just had to quit living off the memories: the war was over, we had to go on to something else. "I'll never believe that," he said. He repeated what the group had said about his expecting so much just because he got wounded in the war. "And I fucking well believe it," he said. "The world *does* owe me a living."

"But, Page," I said as calmly as I could, "nobody asked you to go to Vietnam the first time and certainly nobody asked you to stay after you kept getting wounded." And then he cracked, just sat there sobbing openly, muttering; "Oh God, oh God, I don't know what to do." After he quieted down, he said he would go to a psychiatric clinic the next day and start the counseling his group had advised.

Later, Page gave me a ride out to the airport for my flight up to San Francisco where I planned to leave on the trip back to Tokyo, Hong Kong, Saigon. We talked about what it would be like back in Vietnam. He said for me to go to our old apartment and bring back his big Army searchlight.

As we drove up onto the departure ramp, ready for me to say

good-bye, Page said very coldly: "I'm really jealous of you going back there, Perry Deane. I'd love to go back, only this time I'd make sure I got myself killed." Only then did I begin to understand why Page had been quoted in four or five newspaper stories as saying that Flynn was probably dead. Page only wished for his friend what he wished for himself. For, he had lived to learn the truth of Housman's poem: "Of lads that wore their honors out / Runners whom renown outran / And the name died before the man."

It might heighten the drama of this story for me to leave Page with those words, but the truth is that Page is a survivor in spite of himself. Several months later, after my trip, I saw him in his elegant room high up in the Mark Hopkins Hotel overlooking San Francisco Bay. We smoked joint after joint of super-fine grass, ordered up imported beers and expensive lunches. Our lives were like they had been before. *Ramparts*—its editors entranced by Page's stories on the joy of war—had published a page of his pictures; and *Rolling Stone* had made a sort of folk hero out of him by using him as a character in two stories for which he was taking pictures. That afternoon, he had met two crazy English birds and he was off for an evening with them.

In Hong Kong, I kept delaying the trip, getting drunk in the seamen's bars in Kowloon, playing the same records from four years before: "Those were the days my friend." This time I heard the line about returning to the tavern, finding everyone gone, looking in the mirror (which I did, hearing the words), and asking, "Is that lonely person really me?"

After a few days, I scheduled a flight so early one morning that I would be up and on it before I had time for the fear and dread to set in. I buried my head in a magazine, prepared for everything but the absolute joy I felt when I glanced out the window and once again looked down the coast of Vietnam. We flew straight in over the central highlands and turned left over the old resort town of Dalat, which the pilot described as if it were Bali or Pago Pago.

When he heard that I was coming back, Carl Robinson had written "welcome back to the homeland." He had sent out a Vietnamese driver in a big Chrysler car and he helped me through customs into town. These were the very last days of the full American military presence, and all the officers at MACV headquarters were running around and around the buildings, getting their bodies in shape for the trip home. Others—more vain—were simply lying in bikinis on top of the once usable bunkers around the headquarters.

In a garbage dump at the main gate to the airbase, the Vietnamese had erected a cheap concrete marker, red letters on white: THE NOBLE SACRIFICE OF ALLIED SOLDIERS WILL NEVER BE FORGOTTEN. It had been built right in front of the Chase Manhattan sign—which was removed after so many people took pictures of the two sentences running together.

I began peeling off clothes—jacket, tie, then loosening my shirt and rolling up the sleeves. The traffic was slow and the weather was hot and muggy—in the upper 80's, like Charleston or New Orleans on a clear day. As we moved through the maze of traffic, turned left by the Presidential Palace, right around the ugly brick cathedral and straight down Tu Do Street, everything seemed as it had been. The shock was not that anything had changed, but that it was all so completely familiar to me, as if I had left the day before. At the UPI office, the Vietnamese staff had not changed and "Mister Loc," Anh, Tuyet all came out with big smiles and warm handclasps to welcome me back.

I changed clothes and wandered around the familiar streets, happy as a child in the summer sun: I had come home again. Later, I talked about how good it felt to be back with Joe and Barbara Treaster as we sat in their very comfortable apartment overlooking (through purple bougainvillea on the terrace) the Saigon River and the lush delta beyond. Joe had been in Vietnam three times—once with the U.S. Army and twice as a reporter for the *New York Times.* They both said they loved the place and their lives there and they had no plans for leaving. They too had felt like they were coming home the last time they had returned from a vacation. A friend of Barbara's had written her a poem about yearning to be back in Saigon: "And now the strawberries must be ripe again. . . ."

If the world now regarded Vietnam as a tawdry setting for any real experience, it had nonetheless been the place where a lot of us "came of age." For me, it had been the place where I finally shed the last layers of pretense, got up one morning unafraid to be myself.

But it didn't take long for my nostalgia to sour as I watched unemployed bargirls sorting through street garbage for food; as I listened to a college-educated woman explain that she and her husband made the highest possible salaries but could barely afford to buy rice; as I faced hideously mutilated Vietnamese war veterans every way I looked. The production had changed from *The Wild Bunch* in 1968, to *El Topo* in December, 1972.

I moved among the nightmarish creatures, visiting the places where we had known so much young laughter. The old Cafe Pagode was empty and sad. The Casino Bar was shuttered and abandoned. In truth, there was no way I could restore my friends or my youth to the scene; there was no way I could relive the good times we had known just by coming back to the setting.

When I went into the San Francisco Bar on Tu Do Street, the walls in the men's room had been painted an antiseptic white. The only graffiti was this:

FUCK IT AND LEAVE IT

At the airport in Danang, ten or twelve ragged Vietnamese soldiers fought over who would give me a motorcycle ride into town. It was a five-minute ride at the most, but the young man demanded $5 and threatened me if I didn't pay. Down the muddy road to the old press center, I found the gates but no sign of anything to support the stories I had been telling about the place. The old sleeping quarters were rundown, abandoned, apparently of no use to anybody. I couldn't even find Pootsey, the big old sow who had lived with a large Vietnamese family in a cardboard hootch beside the press center gate.

I found the two or three reporters then stationed in Danang at the Grand Hotel, the most degenerate place I've ever been. On the front steps up to the hotel, there was a collection of beggars that included one three-foot dwarf, two little brothers who had lost left and right legs and so could stand as one, six or eight other varieties of war-deformed men and women, one deaf-mute pimp, and eight or ten dirty toddlers.

The barroom at the hotel was a dank, nearly dark place, inhabited by all those just listed, along with fifteen or twenty working whores. (One showed me snapshots of her four children—all of their daddies had been Americans, but she had no idea who they had been, what their names were.) The women sprawled about on some broken-down plastic couches and some sat up at tables and played cards. There was a cardboard palm tree still in place on the bandstand from earlier days at the Grand. Half the room had been partitioned off with soiled blankets and curtains as a bedroom for the mama-san and off-duty girls.

One night I was sitting in the barroom, talking with two young correspondents who had just arrived in Vietnam. The jukebox was blaring out scratched recordings of Johnny Cash's "Folsom Prison Blues" and other hits of 1967–68. A young veteran hovered over me, begging for more and more money. His right arm had been twisted off just below the elbow and his right leg had been cut off a few inches below the knee so that the two useless limbs dangled inward like clamps. His eyes were also twisted so that neither focused in front of him and his face was set in a fixed grin.

One of the young reporters was asking me how it had been in 1968 and I could only say it had been more active and crazy, not nearly so depressing as it had become. He said it didn't seem so bad to him; he had just arrived and he really loved the whole scene. "Hell," he said, "I'm having a ball. It's my movie." It was a line from a magazine article about our group in 1968.

We drove down to My Tho as friends would set off on an outing from San Francisco to Monterey. We took the same narrow boats and everything seemed as it had been on that trip in late 1968. The towers of the Island of the Phoenix came into sight as we rounded another island in the Mekong, and still nothing seemed changed.

In fact, the place seemed even more fantastic now because the

Coconut Monk had bought a huge old barge from some Korean hauling company and connected it to his island with a high-arched ironwork bridge, replete with more pink and blue dragons.

The holy man had completely renovated the three-story barge, the latest move in his program to lure the peace talks to his island. His octagonal peace table was now in place in a room on the barge's top deck. Comfortable armchairs had been built for dining facilities on the middle deck and sleeping quarters were planned for the first deck.

The Dao Dua himself was seated on a giant porcelain creature—part dragon, part horse, part cow—that, according to Chinese legend, will return to Earth when there is peace. There was also an enormous porcelain urn which depicted the Coconut Monk as the reincarnation of the emperor Minh Mang. His perch was located in a canopied receiving room at one end of the top deck. In a cage beside him, were a bear and a gibbon—further evidence to him that incompatible animals could live at peace. The black bear and the white gibbon wrestled and played without prejudice.

Behind the old man—no longer grinning but sad, distracted—was a huge mural of stormy waters. He said—through gestures and an interpreter—that 1972 was almost past and that meant there were at least nine more years of stormy waters for Vietnam. He said peace had always come—1918, 1945, 1954—in years whose last digits added up to nine. The Dao Dua no longer posed for pictures and he seemed uninterested in his visitors.

We wandered after a long and awkward silence, back onto the island. The monks had stopped the old practice of praying all day and night and none seemed to know when—or even if—the prayers were said. The courtyard where we had prayed before was overgrown by bushes and shrubs. The rest of the island now seemed as unkempt as the rest of Vietnam.

I asked the monk who was guiding us around why all the islanders had big white numbers stenciled on the backs of their robes. He explained that most of the 2,000 young men on the island were deserters (his word). He had been a warrant officer during his first tour of duty; then he had deserted to the island. He was captured and put back in the army, only to desert again to the island. Among the more recent arrivals, he said, was a colonel whose company had been wiped out in the fighting that destroyed Quang Tri. He had vowed never to fight again even if it meant jail.

The monk said government agents had raided the island the previous year and arrested 140 young men. Many were still in the Chi Hoa prison, some had managed to escape back to the island. After the raid, the government simply declared the island a prison, numbered all its residents, and told them they would be arrested if they wandered out of bounds.

We asked the old boatman who gave us a ride back to My Tho what he thought about the Paris talks. Would the ceasefire bring peace to Vietnam? He looked away off down the Mekong, smiled, and gestured. No, there would still be many years of troubled waters.

I had to walk past the apartment we had shared several times a day, since it was on Saigon's main street. Sometimes I would find myself sitting in the coffee shop across the street, staring up at the two big windows as if waiting for a familiar face to pop out of memory (dreams and nightmares) and say, "Hey, man, come on up and let's get stoned."

Four years after all those happy afternoons and evenings, cheap flowered curtains were closed tightly across one window and heavy blue shutters were always locked across the other window. I couldn't even remember the curtains or the shutters because we had always kept them pulled back so we could sit there in the big open windows, chain smoking Flynn's super joints.

I wondered if any of those inscriptions remained on the walls: "Back on your head, Page," "If Flynn was Your Muvver." And what about Mister Long, the opium man. I wondered if he ever stopped by to ask whatever happened to all of us—Flynn and Stone still missing, the rest of us settled into quite different lives a long way from Vietnam.

After several days, I got up the nerve to walk through the

downstairs gate, back through the narrow dingy hallway to the open winding staircase, and up to the heavy wooden door on the first landing. Surely we had engraved our names there at some point, but I couldn't even find a scratch to confirm my romance.

I knocked several times and finally two very proper Vietnamese women answered. They opened the door, but quickly stepped back, glaring at the intruder. They had, of course, refused to learn the language of the Americans. So I spoke to them very slowly in the best French I could muster. I explained that I had lived in this apartment in 1968 and that for sentimental reasons, I wanted to see if it was still the way I remembered it.

Neither woman budged an inch; neither spoke or smiled. I thought it was my French they had not understood. So I repeated the request even more slowly than before. When I kept standing there, one of the women finally snapped at me, "Yes. Yes. We can understand you. But why?" She asked the question that endures:

"Why have you come here?"

FINI BOOK